DOWNSIZING PRISONS

MICHAEL JACOBSON

DOWNSIZING PRISONS

*How to Reduce Crime and
End Mass Incarceration*

New York University Press • *New York and London*

NEW YORK UNIVERSITY PRESS
New York and London
www.nyupress.org

Library of Congress Cataloging-in-Publication Data
Jacobson, Michael, 1953–
Downsizing prisons : how to reduce crime and end mass incarceration /
Michael Jacobson.
p.   cm.
Includes bibliographical references and index.
ISBN 0-8147-4274-2 (cloth : alk. paper)
1. Prisons—United States. 2. Probation—United States. 3. Parole—
United States. 4. Alternatives to imprisonment—United States.
5. Criminals—Rehabilitation—United States.   I. Title.
HV9471.J317 2005
364.6'0973—dc22   2004020592

New York University Press books are printed on acid-free paper,
and their binding materials are chosen for strength and durability.

Manufactured in the United States of America
10 9 8 7 6 5 4 3 2 1

For my Mother and Father

Contents

Acknowledgments

This book grew out of my years working in a number of government positions in New York City, as well as the last several years doing research and teaching at the John Jay College of Criminal Justice and the Graduate Center of the City University of New York. In many ways, my experience as a Ph.D. student at the Graduate Center of the City of New York over twenty years ago began to shape my thinking about criminal justice and criminology. My dissertation adviser, Edward Sagarin, who passed away many years ago, was fervent about making me question and examine strongly held and supposedly commonsense beliefs, my own as well as others'. Most of the things that liberals and conservatives believe about crime were wrong, Ed would always say, and he pushed me relentlessly to justify my positions.

My thinking about crime and corrections policy has gone through a number of metamorphoses as I moved from government jobs in the budget office to Probation and then Correction Commissioner. The last few years in academia have added another dimension to my thinking about issues of crime and public policy. It has been difficult, at times, to reconcile my recent, more contemplative academic experience with that of my former life as a government official. In my jobs at Probation and Correction, there was an almost irresistible urge simply to try to make it through the day without a disaster, never mind to try to effect some long-term structural change. Thankfully, the last several years have given me the opportunity to remain involved in helping policy makers, and frankly myself, try to reconcile theory, practice, and politics.

Along the way, I have benefited greatly from my colleagues (and even bosses) in government and community-based organizations. Ed Koch, David Dinkins, and Rudy Giuliani all allowed me to work in their administrations, and I learned much from each of them. Mindy Tarlow and Katie Lapp, my colleagues in government for more years than any of us want to admit, have always been a source of friendship and support, and their years of expertise (lots of years) have made this book better than it otherwise would have been. Paul Dickstein and Harvey Spector, both of the Office of Management and Budget, were wacky enough to hire a sociology Ph.D. to oversee the city's criminal justice budgets, and I learned from each of them every day.

At Probation, Alfred Siegel was both a friend and colleague and a constant source of knowledge about government, criminal justice, and good restaurants. At Correction, Deputy Commissioners Gary Lanigan and Bernie Kerik were likewise great colleagues and friends, whose vastly different experiences always made my job easier. Despite all my years at Correction and the last several spent studying prison policy, I still don't know what happened in those meetings between Bernie, who has gone on to bigger and better things, and the Deputy Correction Chiefs who worked for us. I do know the more meetings he had, the more those Chiefs looked a little older, and the more overtime went down. Marc Shaw, the First Deputy Mayor in New York City, has been a great friend and sounding board for a host of issues over the years, and though he'll be horrified by even this small mention, it's better than being the subject of a Letterman top-ten list. My numerous conversations with Marty Horn about corrections, probation, and parole, things he knows quite a bit about, have sharpened my thinking over the last several years as well.

To all those at the Vera Institute of Justice with whom I've worked over the years, thanks for your warm friendship and advice; especially to Chris Stone—now a professor at Harvard's Kennedy School of Government—Nick Turner, and Dan Wilhelm. Likewise to Joel Copperman, Liz Gaines, Bob Gangi, Michael Smith, Richard Girgenti, Glenn Goord, Leslie Crocker Snyder, Joseph Gubbay, Judy Greene, Jeremy Travis, Jerry McElroy, and Michael Thompson; I've learned so much from you all. Timothy Hughes at BJS was generous with his time as well as providing valuable data.

To Susan Tucker, Eric Cadora, and Helena Huang (now at the JEHT Foundation) of the Open Society Institute, thank you not only for your generosity in awarding me a fellowship that allowed me to take some time off from teaching to travel around the country, talking to policy makers of various stripes, but also for your advice and counsel on a whole range of issues.

To all my colleagues at John Jay and the Graduate Center who have been both enormously supportive and simultaneously sick to death of this book, I thank you all. Especially to Todd Clear, Jim Levine, Charles

Lindner, Basil Wilson, Gerald Lynch, Zelma Henriques, Robert McCrie, Maki Haberfeld, and John Kleinig at John Jay, thanks for being so accepting, supportive, and kind. I thank all my graduate students who were forced to read chapters, discuss, and listen to endless ramblings on this book—even the ones who said the narrative just didn't work and a couple of my proposed solutions were just wrong. I appreciate your honesty. Good luck in your new jobs as non-tenure-track instructors in Moose Jaw, Saskatchawan. Thanks especially to Carla Barrett, my research assistant at the Graduate Center, who provided assistance of every imaginable kind. Her help was invaluable.

James Jacobs and David Greenberg were kind enough to read drafts and offer thoughtful critiques and comments on the manuscript. Needless to say, any errors that remain are mine alone, though a good case can be made that if they had just read it more carefully, those errors would not have made it into the final version. Special thanks to Eileen Kalish at NYU Press for her support and invaluable suggestions.

My father, Julius Jacobson, would have been enormously happy and proud to see this book. He was a great writer, and any part of the book that seems argumentative and polemical comes directly from him. My mother, Phyllis Jacobson, a wonderful writer herself, taught me to love to read and write, and much of her is in this book as well.

Heartfelt thanks to Joan Gooden-Williams for being the most loving babysitter imaginable and for deftly occupying Alexander, who otherwise would have been using this computer to surf Nickelodeon.

Finally, to Lynn, without whom this book would be inconceivable. She has not only provided the usual love and support attributed to spouses in these pages but also has, in turn, been colleague, editor, proofreader, and critic. That she managed to do all this while finishing her third book and helping to chase around one lively little kid (Alexander, not me) is a testament to the fact that she is a wonderful and generous (and tired) person. She is really smart, but she cannot know all she has meant to the book and to me.

Preface

ON MARCH 15, 1995, while I was the Commissioner of Probation for the City of New York, I was appointed by Mayor Rudolph Giuliani also to run the New York City Department of Correction—the largest city jail system in the United States. Indeed, for the next year and a half, I ran both the city's Probation and Correction Departments. Afterward, for two years, I ran only the much-larger Correction Department, until leaving in 1998 to become a full-time academic at the John Jay College of Criminal Justice.

I think it is fair to say that, until that time, none of my friends or relatives would have predicted—even to the day I was appointed—that I would one day run all the jails in New York City for Mayor Giuliani. I am the son of socialist parents and earned my Ph.D. in sociology in 1985 for the sole purpose of finding a comfortable academic job from which I could write and teach about urban sociology and criminology, my specializations in graduate school. How I went from a full-time graduate student in sociology to Probation and Correction Commissioner is a rather long, convoluted, and ultimately pretty boring story. Suffice it to say that while in graduate school in the late 1970s, a summer internship in the Office of the Deputy Mayor for Public Safety tempered my interest in academia to the point that a government junkie was born. A succession of criminal justice system jobs led to a full-time position in the New York City's Office of Management and Budget (OMB), where I spent almost a decade from 1983 to 1992.

It is probably worth a moment to talk about this particular job, not only because it helped shape and hone my interest in budgets and finance but also since much of what I learned at OMB forms the basis of this book. I wound up in the budget office after Michael Smith, then the head of the Vera Institute of Justice, suggested I apply there to head the unit that oversees many of the city's criminal justice agencies. Frankly, I thought it an odd suggestion, since I considered myself a budding social scientist, albeit inside rather than outside government. Besides, as anyone who has ever worked in government knows, everybody despises those narrow-minded, green-eyeshade-wearing, bean-counting budget bureaucrats. Making matters worse, I really didn't know anything about budgeting or financial management. But Smith convinced me that the Budget Office drove most of the city's important policy decisions (to the endless consternation of agency heads), and that OMB would be even more central as the city went through another financial crisis in the mid- to late 1980s. He said that someone with an interest in and knowledge of criminal justice issues could, and should, learn the technical budgeting part of the job. Combining the two, he said, would allow me to be involved in policy decisions that otherwise would probably not be possible. He was right.

Over the next decade, I had a series of jobs that culminated in becoming a Deputy Budget Director, where I had oversight over the entire city criminal justice system (and a number of other areas as well). Most of those years were ones of fiscal constraint, sometimes rising to fiscal crisis. Though it is always more enjoyable to hand out money than to cut budgets, I spent most of my time at OMB trying to figure out how to save money and simultaneously protect public safety. This was no easy feat in an era when the city jail system was nearly doubling in size, from a daily population of 12,000 in 1980 to a high of almost 23,000 by 1992. The appearance and widespread use of crack cocaine, together with aggressive anti-drug enforcement by the New York Police Department (NYPD), resulted in surging jail populations through the eighties and nineties that required huge expenditures of funds on varied new jail facilities.

We bought and renovated barges that had been used by the British in the Falklands War to house Argentinean prisoners. We commissioned a floating jail (at a cost of well over $100 million) to be built by a shipyard in New Orleans. We converted out-of-service Staten Island ferries to be used as jails. We erected "temporary" reinforced tents, which looked like large white indoor tennis facilities, that had a supposed useful life of five to ten years. These are still in use today. But all this building and extra capacity was still not enough to handle all the inmates, so the Department of Correction would resort to constantly transporting inmates around the city from one facility to another: in effect, the buses themselves became temporary housing. In short, the city spent hundreds of millions of dollars adding jail capacity during the 1980s. For budget officials, this posed problems of how to limit the financial damage to the city that resulted from a seemingly ever-increasing jail population. At that time, attempting to reduce spending on jails, or even to hold it constant, was perceived as utterly utopian.

As the city's economy worsened in the late 1980s, and as criminal justice expenditures continued to grow, it struck a number of us in the Budget Office that this crisis also offered some opportunities (an overused phrase, I know, but apt in this case nonetheless). We convinced then-Mayor Ed Koch, who was strongly ideologically opposed to alternatives to jail and prison, to greatly expand the city's alternatives to incarceration organizations and to create new ones, since it could help control spending on jails. Over the strong objections of the Manhattan District Attorney, Mayor Koch supported an innovative public defender service, based in Harlem, on the theory that it would save money through faster processing of criminal cases. We convinced the Mayor to increase funding for the Department of Probation—a change he opposed even more—in the midst of a fiscal crisis. The lessons from those years remain with me today. First, in an era of fiscal constraint or crisis, politicians are often forced to make very difficult policy choices they would happily avoid if money were not an issue. Second, spending more and more money on incarceration and police does not mean crime will decrease.

The transition from budget official to agency head was rapid but not seamless. In 1992, a couple of weeks after then-Mayor David Dinkins appointed me as the city's Probation Commissioner, I was running the agency. But the transition from someone used to cutting (and, on occasion, also increasing) an agency's budget to someone running that agency was not easy to make. Whatever I had to atone for in a prior life was more than made up for in my first several months at Probation. "Let's increase training," I would say. "Can't, Commissioner. You cut our training budget." "We have to modernize our information technology," I'd suggest. "Can't, Commissioner. You whacked our computer budget." "Can't we at least give these offices a painting and buy a few pieces of furniture?" "We could have before you cut our support services in half." You get the picture. In fairness to the probation staff, it took only a few days before I, too, reverted back to despising those narrow-minded, green-eyeshade-wearing, bean-counting budget bureaucrats who had the audacity to try to cut Probation's budget further, while I was the Commissioner. It was like riding a bike.

As I became more intimately acquainted with the intricacies and possibilities of supervising offenders in the community while at the Probation Department, I began to think more seriously and analytically about the amounts of money used to fund the expansions of jails and prisons, not just in New York but nationally. The reality of being the Probation Commissioner and having the responsibility for supervising about 60,000 adult probationers (almost three-quarters of whom were convicted felons), with a total supervision budget of about $30 million yearly (there was another $40 million for writing presentence investigations and supervising juveniles on probation), was sobering when compared to the city jail system, which had the responsibility of incarcerating a daily population of about 20,000 at a yearly cost of about $800 million. The per-month expenditure on a jail inmate was over $3,000, compared to just over $40 a month for a convicted felon on probation. I began to argue—astoundingly unsuccessfully, I might add—that simply transferring $20 million from the jails budget to probation could radically and profoundly alter the way probation worked. It could lead to significantly more public safety in the form of less crime committed by those on probation supervision, who could be provided with a host of essential services. It would, I argued, make no difference to the jail system, whose budget was so immense that, in all likelihood, the corrections system would not even realize the money was gone. If only those narrow-minded, green-eyeshade-wearing, pencil-pushing budget bureaucrats would have listened. They didn't.

To make matters worse, after arguing for a transfer of resources from jails to probation, I was appointed the Commissioner of Correction by Mayor Giuliani in 1995. Whoops. Again, the Correction staff enjoyed—with the same enthusiasm as had the probation staff—the opportunity to remind me of all the various cuts to the Correction budget I had made while at OMB (while increasing the total amount of funding, I might remind you). In addition, they also got quite a kick out of asking me if it was now all right to move that $20 million out of our budget to Probation. Well, maybe now wasn't quite the right time. (What was that thing I did in that prior life, anyway?)

It took only days at the Department of Correction for me to realize that almost one of every five inmates in the entire system was there as a result of breaking one or more of the rules of being on parole. As applies just about everywhere in the United States, once released from a prison sentence in New York, a person is put on parole or some other form of community supervision with a whole series of conditions.

These conditions might include regular reporting to a parole officer, going to a treatment program, staying off drugs, and getting a job. Violating any one of these conditions could immediately land a parolee back in jail, and then prison to finish out the remainder of his or her sentence.

It seemed to me that New York parole officers were taking liberal advantage of the opportunity to violate parolees under their supervision. The way the process worked in New York was that once a parolee was violated for breaking the parole rules, he or she went immediately to an administrative hearing on Rikers Island. This would take almost four months, and the parolee would either be put back on parole or be sent back to prison, usually for several months. New York parole officers were violating over 10,000 parolees each year.

I remember being amazed that New York City was spending somewhere around $160 million every year to house parolees who were not accused of committing a crime but rather had violated parole. On top of this expense, the state probably spent another $140 million to house most of these parole violators for another several months. New Yorkers were paying around $300 million to house, for several months, thousands of parolees who had not even been convicted of a new crime. The public safety benefits of locking up for only months thousands of people who were not convicted of a crime completely eluded me. Couldn't other good uses could be made of this money, even in pure public safety terms, that would be far more efficient than constantly recycling thousands of people through the jail and prison system for relatively short stays? The more I looked around the country, the more I came to realize how much money we waste on the overuse of incarceration, especially when all my experience and the extant knowledge of what works to reduce crime and recidivism made crystal clear that spending fewer of the government's limited dollars could reduce prison populations and increase public safety.

I have struggled with this issue for the last decade, both inside government and out. And I have struggled with how to convince policy makers and politicians that reducing the numbers of people who go to prison can, if implemented intelligently, not only further reduce crime and help strengthen other essential government services but be politically feasible as well. It remains to be seen whether I have succeeded, but I have consistently felt the potential payoff to be worth the effort.

It is true that keeping some people in prison protects public safety as well as punishes the offender. I am not a prison abolitionist. There are people who, unless removed from their communities, will continue to commit violent acts, or whose offense is so brutal and vicious that no alternative community-based sanction is imaginable or appropriate. But this does not mean prisons should look like they do today, or even that people who have been incarcerated should not receive a second chance after some time and treatment. After all is said and done, the number of people in U.S. jails and prisons—almost 2.2 million at the time of this writing—reflects a public policy gone mad. Prisons and especially long prison sentences should be reserved for the most violent among us. There is no need to lock away for years hundreds of thousands of nonviolent drug offenders or to keep people in prison well past their crime-committing years, effectively turning some prisons into the equivalent of secure nursing homes. Other ways can and should be found to punish as well as change behavior.

Public safety is not the sole province of the criminal justice system. Providing accessible health care protects public safety. Having community-based mental health and child care protects public safety. Having reasonable school class sizes and well-trained teachers protects public safety. Well-funded environmental and transportation agencies protect public safety. If we want to maximize public safety in this country, then we need to shift some money away from the corrections system, where the benefits of locking up nonviolent offenders for longer and longer periods of time are negligible compared to other areas that will result in far greater public safety and healthier communities.

My sense is that, by now, the country's policy makers may well be receptive at last to shrinking state prison systems, because of tight budgets, shifts in public opinion and priorities, and new research that confirms the efficacy of community-based prisoner reentry programs. My experience as someone who ran large probation and jail systems, and also as a consultant who regularly talks to numerous corrections and elected officials across the country, tells me that the United States is in a historical moment of limited duration, when a radical shift away from the mass incarceration of the last three decades can be brought about. It will not be easy, and it will happen in individual states in fits and starts. However, it can be done. Some will argue that these changes, even if possible, might well be only temporary. Once states are in good economic shape again, they will say, levels of imprisonment are likely to rise again—particularly since high-profile crimes that reignite "tough on crime" rhetoric are likely to recur, capturing media attention and inflaming public concerns. This is a fair point, though I believe that the strategies proposed in this book have a good chance of jump-starting long-term structural declines in how prisons are used. These declines, assuming they happen, will not be merely temporary policy changes, doomed to failure as political dynamics shift with the wind, but can be the basis for a long-term restructuring of our prison systems that delivers more public safety at less cost.

Anyway, that's my story—and I'm sticking to it.

Introduction: Bloated Prisons

THERE IS ONLY one way onto Rikers Island. It is a long bridge that connects the borough of Queens to the largest penal colony in the world. Most of the almost 110,000 people who make the trip over the East River to Rikers over the course of a year will spend an average of six weeks there before they are released back to their communities. Many will have made bail; others will have had their low-level cases dismissed or have completed their short sentences; some will be found not guilty; and many will be sentenced to serve their time on probation. However, almost 10,000 of these people will plead to or be found guilty of a felony crime and will be sent to the New York State prison system thereafter. This mammoth system of sorting and punishing exists in different forms in every city and county in the United States. Nonetheless from Los Angeles, California, to Fargo, North Dakota, to Clinton, New York, criminal justice systems perform remarkably analogous functions: deciding who stays home and who goes to prison. It is the latter decision on which this book concentrates.

The United States now locks up a higher percentage of its population than any country in the world. The more than 2 million people who are incarcerated today make up roughly eight times the number in 1975. Moreover, those in prison are disproportionately African-American and Latino, and much of the increase in prison population over the last decade and a half has been driven by those sentenced for nonviolent drug or property crime. An emerging body of research documents the harm to family members and communities of what David Garland, a sociologist well known for his work on punishment, calls "mass imprisonment."[1] By now, these facts and figures are known and largely accepted. Over the last two decades, a host of criminologists and analysts have pointed to an array of problems in the size and scope of the U.S. penal system and have argued strenuously for the system's reform.[2] Many writers have called for less spending on incarceration and, as an alternative, more spending on economic or community development, preventive, educational, or early childhood development programs. The argument is that spending now on prevention will result in greater social justice, reduced incarceration, and less spending on criminal justice and corrections down the road. Yet, despite such overwhelming and persuasive criticisms, the growth of prisons and prison spending has continued.[3]

For the outpouring of intellectual and academic criticism has not been able to halt the momentum toward greater incarceration created by the last two decades of uncontrolled spending on corrections, driven by longer and mandatory prison sentences, huge increases in the number of those incarcerated for drug offenses, the introduction of private capital in the form of correctional privatization, and the growth of exceedingly powerful corrections unions. These structural forces, combined with a remarkably simplistic and inflammatory public and political discourse on the value of prisons, have all but ensured the continued growth in incarceration.

The purpose of the book is not merely to echo valuable work already done on the shortcomings of the U.S. prison policy. Rather, my goal is to make a substantive and political case that policy makers can begin to reverse 30 years of prison growth in a way that protects public safety while ameliorating pressing problems of health care, education, and deteriorating state budgets. We actually know quite a bit about "what works" in corrections. Although much of the academic work on corrections has been concentrated on the many shortcomings of our corrections policy and, at times, can take on a certain "preaching to the choir" tendency, there is also a growing body of work on effective programs and interventions that can reduce crime, decrease recidivism, and protect public safety.[4] This book will try to make the case that resources can be made available, through reforming our corrections system, that can not only fund these efforts at creating long-term public safety but also help ameliorate the structural underfunding of our education and health care systems. In making this case, I draw heavily on my own background and experience.

I have personally made that trip to Rikers Island more times than I can remember. From 1995 to 1998, I was the Commissioner of the New York City Department of Correction, the largest city jail system in the country. While in that job, and afterward, I spent a good deal of time and energy trying to figure out how to make the city's correction system smaller and safer, always keeping public safety in mind. Because I was the city's Probation Commissioner for the three years prior (and one year during) my tenure as Correction Commissioner, I always thought that probation and other alternatives were far more appropriate than incarceration for certain groups of offenders. Though probation is probably the most poorly funded part of the nation's criminal justice system, along with other types of diversion programs it has the potential to provide meaningful and serious supervision for many people, especially drug offenders, now in prison.

None of what I am proposing in this book can be accomplished without the reallocation of resources from corrections to other parts of the criminal justice system and to other parts of government. I spent a decade at the New York City Office of Management and Budget (OMB), leaving a Deputy Budget Director position in 1992 to become the Probation Commissioner. If I learned anything from my time at OMB (other than that budget analysts are not the most popular people in the world, especially during a fiscal crisis), it was the following. While fiscal crises and severely constrained economies are painful and frequently require service reductions and even layoffs, they are also an opportunity for policy makers to make extraordinary decisions. During periods of fiscal constraint, the pressures to keep spending in line with revenues can create an environment where budgets trump politics. This is why, during the late 1980s, New York City was able to hugely expand alternatives to incarceration and to fund after-school programs even while the city was in one of its worst periods of economic hardship. Yet the Mayor and city legislature were willing to transfer funds away from the jail system into alternatives to incarceration. Millions of dollars were thereby saved, allowing the city to fund other desirable services; for instance, a portion of saved monies went to after-school programs for children. Without the pressures of declining revenues and the need to balance budgets, though, such decisions would have been politically impossible. Because of this experience, both as a budget analyst and as a criminal justice system administrator, I was particularly cognizant of Realpolitik considerations when writing this book—namely, that large-scale proposals for governmental reform must be accompanied by an achievable fiscal and political strategy if they are to be at all successful.

Stemming from my past experiences, too, is one of this book's major arguments: the tremendous growth of incarceration over the last few decades relates directly to this country's present difficulties in adequately funding its education and health care systems. Money spent on spiraling corrections costs, especially in light of many states' tax cuts during the prosperous 1990s, came at the expense of other crucial governmental services. It will take more than transferring funding from corrections to health care and education to fully address the overwhelming needs in these areas. However, significantly reducing corrections spending so that funds can be made available for these (and other) priority areas of government can make a huge difference in millions of people's lives. The country's recent recession, and most states' dramatically deteriorating fiscal health, has only compounded this crisis. While the national economy has shown some recent signs of ending years of stagnation and job loss, state economies will continue to be constrained for years, as states economies lag well behind the national economy in recovery, as pressures to fund Medicaid and primary and secondary education continue, and as the full effect of years of cumulative tax cuts are felt. Yet it is precisely these factors that can set the stage for a significant decrease in corrections expenditures.

Of course, health and education needs could also be addressed in other ways. For instance, states could raise taxes, or the federal government could assume the entire cost of Medicaid, thereby freeing up funds for state budgets. However, my argument is based on research and experience that strongly shows that the United States is presently incarcerating too many people and spending too much money on imprisonment—funds that could be more sensibly and productively used elsewhere. It might well be necessary to raise more revenue or to pressure the federal government to absorb more Medicaid costs, but in either case it certainly makes sense to redirect unnecessary monies now being spent on prisons.

A fiscal and political climate now exists that can make policy and law makers receptive to altering criminal justice policy, especially regarding the use of prison. This book will essentially frame and present the political, fiscal, and substantive case that can be used by states to begin the process of reversing the last 30 years of prison growth. These budget savings can then move to other parts of the budget—quite literally, as I will show through illustrations peppered throughout this volume and through the case studies of California, Connecticut, and Louisiana that comprise the bulk of Chapter 6.

I have spent a good portion of the last few years working with a number of states that are trying to control and reallocate prison expenses. Some have had more success than others, but the number of states now actively struggling with seemingly uncontrolled prison expansion increases each year.

I argue that change is both challenging and possible. A strategy can be built that includes more funding for education and health care, along with an aggressive fiscal strategy that moves resources over the next several years away from corrections. The tools for this strategy include making use of severely constrained and, in many cases, deteriorating fiscal conditions of states and the strong public desire for more investment in education and health care. Recent public opinion polling not only indicates far more importance placed on education and health issues than on crime but also a much more complex and "progressive" attitude about using alternatives to prison. The combination of states' experience of massive declines in revenues, public demand for service enhancements in health and education systems, and the declining relative importance of crime as a public issue provides a basis for arguing for large-scale reductions in the size of the U.S. prison system. Thus I am proposing a strategy that recognizes and takes advantage of larger political and economic realities to counter the charged tenor of criminal justice discourse and accompanying policies of the last 30 years.

This strategy grows from a sense of urgency about an uncertain national economy that has had disastrous fiscal consequences on state budgets. Though recessions are cyclical occurrences in a capitalist economy, the long-term picture for many states remains bleak. Even with a slowly recovering national economy, states simply do not (and will not) have the revenue to continue prison expansion while simultaneously supporting Medicaid, maintaining low tax rates, and adequately funding education and health systems. The overall severity of the early twenty-first-century economic crisis will abate, but states will still have to make hard choices; they will be forced fundamentally to reexamine, among other priorities, the size and scope of their corrections systems.

In addition, the strategy I propose emphasizes the importance of making structural reforms in how most states' probation and parole systems operate. Here, I discuss a dramatic increase in the number of "technical" parole violators who are being sent back to prison not for committing new crimes but for breaking one or more of the many conditions of parole or probation. The book will concentrate primarily, though not completely, on parole as opposed to probation violators. The main reason for this is that parole agencies, more so than probation, have the extraordinary ability to send parolees back to prison or jail immediately while they await their administrative or court hearings. Additionally, the structure of parole is quite similar in every state (unlike probation, which can be a county, judicial, or state function), and it is parole violators who are being reincarcerated in record numbers. This said, I discuss probation as well, especially in Chapter 6, where I discuss the issue of probation violators in Connecticut and Louisiana in some depth.

In addition to parole and probation reform, I advocate for the importance of large-scale prison diversion programs for nonviolent offenders, along with different types of sentencing reform, much of which has already begun in different degrees in many places around the country.

Moreover, this book contends that reforms can occur at the same time that public safety is protected and even enhanced. Policy makers, as well as the general public, reasonably require assurances that reducing the size of prison systems will not increase crime. Quite the contrary is conceivable, though: I argue that reforms, if thoughtfully enacted, will not increase crime and may actually improve public safety. By way of documenting this point, Chapter 4 presents a case study of New York City. During the 1990s and into the 2000s, New York City led the nation in crime decline while substantially decreasing its use of prison.

Overall, then, I contend both that correctional reform needs to happen and that current political and economic imperatives make this a propitious moment to bring about a long-overdue policy reversal. Law makers and politicians, until recently terrified of any serious change in criminal justice policy, are now operating in a very different environment to that of the last two decades. They must now consider the tightened state economies and unrelenting public desires for improvements in education and health care (coupled with their always strong desire not to raise taxes). What law makers need, then, is a substantive approach that allows them to address other pressing governmental needs while assuring the public of its safety.

Though this book is obviously a case study involving U.S. criminal justice policy, it has relevance beyond American borders. In Western Europe, Australia, and South Africa especially, the use and size of prison systems is expanding. For instance, from 1992 to 1998 the prison systems of Germany grew by 37%, Spain by 27%, the Netherlands by 80%, Australia by 32%, and South Africa by 27%. Additionally the prison systems in Italy, Spain, South Africa, France, and Australia are crowded well over capacity.[5] Great Britain saw one of the largest percentages in prison population increase in the world, from 44,570 in 1993 to 65,300 in 1998, an increase of 47%.[6] Finally, a longer-term view of some of these countries' prison growth reveals that from 1983 to 1997 the Netherlands increased by 240%, Spain by 192% and Portugal by 140%.[7]

With a tight global economy exerting tremendous budget pressures on most countries, the stringent fiscal and budget-balancing requirements for countries now in or trying to enter the European Union, and the faltering economy of South Africa, all these countries are experiencing similar, though perhaps less pronounced, pressures to those in the United States. As prison populations increase, especially during periods of tightening economies, other essential services of government suffer as law makers feel compelled to fund spiraling prison costs. While the political cultures as well as the specific criminal justice problems of European countries differ from those of the United States, the solutions to out-of-control prison expansion may contain similar elements. Like their U.S. counterparts, law makers in other countries require coherent analyses and strategies to bring down prison use and costs while protecting public safety and redirecting funds to other needed services.

Other reasons for downsizing prisons need to be cited as well. One of the lessons of Abu Ghraib is that in the absence of strong, committed ethical leadership, prisons can easily deteriorate into brutal harmful places for both prisoners and staff. Any institution that operates with the constant threat of, and ideally only the occasional use of, force is one that should house as few people as possible. Prisons should provide humane care and have the ability to prepare those who leave not to come back. But even the most efficient and effective prison systems should be as small as possible. People who pose a real threat to public safety or who have committed violent acts should be in prison. Prison should not be the default for our failure to use other methods of social control, community or restorative justice. It is too expensive, too punitive, and the potential for harm to prisoners, their families, and communities too great to overuse it in the way that we do.

Obviously, this book is an attempt to provide a detailed argument and a concrete strategy in the distinctly American context. To meet this goal, I have organized the chapters as follows. In Chapter 1, "Mass Incarceration," I continue with the overview started here by way of introduction. More specifically, I explain why changing criminal justice policy in the corrections arena is especially difficult and distinctive. At the same time, the chapter details four recent developments, to which I have already alluded, that make the current moment especially opportune for proposing changes in prison and sentencing practices.

Chapter 2, "Unintended Consequences," discusses a set of cultural, political, and economic factors that have made reform appear a nearly insurmountable task. Among these factors, the emergence of a punitive discourse makes it seem that politicians have everything to gain from a "get tough" approach and everything to lose from taking more progressive positions. In addition, change has become more difficult in the context of recently emerging private prisons and of private capital influential in encouraging new prison building. Moreover, public corrections unions now play a powerful role in pushing for increased spending on prisons. In this respect, and probably in this respect alone, their organizational interests have coincided with those of the private prison industry: both have financial and political reasons to maintain and expand the country's prison system. Chapter 2 also examines the relationship of prisons to economic development, focusing especially on problems in rural areas, where prisons are perceived as vital to a region's financial survival.

Chapter 3 analyzes two of the four developments alluded to above: deteriorating state budgets and changing public opinion. This chapter explores the difficulties states are now facing in balancing their budgets amid declining revenues and increasing demands for service in education. These pressures continue to exist in a political environment that mitigates against tax increases of any sort. As corrections budgets continue to rise and consume larger proportions of state budgets, for the first time in decades law makers are finding themselves under increasing pressure to cut corrections budgets. I cite specific examples of budgetary measures many states have started to enact to balance their books, including closing prisons and repealing mandatory minimum sentencing laws to reduce corrections costs. Such state-level fiscal pressures have created an environment wherein corrections budget reductions and sentencing changes, impossible just two or three years ago, may now be viewed as acceptable and even necessary.

The second new development examined in Chapter 3 is the changing nature of U.S. public opinion on crime and corrections issues. Several national polls provide evidence that the public may well be ready for a shift in corrections policy, especially in tough economic times.

Additional verification comes from the State of California specifically, where a public proposition was put on the ballot to fund treatment for nonviolent drug offenders in lieu of prison. This referendum,, Proposition 36, passed overwhelmingly by a 61% to 39% margin, in a state that only several years earlier passed the toughest "three strikes" law in the country.

Chapter 4 is a case study of New York City, which, since the mid-1990s, has experienced the largest ongoing crime drop of any large city in the country while simultaneously sending fewer people to prison than it did before this decline. In this chapter, I document changes that resulted from increased use of up-front or pretrial short-term incarceration and the substantial decrease in the use of prison sentences. I make the case that, based on the New York City experience, the increased use of prison is not a necessary component of crime reduction strategies: in fact, at the same time prison use declines, public safety can be enhanced. Nor can it be said that what has happened in New York City will not interest law makers in the South or Midwest. On the contrary, the "New York miracle" has attracted favorable attention from policy makers all around the country. Thus law makers elsewhere may find it useful to learn that an increased use of prison played no demonstrable role in the city's crime drop.

Chapter 5 focuses on how states can begin to turn the tide of prison expansion. In particular, it centers on parole and probation technical violations and their contribution to the size of the country's prison system. I document how, in several states, as much as 20% of the prison population is made up of technical violators. In addition, I describe a number of incentives that currently exist for parole officers to send as many technical violators as possible back to prison. Finally, this chapter offers several policy options for restructuring parole systems to drastically reduce the flow of technical violators back to prison while maintaining and even increasing public safety. As I argue, parole officers need to be given options other than prison as ways of reacting to violations. A more drastic policy of eliminating postprison supervision entirely and replacing it with a voucher system will also be discussed as a policy option.

Chapter 6 is a detailed analysis of three states' experiences—those of California, Connecticut, and Louisiana—using data from these states to examine problems of, and potential for, reform. These states were chosen on the basis of their differing size and political cultures but also because each has experienced corrections growth amid severe budgetary crisis; important, too, is that I have worked as a (now academic) consultant with policy makers who have been attempting actual reforms in two of these states.

Each case study proceeds with four analogous sections. First, I analyze the causes of recent prison growth in California, Connecticut, and Louisiana, respectively. Second, I paint a picture of each state's political context. Third, I depict the condition of each state's budget. Finally, I offer "proposed plans of reform" designed with each state's particular circumstances in mind. My goal in this chapter is not only, or even primarily, to focus attention on these individual states' problems. Rather, I have tried to provide a model of how most states could function better if their prison systems were diminished in size at the same time that public safety needs continued to be met. In a time of ongoing state budgetary shortfalls, and when most Americans are clamoring for better-funded health care and education, these concrete proposals may be timely indeed. Thus the goal of Chapter 6, and of the summary Chapter 7 that follows by way of conclusion, is to demonstrate precisely that "real world" reforms are both desirable and achievable.

I

Mass Incarceration

IN 1993, DURING a slumber party, 12-year-old Polly Klaas was abducted from her home in Petaluma, California, and killed by a sex offender on parole named Richard Davis. The viciousness of the crime, the purity and innocence of the victim, and the psychotic unremorseful persona of Davis—who claimed at his sentencing hearing that Polly said before he killed her "just don't do me like my dad"[1]—all combined to fuel a supercharged political environment that propelled Californians in 1994 to vote overwhelmingly for the now-famous "three strikes" law, requiring life in prison after a third felony conviction.

In 1994, 7-year-old Megan Kanka was lured into her neighbor's house by a twice-convicted child molester who said he wanted to show her a puppy. He then sexually molested and murdered her. Less than two years later, President Bill Clinton signed into law the federal Megan's Law, requiring that communities be notified when sex offenders were returning to their neighborhoods. By 2002, every state had some version of a sex-offender notification law.

In 1997, Jenna Grieshaber, a nursing student in Albany, New York, was murdered by a parolee previously convicted of a violent crime. One year later, Governor George Pataki signed Jenna's Law into effect. This law ended discretionary release on parole—namely, the ability of a parole board to grant a prisoner early release—for all those convicted of a violent felony in New York.

That high-profile events affect and help shape public policy is not particularly new or surprising. Yet the frequency with which such events serve as a catalyst to influence criminal justice policy differentiates this realm from other policy arenas. Many writers have commented on a dialectical relationship between high-profile events and criminal justice policy. A number of sociologists and criminologists, including David Garland, Katherine Beckett, Michael Tonry, Edwin Sutherland, and Stanley Cohen, have noted the powerful impact and political use of such events in shaping public opinion and policy.[2] While the events themselves cannot entirely explain wholesale shifts of direction in policy in the absence of larger political and social trends, their impact has nonetheless been significant. Simply naming laws after victims cements the relationship between law and heinous high-profile crimes. In an era when conservative and retributive positions on crime dominate policy and public discourse, the "value" of such high-profile cases is high, for law makers and politicians.

For what better way to bring home the need for more and longer prison sentences than a real-life horrible and tragic crime such as the murder of Polly Klaas? Such cases become metaphors for all that is wrong in society, and the powerful emotional responses they elicit can be used as leverage to further toughen up the criminal justice system. In fact, high-profile events serve multiple political purposes that combine to increase the harshness of contemporary punitive policies. As Beckett notes, "Emphasizing the pathology of criminals and the utility of punishment, for example, obscures the role of social inequality in the generation of crime. Political outcomes such as three strikes legislation are thus best understood as a product of symbolic struggles in which actors disseminate favored ways of framing social problems and compete to have these versions of reality accepted as truth."[3]

Many significant changes in criminal justice policy over the last 10 to 15 years have followed one or a series of high-profile crimes. It requires only a few horrible crimes to be committed by individuals on probation for all 700,000 parolees and the 4 million probationers in the United States to be affected.[4] By 2000, 16 states had completely eliminated discretionary release on parole, and an additional 4 states had abolished discretionary parole for selected crimes.[5] Twenty-four states now have some kind of three strikes legislation.[6] Hence it is not surprising that many of these states have named their newly altered laws after the victims of high-profile crimes.

As previously noted, high-profile crimes do not happen in a vacuum but in a social environment that is already laced with both contempt for and fear of those who are living in poverty, which can all too easily translate into excessive and overly harsh responses to crime. Analyzing the sociological phenomena that lead to a social climate of vindictiveness, criminologist Jock Young writes:

> Relative deprivation downwards, a feeling that those who work little or not at all are getting an easy ride on your back and your taxes, is

a widespread sentiment. Thus whereas the "contented" middle classes may well feel sympathy towards the underclass and their "relative satisfaction" with their position translates into feelings of charity, those of the much larger constituency of discontent are more likely to demand welfare to work programmes, stamp down on dole "cheats," etc. Such a response, whatever its rationality, is not in itself punitive: it is at most authoritarian but it is not necessarily vindictive. But tied to such a quasi-rational response to a violation of meritocratic principles is frequently a much more compelling subtext which seeks not only to redress a perceived reluctance to work but to go beyond this to punish, demean and humiliate.

The key features of such resentment are disproportionality, scapegoating, and stereotyping. That is the group selected is seen to contribute to the problems of society quite disproportionally to their actual impact (e.g. teenage mothers, beggars, immigrants, drug users) and they are scapegoated and depicted as key players in the creation of social problems. Their portrayal is presented in an extraordinarily stereotypical fashion which bears little relationship to reality.[7]

Thus, a social climate already exists in the United States that is filled with resentment toward the poor, made worse by the stresses and massive economic insecurity felt by the millions worried about hanging on to their jobs in an era of fiscal retrenchment.

Moreover, as philosopher Nils Christie notes, highly stratified societies seem to find it easier to inflict pain and punishment on groups who are less fortunate.[8] Perhaps, then, it is not surprising that crime is more susceptible than other areas of government to the influence of high profile incidents. In an already emotionally charged punitive social and political environment, the commission of a high-profile crime, especially one of violence, becomes a catalyst for a series of complex emotional and political responses that can have an almost immediate effect on public policy.

In varying degrees, most people are already frightened by the specter of violent crime. Almost everyone knows someone who has been a crime victim. Most people have strong opinions about crime and what to do about it. No expertise is needed to feel strongly about capital punishment or rehabilitation versus retribution. No specialized knowledge is required to think "this could have been me or my child," or to become frightened and angry on hearing the awful stories of the crimes committed against Polly Klaas or Megan Kanka. On a visceral level, it seems natural to want to extract revenge against someone like Richard Davis, who could so brutally take the life of a small child. Moreover, expressing anger about crime may feel socially acceptable in an environment already oriented toward retribution and punishment.

Such visceral reactions on the part of the public and law makers alike set criminal justice policy apart from other areas of public policy. For instance, in the medical arena, a hospital may make a tragic mistake during a routine operation on a patient's appendix, or a doctor may operate on the wrong side of a patient's brain. In response, investigations by oversight health agencies, lawsuits, and remedial actions are likely to ensue, yet it is hardly likely that the medical procedures themselves will be changed or abolished.

Similarly, it is not unusual for some high school graduates to leave school without knowing how to read or write at or above grade levels. While this may outrage parents and educators, hardly will anyone call for abolishing, say, the twelfth grade in the same way that many will call for the abolition of parole after one or several tragic high-profile crimes. More conceivable is that high school will continue while educators and parents struggle with how to improve our system of public education. Other counterexamples come to mind: a bridge may collapse due to poor maintenance or design, a water sewage system may fail; a NASA spaceship may explode; the military may accidentally drop bombs on civilian targets. Yet all these governmental operations will continue with, perhaps, some modifications implemented as a result of expert analyses. Horrible as each of these social problems may be, especially to those immediately affected, none is likely to result in the kind of spontaneous public and political reaction and basic change in service delivery that have followed incidents of brutal crimes committed by parolees.

On its face, these examples might seem comparable more to errors of technology (a spaceship exploding, a bridge collapsing, and even teaching a child to read) than to value-laden judgments about crime (should a criminal go free or remain incarcerated for as long as possible?). But the analogy may be closer than at first glance appears. For most criminologists know and agree about the risks that different types of people pose to society once they leave prison. Experts in this area concur that the overwhelming majority of people stop committing violent crimes once they pass through their thirties and have significant relationships and children. It is well known that staying drug free and being employed greatly reduce the risk of future criminal activity, and that appropriately targeted rehabilitation programs reduce crime and recidivism.

Yet, the other unique characteristic of policy making in the area of corrections and punishment is that the role of academic experts and researchers has declined over the last 30 years, largely replaced by the growing influence of legislators and politicians.[9] Again going back to the examples of education, health, transportation, environmental protection, space administration, and the military, the majority of substantive decisions in these areas tend to be made by experts in a respective field; important decisions are usually based on, or at least informed by, research. This is not to say that legislators play no role outside the criminal justice arena; obviously, they do. But to the extent that legislators get involved in the details of, say, bridge construction, they may debate the utility of having a bridge in a particular location, or the overall budget for the bridge, or whether the bridge should be tolled. But I know of no case where a state legislature has decided to legislate the engineering and placement of structural supports for the bridge itself.

Moreover, while the issue of health care delivery and managed care has been a hotly debated political issue in the United States for the last decade, the actual delivery of the basic medical service is usually, though not always, left to doctors. The ongoing political debate about ending the practice of partial-birth abortions is an example in a medical context of the type of debate that happens in criminal justice all the time. Nevertheless, in these areas, both the public and politicians recognize that experts in the field, knowledgeable about the findings of well-regarded research, are crucial in determining how basic services are designed and delivered.

In the field of corrections policy, a different situation has prevailed. As David Garland writes in his excellent analysis of the impact the dramatic reconfiguration of the U.S. penal system has had on practitioners and researchers through the last few decades:

> Hierarchies shifted precariously; settled routines were pulled apart; objectives and priorities were reformulated; standard working practices were altered; and professional expertise was subjected to challenge and viewed with increasing skepticism. The rapid emergence of new ways of thinking and acting on crime, and the concomi-

tant discrediting of older assumptions and professional orientations, ensured that many penal practitioners and academics lived through the 1980's and 1990's with a chronic sense of crisis and professional anomie.[10]

In fact, over the last 30 years, the role of corrections experts and administrators has largely been supplanted by the increasing power of governors and state legislators. In the early 1970s, corrections experts both in and outside government continued to emphasize two major goals: they were concerned about rehabilitation and about stabilizing the size of the U.S. prison system. Indeed, Garland quotes a 1973 National Advisory Commission report that recommended "no new institutions for adults should be built and existing institutions for juveniles should be closed" and concluded that "the prison, the reformatory and the jail have achieved only a shocking level of failure."[11] Indeed, if one examines the policy positions of the American Correctional Association (ACA), the official association for prisons and jails in the United States, these have regularly included the following: support for community corrections and intermediate sanctions, support of rehabilitative and prevention services, early release and community supervision of nonviolent offenders, and effective drug treatment programs.[12]

Yet these recommendations, ensuing from research sponsored by the government and from a correctional group that can scarcely be labeled liberal, did not become the basis of American prison policy in subsequent years. Instead, since the early 1970s, the U.S. prison population has increased eightfold, a policy completely antithetical to the Commission's recommendations. Thus the direction advocated by legislators and politicians—increasing rather than decreasing the use of prisons—has taken precedence over the advice of criminal justice experts. Quoting Garland again: "Rereading the government documents, research reports and expert commentaries of that period [1970], one finds a set of assumptions and expectations that have been completely confounded by subsequent events."[13]

In some cases, law makers have used the writings of academic "experts" to justify policy shifts toward greater retribution and increased reliance on prisons. One such article, Robert Martinson's now-famous "What Works? Questions and Answers about Prison Reform," was written and broadly disseminated in 1974. Martinson took issue with the emphasis on rehabilitation that reigned in the sixties and seventies, surmising, "With few and isolated exceptions, the rehabilitative efforts that have been reported so far have had no appreciable effect on recidivism."[14] His findings, which have been abbreviated "Nothing Works," became well known in policy circles, despite the fact that within a few years Martinson had greatly modified his earlier findings to argue that many well-structured and targeted recidivism programs were successful.[15] These later findings were completely ignored by the same law makers who eagerly cited his initial article.

A more contemporary example of this striking divergence between research and penal policy is correctional education. In 1994, as part of a much larger crime bill proposed by then-President Bill Clinton (discussed in further detail in Chapter 2), Congress eliminated the Pell Grant funding that reimbursed college courses for prisoners; soon thereafter, a number of states followed suit, eliminating college courses from the programs they made available for prisoners. By 1995 only 8 of the 350 college programs in prison nationwide remained in existence.[16]

Compare this popular trend of eliminating college programs for prisoners with the findings of research about the value to prisoners of a college education and/or other professional training. Research indicates that college education reduces recidivism rates;[17] this research is especially well known to practitioners.[18] Specifically in this vein, a recent survey report on prison programming by the Urban Institute concluded: "In general, participants in prison-based educational, vocational and work release programs are more successful—that is they commit fewer crimes and are employed more often and for longer periods of time after release than are non-participants."[19] Another study done by the New York State Department of Corrections for the Graduate Center of the City University of New York found "Women who attended college while in prison were significantly less likely to be reincarcerated (7.7%) than those who did not attend college while in prison (29.9%)."[20]

This finding makes intuitive sense. Coming out of prison with a felony conviction (sometimes more than one), and likely with no stellar record of past employment, a college education is one powerful sign that a person has decided to change substantially and that she has acquired the skills necessary to perform particular jobs. Of course, even with a college education, ex-prisoners find it difficult to procure employment; imagine how much harder this task becomes without a degree or equivalent certification. Given that we know a college education reduces recidivism, and that it increases employment rates for ex-prisoners, who then contribute money back to the government through income and sales taxes, college courses should be widely available in U.S. prisons.

Yet it appears that policy is based much more on politics than on extant research, even as measures such as eliminating the Pell Grants may be justified on seemingly nonpolitical grounds—e.g., by citing funding constraints. But states in financial distress could have recouped their funding for these programs in the form of reduced recidivism and attendant savings in police, court, and prison costs, as well as through tax revenues collected from employed ex-prisoners. Consequently such apparently rational explanations—budgetary problems—may be outward rationalizations for a deeper, more emotionally based unwillingness to fund programs for prisoners in the punitive context of the last several decades. In this environment, substantive arguments about the positive effects of college education have been trumped by political objections against college education that may take the form of "I have to work two jobs to pay for my kid's college education but I have to pay for some convicted violent felon's education? No way!" This convergence of an overall retributive environment and of many people's own understandable economic insecurities (including financial burdens they may feel with regard to paying for their own children's college education) has created a political atmosphere in which research findings about recidivism rates and prison programs are simply overwhelmed.

In the last several years, many state legislatures have actually gone so far as to mandate specifically how a prison should look and operate —an intrusion into expert territory that even 20 years ago was unthinkable. In some states, weight-lifting equipment has been banned either because legislators felt that inmates would become too strong or because this activity was seen as too leisurely. (In contrast, the advent of weight-lifting machines means that staff and inmates are not endangered in the manner they were by free weights' use). In some places, television has been eliminated. Chase Rivelend, the former Corrections Commissioner of Washington State and Colorado, has written about the influence of both state and federal legislatures on prison operations. As Rivelend describes:

> Work and educational opportunities have frequently not kept pace with population growth, and in some instances have been intention-

ally reduced, most frequently due to the actions of legislative bodies. Access to courts previously available to inmates to challenge conditions of confinement has been limited by congressional passage of the Prison Litigation Reform Act, and in some jurisdictions by changes in state laws. Public sentiment and political rhetoric have often limited prison administrators' ability to manage overcrowded prisons in ways and with tools that sound professionals suggest are appropriate. Weights, televisions and other "amenities" have been removed from prisons in many jurisdictions. Overcrowded prisons frequently have not been provided sufficient additional staff to handle the excess population. Some of the volatile conditions that existed in the 1970's exist today.[21]

Such "intrusions" from outside are part of a "get tough" environment that includes, among other elements of a larger agenda, efforts aimed at enacting longer sentences. Creating and changing criminal sentences is a basic and proper function of state legislative bodies, whether or not one agrees with the end result. But not so with other, Foucauldian-sounding measures, aimed at dictating precisely how prisons should operate and what kinds of recreation, programs, and food they should provide, that show exactly how limited the role of corrections experts has become. This intrusion may be felt as especially egregious given that corrections professionals still believe prison programs to be useful for both rehabilitative purposes and the safe management of prisons.

None of this is meant to imply that the decline of influence of correctional experts and the rising influence of state and federal legislators is a purely negative phenomenon. American penal history is full of examples of everyday brutality as well as high-profile events like the Attica riots, caused by horrid conditions and prisoner maltreatment at the hands of corrections practitioners. In many ways, greater legislative involvement in corrections has been exceedingly beneficial to the field; in particular, the oversight of the federal courts has forced state prison systems to be more humane and less overcrowded. No one can argue that greater legislative attention to the horrible abuses perpetrated at the Abu Ghraib prison in Iraq will result in anything but positive changes to at least how the United States military operates prisons and will likely lead to improvement in state systems as well. Indeed, later in this book, I suggest that greater legislative oversight of parole can also contribute mightily to prison reform. In fact, one of the ways that serious prison reform can happen is to have greater oversight and legislative involvement in demanding that prisons adequately prepare prisoners to successfully reenter their communities.

However, when it comes to academic and other expert input into the making of corrections policy (especially sentencing and the amount and kinds of prison programs), greater balance is needed. It is precisely in the area of sentencing—and, in particular, mandatory sentencing—that state legislatures have acted precipitously and with little regard for extant research. A growing and substantial body of research on corrections and sentencing, and on the consequences of mass incarceration, has appeared through the last two decades. Partly as a result of the research attention their field has been getting, as a rule, state correction directors are becoming more highly educated and sophisticated about the field. Thus, it makes a great deal of sense to allow these groups more input into policy making than they now possess. At the same time, legislators should take more of an interest in what actually happens in prisons and parole agencies as well as what happens to those who leave prisons.

In sum, the politics of crime, including charged public reactions that have rapidly become translated into law, provides a key explanation for why contemporary corrections policy has gone in virtually the opposite direction to that advocated by academic and governmental experts and practitioners. Over the last several decades, excellent work in criminology and public policy has been done on the harmful effects of prison to prisoners and their communities;[22] on the hugely disproportionate incarceration of minorities;[23] on misguided sentencing policies in the form of more mandatory and longer prison sentences;[24] and on the value of rehabilitative programs and alternative sanctions to prison.[25] Despite this impressive body of research, prisons and the funds devoted to them continue to grow. As the case of college education for prisoners demonstrates, then, detached analyses have offered little match for the "real world" concerns and constraints that have lately preoccupied governors and legislators.

Indeed, for some law makers, expert research comes across as virtually otherworldly when compared to the power of the crime issue in an environment already punitive toward the poor (who, not surprisingly, commit most "street" crime), and as reflected in the outcries of and stories told by crime victims. These stories, coupled with this underlying animosity toward the poor, the public's fear of crime (until recently on the rise), and the benefits perceived by politicians in appearing tough on crime, have played an enormous role in driving contemporary corrections policy. These factors also constitute the contextual backdrop that must be recognized, and addressed, if significant changes are to ensue.

TAKING THE POLITICS OF CRIME INTO ACCOUNT

Any attempt to have a substantial impact on American correctional policy must take into account—certainly not ignore—the close relationship between crime politics and the sentencing and prison policy processes just described. Of course, this is more easily said than done: the practical issue of how to turn the tide of increased prison populations is one of the most complex political issues facing policy makers today. Because the growth in correctional populations has been spurred by public fears, and by the beliefs of politicians of both parties that increasing prison sentences makes good politics, reversing a 30-year punitive trend has proved nearly impossible.

Compounding this dilemma are several concrete realities. More than 600,000 convicted felons annually leave prisons and return to the community. Since almost everyone who goes to prison leaves (except for the 5% whose sentences are death or life in prison with no parole), the number of people who exit rises yearly. However, based on the rate at which those released from prison are known to return, 67.5% of those who leave prison will be rearrested, and 51.8% will be behind bars again after three years.[26] One reason for this is that parole agencies are aggressively returning parolees to prison for violating the conditions of their parole: parole violators make up the largest-growing group of prison admissions across the country. In fact, from 1990 to 2002 new admissions to prisons have increased by 22% compared to 55% for parole violators.[27] Moreover, about half of these parole violators are returned to prison not for committing new crimes but for breaking one of the many conditions of parole.

Consequently, a powerful tautology is at work in the U.S. correctional system. New laws are constantly being passed and policies enacted that ensure more people will serve prison time each year. More people going to prison means more people coming out of prison. As greater numbers are released, almost half will wind up back in prison three years later. The result is that the politics of punishment, combined with the day-to-day workings of the correctional system, poses an apparently insurmountable obstacle to the task of reversing present trends. Further compounding the difficulty is not just the sheer size and scope of the American corrections system, with over 2 million people incarcerated, but also the growing power and influence of private corrections institutions and corrections unions and the nearly $60 billion annually spent on corrections.[28] This self-perpetuating system seems almost unstoppable. Yet it can be changed.

Social policy usually changes in one of two ways. One possibility is that powerful social movements exert tremendous pressure on elected officials to radically alter public policy. The other is that differences are effected through the "normal" structured policy-making process of the federal and state government. At the state level, for instance, governors' offices and legislators regularly propose new executive rules, programs, laws, and revisions to policy, based on a host of substantive and political concerns. Of course, these ways of bringing about change are often interconnected; frequently, a symbiotic connection builds between the force of social movements and the more "inside baseball" political processes through which new laws and policies are forged. Successful social movements may find that policy makers have made subtle accommodations to their radical agendas. Alternatively, the results of the normal policy-making process can be a catalyst for creating new social movements if newly adopted measures or laws are viewed as problematic by one group or another.

This book focuses on how change can be effected on the governmental level of the policy-making and legislative process. My argument is not designed to mobilize huge numbers of people to protest prison policy so much as to make a broad case that governmental actors, as well as the larger public, have good reason to reverse the punitive trends of the last 30 years. Of course, this goal can be aided by the creation and success of existing grassroots organizations that also seek to effect change. Moreover, as policy changes are implemented that coincide with many existing groups' goals, these changes can strengthen movements and assist in widening their appeal, thereby further providing an impetus toward institutional reform. For this reason, it seems useful briefly to discuss the role of social movements in changing policy in general, as well as the current state of several community-based prison and sentencing reform efforts.

SOCIAL MOVEMENTS

The U.S. civil rights and feminist movements may be the two most important recent examples of large-scale grassroots efforts to protest against and significantly change government policy. Huge numbers of people were mobilized to protest myriad governmental laws and policies that discriminated against minorities and women; in a relatively short time period, these movements succeeded in realizing major legislative and governmental reforms. In terms of achieving the most radical changes in social policy in the shortest period of time, then, large-scale social movements may be the most effective way to bring about change.[29]

Though the issue of mass incarceration has not risen to the level where huge nationwide pressure is being exerted on law makers to change America's penal policy, some local movements around the country have succeeded in calling attention to the problem and in many cases have played a key role in getting laws passed that ease the severity of some criminal sentences. Some of these groups have also managed to get policy makers to reverse plans to build new prisons and detention centers. Among such social movement groups are the Drop the Rock effort in New York State, whose goal is to change the Rockefeller Drug Laws, and the No More Prisons group that works to limit prison growth and deflate support for private prisons and for companies such as Sodexho Marriott that have been large shareholders in private prisons and also provide food service on college campuses. One group largely centered in California, Critical Resistance, has been active in prison and juvenile justice reform. Another group, Families Against Mandatory Minimums (FAMM), has been especially active and successful in community organizing and pressuring legislators in Michigan to roll back mandatory minimum drug sentences.

As the American prison system has grown and the proportion of minorities incarcerated has increased, more of these grassroots groups have sprung up around the country. It is not surprising that diverse protests would spring up around criminal justice issues when the total incarceration rate for whites in the United States is 681 per 100,000 compared to 1,778 per 100,000 for Hispanics and 4,834 per 100,000 for Blacks,[30] and when approximately one-third of all Black men between the ages of 20 and 29 are under some form of criminal justice control.[31] Shocking, too, is that if incarceration rates remain unchanged, the statistical chances that a Black baby born in 2001 will go to prison are 32.2%.[32] These statistics, and the inequalities they approximate, have motivated many of the groups discussed above to feel that social action is needed.

Making it difficult for mass incarceration to become a full-blown social movement issue, though, is that the group under discussion are largely convicted felons or, in the case of jails, people charged with crimes. And, whether convicted or just charged, "criminals" have not historically engendered much sympathy with the American public. As the public becomes more educated about class and racial inequalities manifested in conviction rates, and about the large percentage of people who are nonviolent drug offenders, many may also become more sympathetically disposed to reform.[33] Nevertheless, the incarcerated are one of the most demonized groups on the American cultural landscape. Grassroots groups hoping to build a mass nationwide anti-incarceration movement face daunting challenges. Yet perhaps these movements can be strengthened to the extent that they put forward specific proposals that state legislators can reasonably and practically support.

CHANGING POLICY

Before turning to a specific discussion of how official policies and sentencing laws can be altered, some clarification is needed. Although many writers and analysts refer in passing to the "U.S. prison system," this system is actually composed of 51 separate and distinct units. The overwhelming majority of people in prison in the United States live in one of the 50 state prison systems, along with Washington, D.C., that collectively house slightly more than 1.2 million prisoners.[34] The great majority of crimes are state crimes, breaking one or more of the penal laws created by state legislatures. Moreover, some defendants receive time served for violating specific state laws that, in other states, might not be crimes at all. By contrast, the federal prison system, run by the Federal Bureau of Prisons, houses 159,000 prisoners, though the federal prison system is increasing far more rapidly than state systems.[35] A crime rises to the level of a federal offense when it breaks one or more of the federal penal codes passed by Congress. Examples of federal crimes are kidnapping, bank robbery, and securities fraud.

From a policy perspective, these facts have complicated repercussions. Reversing 30 years of incarceration policy means that significant changes must take place in most, if not all, of the 50 states. While the governance of the prison system is the same in every state—the governor almost always runs the prisons—the similarity ends there. States diverge greatly in their respective political cultures, ideologies, public concerns, and governmental priorities (including how much importance they accord public safety). For example, Iowa has a rural, farm-based economy, a part-time citizen legislature, and a relatively homogeneous population. This is quite different from diverse California, with its multifaceted economy, large cities, and full-time professional legislature.

Then, too, state correction systems differ in terms of the functions they perform. Though each state oversees its own prison system, some also contain probation and parole agencies (e.g., North Carolina and Louisiana); others contain parole agencies but not probation (e.g., California); still others do not run either probation or parole at the state level (e.g., New York). In some states, probation is operated at the county level (e.g., Texas or Arizona), while in others it is a state function alone (e.g., Michigan or Washington). One way of visualizing these differences is to look at sharp divergences in the recent growth rate of many state prison systems since 1990, as Figure 1.1 indicates.

Though the average rate of growth for the U.S. was 86% from 1990 to 2002, within individual states, rates of increase ranged from 22% in New York to 224% in Texas. Some rates of growth seem unexpectedly high. Though the increases in the California and Texas prison systems are fairly well known, the astounding 216% increase for Idaho and 114% increase for Hawaii were barely discussed in the media and by the public. Then, too, these differing rates of growth reflect a myriad of state-specific issues. The California system may have grown because mandatory minimum sentences for repeat felony offenders were created, and as a result of changes in parole policy. In Rhode Island, though, increases may reflect the impact of long probation sentences and the returning to prison of many probationers for long periods if, or when, they violate the terms of their probation. Every state seems to have its own story, and complicated reasons, for the increases in incarceration it has experienced.

Consequently, affecting national incarceration rates would involve the difficult task of changing most states' diverse prison and prison-

Figure 1.1
Percentage Increase of Sentenced Prisoners under Jurisdiction of
Correctional Authorities, Selected States, 1990–2002

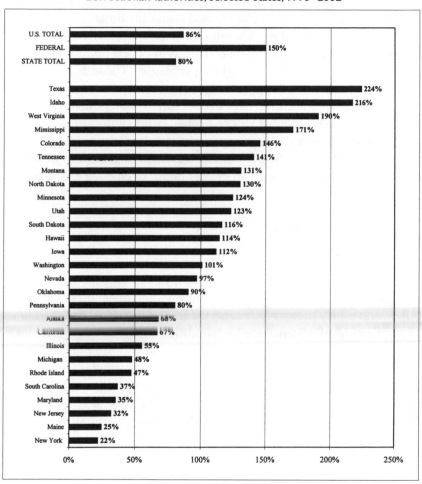

Source: Bureau of Justice Statistics, *Prisoners in 2000*, and BJS File Corpop02: Prisoners under State or Federal Jurisdiction.

related policies. Yet Figure 1.1 also underscores an overarching similarity among all the states: every state increased the size of its prison system over the last decade. While the states did so at very different rates, not one state system remained at the same level from 1990 to 2002, and no state came close to decreasing its system's size. Ironically, this may create a commonality among state legislatures and governors that can become a ground for arguing for change. For as prison systems have increased, so have the percentages of state budgets devoted to this governmental function. States therefore share the problem of how to meet all their budgetary needs in constrained economic times.

Over the last several years, a number of national, state, and local developments have occurred in the economy, in public opinion, in criminal justice policy, and in crime fighting strategies. These developments have created a window of opportunity to reverse the huge growth in incarceration that has occurred over the last three decades; taken together, they provide the building blocks of a coherent and substantive political strategy that can alter the way we punish offenders while carefully safeguarding public safety. Below I briefly summarize these four developments before discussing them in greater depth in ensuing chapters.

TAKING ADVANTAGE OF FOUR RECENT DEVELOPMENTS

In very different ways, four recent developments suggest that stronger arguments can be made today than at previous times to persuade the public and policy makers to reverse the tide of increased incarceration. These four developments are the condition of the states' economies, changes in public opinion, the success of New York City and other select states or cities in reducing crime without substantially increasing the use of prison, and the huge increase in technical parole violators' return to prison, which offers a relatively easy way of reforming the criminal justice system and freeing badly needed funds for other state functions.

The Economy

During 2001, the United States officially entered a recession.[36] The economic boom of the 1990s began to seem like a distant memory amid the highly visible collapse of the dotcom sector that earlier created young millionaires and an entire class of aspiring entrepreneurs. The misfortune of this technology sector was a metaphor for the national economy. When national unemployment rates increased from 4.9% to 5.4% over September–October 2001, and as the one-year decline in industrial production continued into November 2001, economists at the

National Bureau of Economic Research declared the United States to be in a recession.[37] The terrorist attacks of September 11, 2001, aggravated unemployment even further, as hundreds of thousands of jobs were lost in the tourism and financial sectors of the economy.[38] Nowhere were the effects of the deteriorating national economy felt more than at the level of state budgets.

By 2002, many states were experiencing such drastic revenue short-falls that they started to implement dramatic spending reductions and program retrenchment. During 2002, 44 states had significantly declin-ing revenues and 36 were cutting back on core state services. Together, in that one year alone, states had revenue shortfalls of over $40 billion.[39] The country's largest states, California and New York, struggled with budget deficits of $8 billion and $11 billion, respectively.[40] Almost over-night, it seemed, states that were once thriving and driving the national economy were in desperate fiscal condition. Moreover states that expe-rienced surpluses in the late 1990s, allowing for expanded services and the delivery of tax cuts, now had to make extremely difficult choices about cutting services or increasing revenues through new taxes or fees.

By 2003, more than a year and a half after the end of the national re-cession, and with some improvement in national economic indicators, the fiscal situation of states continued to deteriorate. On top of huge deficits in 2001 and 2002, 37 states continued to cut their budgets by al-most $15 billion, the largest spending cut since 1979.[41] These cuts came on top of almost $13 billion in reductions made in 2002. Though econo-mists are encouraged by recent signs of improvement in the national economy, the near-term fiscal outlook for states is still bleak, given the cumulative effect of tax cuts, uncontrollable growth in Medicaid costs, and huge outstanding financial needs in the areas of education and health care.

In 2004, with the national economy slowly improving, state law makers nevertheless continue to develop their budgets with extreme care since many states are still in very precarious fiscal condition, and the majority of states continue to struggle with funding essential services.

As state legislatures and governors around the country scoured their expenses, an interesting and almost universal trend became appar-ent. Over the 13-year period from 1988 to 2001, the only core function of state government that grew as a total percentage of state budgets was corrections.[42] The other state expenditure to grow as a proportion of state budgets was Medicaid, but states have little control over the nationally mandated costs of that entitlement program. In contrast, while corrections and Medicaid grew, every other basic service provided by state governments—primary and secondary education, transportation, environmental protection, and public assistance—declined as a percentage of state budgets from 1988 to 2001.

The combination of declining or no growth revenues generally and disproportionate spending on prisons specifically can be a key component of a state-based strategy to reduce spending on corrections. This is especially relevant now, as many states are beginning to eye prisons as a possible source of spending cuts, a development unfamiliar only three years ago.[43] Even with the country now slowly emerging from its recession, according to economists, state economies are likely to be exceptionally constrained over the next few years as they cope with deep declines in revenues and service cuts they have been forced to enact over the last several years.[44]

Changing Public Opinion

While states have disproportionately funded prisons in comparison with other state services, national public opinion on crime and fear of crime has slowly but surely altered. According to the annual national Harris polls conducted over the last twenty years, crime no longer dominates all other issues as the one about which Americans are most concerned.[45] Instead, crime dropped substantially from its place as the most urgent issue Americans thought government should address from the mid-1980s through 1994. In 1994, 36% of Americans thought crime and violence was the number-one issue that government needed to address; by 2003, this number was less than 0.5%.[46] Crime has been replaced by education as the state-specific issue most frequently rated as Americans' primary concern over the last seven years, even though the amount of funding devoted by states to education has proportionately declined.[47] This disjuncture—public concerns about education rising as public funding has declined—has not been lost on governors and legislators and is a central part of the overall strategy and argument I propose here.

In addition to the Harris poll, a national poll conducted in 2002 by Peter D. Hart Research Associates[48] found a somewhat surprising turnaround by Americans on the issue of punishing criminal offenders. Two-thirds (65%) of the respondents thought America needed a tougher approach to the causes of crime, compared to one-third (32%) who favored a tougher approach to crime in the form of longer sentences and less parole.[49] In 1994, the country was equally split on this issue. In addition, more than half of Americans (54%) now think the number-one goal of the criminal justice system should be prevention and rehabilitation, compared to 39% who think punishment and enforcement should be the criminal justice system's top goal.[50]

All told, these polls suggest that a shift in public attitudes toward crime and criminal justice has taken place in the last seven or eight years. No doubt, one reason opinions have changed relates to the national drop in crime since 1993. According to the Federal Bureau of Investigation, violent crime plummeted by 26% between 1993 and 2002;[51] fear of crime seems to have dropped as well. (The question of how prison expansion has contributed to this decline will be more fully discussed in Chapter 4.) Nonetheless, Americans have started to think about crime differently than in prior decades, and these opinions, while not fully recognized by the country's policy makers, are likely to affect U.S. correctional policy over the next decade.

Thus, pressure on state law makers to reduce overall spending as prison spending continues to grow, and the shift of public opinion away from crime toward education, can constitute important elements in building a case for change.

The Case of New York City

Seemingly unrelated to the broad developments just discussed, New York City's recent crime-reducing experience nevertheless is germane to sentencing and prison policies on the national level. I will use this experience as a lesson not in public order or zero-tolerance policing strategies but in how New York managed so dramatically to reduce crime while simultaneously reducing its use of prison.

From 1993 to 2003,[52] violent crime in New York City declined by a remarkable 64% and homicides by 69%.[53] This represents a decrease of more than twice the national average; New York City's decline in violent crime is responsible for 16% of the national drop in crime from 1993 to 2001.[54] Because New York City has therefore garnered a national and even international reputation for cutting its crime rate to a fraction of what it was less than a decade ago, debate has ensued over the causes of the city's success. Should the decrease be credited to new policing strategies, to changing demographics or drug markets, or to some combination of the three? For this book's purposes, though, ascertaining the causes of New York City's crime decline is a side note. What I am most interested in here is how the case of New York City is potentially relevant to the making of criminal justice policy on the national level. How has New York managed to achieve such substantial decreases in crime while also significantly decreasing the numbers of people sent to prison during the same period?

Despite the fact that the New York Police Department (NYPD) made a record number of total arrests and had a relatively constant and then slowly declining level of felony arrests during these years, almost half the number of people from New York City sentenced to prison in 1993 were sentenced in 2001.[55] Also noteworthy is that this decrease began immediately, in 1994, and continued steadily through the remainder of the decade. Thus, the largest and most well publicized crime decrease in the country was accomplished with not an increase but a decrease in the use of prison. And consequently, while for some it may make intuitive sense that a toughening-up of the criminal justice system by sending more people to prison for longer periods would be required for any crime reduction effort to be successful, this was simply not true in New York City.

The potential national ramifications of this observation should not be underestimated. Though New York may have been regarded with suspicion in other areas of the country, the city, and especially its Mayor during the crime decrease, Rudolph W. Giuliani, received attention and accolades for anti-crime efforts from virtually every part of the United States. It has become common for city and state officials from around the country to visit in order to learn how the city managed this "New York miracle." That this feat was accompanied by less rather than more prison use is a largely unrecognized and unreported fact that nevertheless has clear implications for public safety and corrections policy. Indeed, the experience raises a key question that state policy makers should be forced to answer: If New York City managed to reduce violent crime and murder so substantially without increasing its use of prison, why do we have to keep building and spending money on prisons in our own backyards?

After New York City, San Diego had the largest crime decrease of any major U.S. city over 1993–2001.[56] While San Diego and New York are obviously very different and have used quite different law enforcement strategies, this California city also achieved crime reductions while reducing the number of people sent to prison. Statistics from other states' experiences, too, may help spur renewed political debate about rising prison populations: in particular, no apparent relationship seems to exist between increased use of prison and crime reductions. In this regard New York State, which increased its prison population by 9% from 1992 to 2002 as violent crime fell by 53%, can be compared with West Virginia, which increased its prison population by 171% even as crime increased by 10%.[57] Such comparisons may provide important and useful information to state policy makers.

Technical Parole and Probation Violators

This issue suggests both a need for a new strategy to reduce the size of the U.S. prison system and a central component of that strategy. Only a handful of people in the criminal justice system know that striking increases in the number of parolees sent back to prison on technical violations have been driving the size and cost of the current prison system. Every parole and probation agency in the United States has a number of conditions that must be met while the parolee or probationer is under supervision. The standard conditions usually include having a job, regular reporting, not consorting with other felons, abstinence from drugs, and attending all court-assigned programs. In some cases, additional conditions include community service, drug treatment, or vocational training programs. Not meeting one or more of these conditions is considered a technical violation of parole or probation. In the case of parole, this can result in a parolee being immediately returned to prison or jail to serve the rest of his or her sentence, if the parole officer files a violation order with the paroling agency or court and a judge or parole official finds that a technical violation indeed occurred.

Important to emphasize is that technical violations do not include any new crime(s) committed by a parolee or probationer but simply nonviolent infractions of someone's terms of supervision. Thus it seems telling indeed that, from 1990 to 2002, new admissions to prisons have increased by 22% compared to 55% for parole violators.[58] About half of all these parole violators are returned to prison for violating one or more of the many conditions of parole, not for committing new crimes.

In fact, of the 52% of all prisoners who return to prison after their release, over half, or 26% are returned for technical parole violations.[59]

In many states, technical parole violators make up the largest single category of prison admissions. For instance, of the 128,000 prison admissions in 2001 in California, 74,000, or 58%, were technical parole violators.[60] Furthermore, California has approximately 115,000 people on parole at any one time.[61] For the last several years until 2002, California parole agents have "technically violated" the parole of almost 70,000 of those parolees each year and sent them back to prison. Again, these violations are not for new crimes but for infractions such as drug use (or, in the parlance of the criminal justice field, "dirty urines"), nonreporting, and not attending treatment programs. On average, these 70,000 parolees were sent back to prison for 160 days. This means that technical violators were occupying almost 30,000 prison beds at any one time, at an annual cost to California taxpayers of almost $1 billion.[62]

In Chapter 5, I examine in depth why California and other states' parole officers have been technically violating such large numbers of parolees. For now, suffice it to say that both parole and probation are among the most poorly financed agencies in government, and certainly in the criminal justice system. As a result, parole officers have few or no resources at their disposal to address violative behaviors such as drug use, not attending treatment, or irregular reporting or nonreporting. Faced with a decision either to ignore violations of the conditions of parole or to use the only other option available to them—prison—parole officers consistently choose prison. In a political era dominated by toughness on crime and risk avoidance at all costs, the decision to send huge numbers of technical parole violators to prison for several months because there are no other alternatives may end up being rational in an irrational environment. But a different way to proceed is conceivable and appropriate. In lieu of prison, creating intermediate sanctions for technical parole violators would protect public safety as much as, if not more than, prison, and at a far lower economic cost for the American public.

Technical parole and probation violations tend to take place far from public view and thus are a little-understood aspect of the criminal justice system. Few state legislatures realize the extent of this problem in their own states, much less the reasons why parolees have been sent back to prison on technical violations. This is partly because technical violations take place in "private," with only a few parties aware of what has occurred. But compounding the problem's invisibility is also that little detailed national or even statewide data have been collected about the issue. Existing data on the federal level tends to be aggregate-level information by state that, while differentiating technical parole violations from violations as a result of new crimes, has exceptionally little detail about the specific reasons for violations or the length of time spent in prison for different violations. There are also self-reporting data from interviewed prisoners that cannot be disaggregated down to the state level.[63] The national data on probation are even worse, since in many states probation is a county function and in others a state or judicial function. Establishing uniform and detailed data collection for all these different probation agencies has proven very difficult. Moreover, the problem tends to be tautological: the reason little national information exists on technical parole violations is that there are scarce state-level data for the federal government to collect.

Therefore, at present, increases in the correctional system are driven by factors that are neither transparent nor subject to oversight by policy and law makers. In addition, political and organizational incentives conspire to encourage this system of maximizing the numbers of people sent back to prison for technical violations. The good news, though, is that this system is ripe for reform, and that change need not involve the complicated process of rewriting or repealing legislation. Here it is helpful that parole is a government function controlled by the state executive and (nominally) overseen by legislatures; this means that changes can be made, if necessary, within the purview of executive policy, without new legislation having to be passed. Moreover, in the context of the budgetary deficits states are facing, most governors and state legislatures, even quite conservative ones, are likely to be interested in reexamining this mysterious process that is driving U.S. incarceration rates.

None of these developments ameliorates the harsh attitudes that much of the country harbors toward those who are poor. If anything, the recent state of the U.S. economy, characterized by layoffs, retrenchment, and economic insecurity, may have worsened those attitudes. However, I argue that these developments provide a significant (though perhaps temporary) counterweight to, in Young's words, "a sociology of vindictiveness."[64] This counterweight can become the basis for a strategy to downsize prison systems even in a still powerfully punitive environment.

2

Unintended Consequences

WHEN RAY KRONE was released from an Arizona prison in April 2002 (after DNA evidence proved he was not responsible for the 1991 murder of a Phoenix bartender), he became the one hundredth person exonerated and released from death row since 1973. All told, as of December 2003, 112 prisoners were found innocent and released from death row. More than half these releases happened during the last decade.[1]

Then, as a result of the sheer number of high-profile exonerations over the last decade and the 2000 moratorium on capital punishment declared by Illinois Governor Ryan, public opinion on the death penalty began to change. In 1995, national polls showed that 13% of Americans were not in favor of the death penalty for a person convicted of murder. By 2003, more than twice as many, or 28%, opposed capital punishment.[2]

Public opinion polls also began to show a decline in the relative importance of crime as an issue of concern for Americans as well as a willingness to use alternatives to prison for nonviolent criminals.

Dramatically different, too, was that 26% fewer violent crimes had been committed in 2002 than in 1992.[3]

But one thing that did not alter alongside these significant criminal justice events and shifts in public opinion on crime was that each year more people have gone to prison and jails than the year before. In short, crime has gone down and our attitudes have changed, but our incarceration practices have not.

Indeed, as the number of people incarcerated has grown eightfold over three consecutive decades, many academic and policy observers have objected vigorously. Yet, despite an array of critical voices, most state prison systems have continued to swell. Why? It may be that several political, social, and economic factors—operating together and considered here, when taken together, as "structural impediments" —made it difficult for diverse critiques, however legitimate, to be addressed.

Central to this chapter's purpose is the contention that any serious effort to promote a reform strategy must anticipate and answer, rather than avoid, the problems and counterarguments that have stymied efforts to significantly "downsize" the prison system. Let me begin, then, by summarizing the various critiques of the prison system that have been lodged, for good reason, to date.

THE INEQUITABLE USE OF INCARCERATION

Perhaps the most well known critique of current punitive trends is that racial and class biases skew who goes to prison. The incarceration rate of Caucasians is about one-eighth that of Blacks and approximately one-third that of Hispanics.[4] Perhaps the most disturbing statistic in terms of the racial imbalance of who goes to prison is that if current incarceration rates stay constant, 1 in 3 Black males can expect to go to prison in his lifetime, compared to 1 in 6 Hispanic males and 1 in 17 white males.[5]

Also striking is that the overwhelming majority of prisoners are poor, and that their prior employment levels are exceptionally low.[6] Related to these observations are criticisms of the criminal justice system for being racist in its day to day operations of arresting, indicting, convicting, and sentencing offenders.[7] For example, research shows that rates of illegal drug use for whites and Blacks are similar, with almost 9% for white and almost 10% for Blacks,[8] yet this proportion is not remotely reflected in the demography of the nation's prison population. Other critics have spurred debate over decade-long disparities in federal criminal penalties for powdered cocaine (used predominantly by whites) as opposed to crack cocaine (used predominantly by Blacks). For instance, the 1986 Anti–Drug Abuse Act set exactly the same minimum penalty—five years—for selling 500 grams of cocaine as for selling 5 grams of crack. This fact alone has generated controversy and provided understandable fuel for advocates of federal sentencing reform.[9]

In addition, critiques of racial and class inequities go beyond relatively narrow discussion of how and why minorities are disproportionately incarcerated to larger issues of state control over populations for whom neither jobs nor a decent standard of living has been available. Punishment through incarceration has often been indicted as a social control mechanism for containing a potentially problematic population;

moreover, the prison system has been characterized as functional in driving down national unemployment rates (since state prisoners do not show up as unemployed while incarcerated).[10] Furthermore, current U.S. Census rules require that prisoners be counted as residents of the county in which they are incarcerated. Since state prisoners are overwhelmingly poor minorities from urban areas, and prisons tend to be in white suburban or rural areas, these suburban or rural communities have their congressional representation strengthened while poor and minority urban communities find that their numbers have diminished.[11]

Michael Tonry, perhaps the leading scholar and critic of sentencing policy in the United States, lays much of the blame for disproportionate rates of incarceration on the War on Drugs that unfairly targeted young, urban minority males for arrest and imprisonment (and for whom replacements were always ready to step into the drug-dealing jobs they vacated). He also is highly critical of the underlying politics behind this "war":

> The evidence on the effectiveness of recent crime control and drug abuse policies, as the first section [of his article] demonstrated, cannot justify their racially disparate effects on Blacks, or, as this section demonstrates, can the claims that such policies merely manifest the people's will or respect the interests of Black victims. All that is left is politics of the ugliest kind. The War on Drugs and the set of harsh crime control policies in which it was enmeshed were adopted to achieve political, not policy, objectives, and it is the adoption for political purposes of policies with foreseeable disparate impacts, the use of disadvantaged Black Americans as means to the achievement of White politicians' electoral ends, that must in the end be justified. It cannot.[12]

Loic Wacquant, a sociologist who has written about prisons and corrections policy, says in a more radical and controversial critique of America's penal policy that the astoundingly high Black incarceration rates over the last 30 years can be explained "as a result of the obsolescence of the ghetto as a device for caste control and a correlative need for a substitute apparatus for keeping (unskilled) African Americans 'in their place' i.e. in a subordinate and confined position in physical, social and symbolic space."[13]

Not surprising, then, are the numerous critiques, from a myriad of perspectives, of the most striking aspect of incarceration in the United States: the astounding racial imbalance found in our prisons and jails.

UNFAIR AND SHORT-SIGHTED SENTENCING POLICY

A second common objection to current trends emphasizes the rapid rise of harsh mandatory minimums and "truth in sentencing" laws. Truth in sentencing refers to the replacement of indeterminate sentencing schemes that provided a range of years someone could spend in prison (along with the possibility of early release on parole) with a determinate or "straight" sentence (e.g., five years) that did not allow for the possibility of early release on parole.[14] Along with three strikes legislation and the abolition of parole, such laws have greatly fueled America's three-decade-long incarceration boom. Over this period, as critics have pointed out, criminal penalties became harsher for virtually all categories of crime. Moreover, federal sentencing guidelines significantly restricted judges' discretionary power in meting out criminal penalties, proscribing specific penalties based on prior criminal history and current offense. Thus three strikes laws, in effect in nearly half the states, require up to life in prison after a third felony conviction; in some states, this third felony must be a violent conviction, while in others any conviction counts.[15]

Various other trends have been thoroughly documented as well, focusing critical attention both on whether punishments are proportional to offenses and on whether any general or specific crime deterrence functions are served by such increasingly punitive measures.[16]

Also influential in most states is a recent movement that requires offenders, especially those convicted of violent crimes, to serve at least 85% of their sentences.[17] Then, too, the total or partial elimination of parole in 20 states has contributed to longer times served, as have the increased penalties attached to the use and sale of illegal drugs. In fact, from 1980 to 2001, 25% of the increase in the U.S. prison population has been for nonviolent drug convictions.[18] Though New York State's Rockefeller Drug Laws are probably the most well known example of severe sentencing for drug offenders, clearly the trend to incarcerate those who use and sell drugs has been a national one.

One result of this plethora of sentencing changes, which taken together have greatly increased lengths of prison stays, is that the U.S.

prison population has begun to age.[19] One effect of this aging population (in addition to increased medical costs) is that people are being
kept in prison well beyond the crime-committing ages (16–35) when the
overwhelming number of offenses is known to occur. In fact, as the
prison population ages, many states are opening geriatric prisons.

In summing up the weight of the evidence on how all the sentencing changes over the last 25 years (more mandatory sentences, more determinate as opposed to indeterminate sentences, generally increasing
sentence lengths, and more three strikes laws) have affected the crime
rate, Michael Tonry writes:

> No one doubts that having some penalties is better than having none.
> What is widely doubted is the proposition that changes in penalties
> have any significant effects on behavior. Most crime-control scholars
> are doubtful because that proposition is refuted by the clear weight of
> the research evidence and because every nonpartisan expert body in
> the United States, Canada, and England that has examined the evi-
> dence has reached that same conclusion.[20]

UNINTENDED CONSEQUENCES OF INCARCERATION

In the last several years, a critical literature has also burgeoned about
socially detrimental "unintended" consequences of incarceration.[21] In
this vein, concerns have been expressed about how mass incarceration
affects the communities and family members of those incarcerated, let
alone the lives of prisoners themselves after they have been released
from prison. For example, some research suggests that, after losing a
large number of young men to prison, communities may experience a
"tipping point": specifically, Dina Rose and Todd Clear found that several Florida communities suffered an increase in crime once the proportion of people sent to prison passed a particular level.[22] Rose and
Clear argue that, once the percentage of incarcerated young men exceeded that point, social disorganization increased as many families became single-parent-headed; thereafter, foster care placements and juvenile crime also tended to rise.

Other detrimental consequences of incarceration have been noted.
For instance, a diverse group of researchers and analysts have become
increasingly concerned about problems of "prisoner reentry." This term

refers to hefty barriers encountered by ex-prisoners as they attempt to reintegrate themselves back into their communities. Such barriers are sometimes exacerbated over the course of lengthy prison stays, during which, in some cases, little or no remedial programs may have been offered.

The structural barriers to successful reentry include federal policies that deny housing and welfare benefits to some convicted felons, a lack of job training and placement for a hard-to-employ population, exceedingly limited drug treatment and mental health programs, and an almost complete absence of transitional housing for the significant number of prisoners returning with no place to live. When the hundreds of thousands of returning prisoners are confronted with these kinds of impediments in trying to live a crime-free life, it is not surprising that recidivism rates stay remarkably high.

In addition, two-thirds of women who are imprisoned are mothers.[23] Since many were single parents to begin with, imprisonment further aggravated problems these women were experiencing, sometimes leading to increased foster care placements. Indeed, preliminary research on children of incarcerated mothers shows a whole range of negative behavior and attachment issues that can ultimately result in higher rates of crime as well as large financial costs.[24] In addition, 55% of incarcerated men in state facilities are fathers[25] who are unable to see, support, or at a minimum make child support payments to their children. More than half of all incarcerated mothers and fathers never have a visit from their children, a figure that is particularly disturbing when 1.5 million children in the United States have a parent who is in prison.[26]

Incarceration also has a significant effect on the employment prospects for those released from jail or prison. The stigma attached to having been incarcerated, especially for a felony conviction, significantly lowers the long-term employment and earning potential for those leaving prison. Since those who leave prison are overwhelmingly young minority men, these effects are felt by those with the least power in the labor market. Bruce Western and Katherine Beckett found that adult incarceration lowers paid employment by around 5 to 10 weeks a year, and the effect of having over a million men in prison and jail "generates the equivalent of a full year of unemployment for more than 200,000 American men. In the long run, incarceration thus significantly undermines the productivity and employment chances of the male workforce."[27]

In their excellent edited volume on the collateral consequences of imprisonment, Mauer and Chesney-Lynd detail "invisible punishments" for current and former prisoners, including the denial of welfare benefits to drug offenders; the impact on families and children; the huge moral, legal, and practical effects of felony disenfranchisement laws in many states that bar ex-prisoners from voting; and the negative influence on communities that send large numbers of their young people to prison.[28]

UNDERUSE AND UNDERFUNDING OF ALTERNATIVES TO INCARCERATION AND REHABILITATION PROGRAMS

Still another valid criticism of current policies is that alternatives to incarceration programs have been underused and underfunded, despite their promise or proven records of success. There are several reasons why this critique is quite important, and why greater investments in alternatives to incarceration, including what Todd Clear and others have referred to as a community justice–oriented approach, would likely yield significant public safety, cost, and moral benefits.

One reason involves sheer scale: most convicted criminals in the United States are not in prison or jail; in fact, of the 6.7 million people under criminal justice supervision in the United States in 2002, approximately 71%, or 4.7 million people, have been either sentenced to probation (4 million) or are on parole (750,000).[29] Though prisons have received far more public, academic, and policy attention than probation or parole, and have been the recipients of much more funding, community-based sanctions clearly have the numbers to merit paying attention to them. Yet the lack of attention that has actually been paid probation and parole is rendered especially disturbing by the fact that 52%[30] of all probationers have been convicted of a felony, as have all 750,000 of the country's parolees.

Second, devoting adequate resources to probation and parole is simply a far less costly proposition than spending money on prisons. The cost of supervising one person per year on probation or parole is about $200,[31] compared to over $20,000 for prison.[32] With funding disparities like these, it is little wonder that probation and parole have been the brunt of tremendous criticism over the last few decades. Of probation, David Rothman has said, "Investigative committees of all types, whether comprised of legislators, social workers, blue ribbon grand jurors, or concerned citizens returned a similar verdict: probation was implemented in a most superficial, routine, and careless fashion, as a 'more or less hit-or-miss affair' a 'blundering head.'"[33] On parole, Samuel Walker has commented, "Parole supervision, whether regular or intensive, suffers from the same basic problem: the superficiality of the 'treatment' often involving routine monthly meetings with parole officers and little in the way of meaningful services."[34]

Yet community corrections agencies have been relatively starved for resources while more popular and highly visible prison systems have received the bulk of most states' corrections funding. Nor is it surprising, given that probation and parole have been so severely underfunded, that these agencies' caseloads have ballooned out of control over the last several decades. Whereas the 1967 President's Crime Commission recommended that the ideal caseload for both probation and parole would be 30 cases for each officer, the national average for probation is about 150:1 and parole 80:1.[35] In many jurisdictions the caseloads are far higher than this national average: in New York City, probation caseloads approach 250:1,[36] and in Los Angeles, most probationers are on caseloads of 1000:1.[37]

The third reason this critique is so important is that, even amid this bleak situation, a number of community corrections programs have been remarkably successful. As Joan Petersilia, one of the country's foremost experts in this area, has noted, "community correctional programs do work. When probation and parole programs are targeted to appropriate clientele, and when the programs are delivered consistently over several months and incorporate treatment and surveillance activities, offender recidivism can be reduced."[38] Indeed, innovative probation/police and community programs such as Boston's Operation Night Light, Washington's SMART Partnership for police and community corrections, and Chicago's Project Safeway have received high marks from evaluators for their performance in bringing down crime and controlling costs.[39]

Moreover, despite the pessimistic interpretation of Martinson's 1974 "What Works?" article—namely, that relatively few rehabilitation programs have resulted in declining recidivism rates—other analysts have reached far more positive conclusions. Canadian researchers have conducted much of the research over the last 15 years on the effectiveness of program interventions, and their findings are promising. As Paul Gendreau, Francis Cullen, and James Bonta write about the results, taken together, of these studies:

> First, if one surveys all the treatment studies that had control group comparisons, as Mark Lipsey (1992) did for 443 studies, 64 percent of the studies reported reductions in favor of the treatment group. The average reduction in recidivism summed across the 443 studies was 10 percent. Secondly, according to Lipsey, when the results were broken down by the general type of program (e.g., employment), reductions in recidivism ranged from 10–18 percent.[40]

In a recent review of correctional treatment programs, Gerald G. Gaes et al. assessed the value of rehabilitation programs in somewhat more reserved but still largely positive terms. According to this group of researchers, "correctional treatment for adults has modest but substantively meaningful effects. Even though the level of recidivism is modest, even small reductions can produce future reductions in criminality."[41] Finally, critics of current trends have also proposed innovative alternatives in the form of community justice and restorative justice approaches. While these suggestions are more broadly philosophical than the specific programmatic initiatives mentioned above, they share with them a commitment to attempt to resolve crime-related problems outside prison walls. According to Todd Clear, community justice is "different from traditional criminal justice in three important ways: It is based on the neighborhood rather than on legal jurisdiction; it is problem solving rather than adversarial; and it is restorative rather than retributive."[42] Community justice, as opposed to traditional criminal justice, encourages and presupposes active community participation in planning and participating in programs to prevent and address offending.

At the heart of the concept of community justice is the realization that some neighborhoods or communities have a much higher concentration than others of ex-prisoners and persons currently under parole or probation supervision. Higher-than-average proportions of residents in these communities end up in jail or prison, and it is to these same neighborhoods that they will return after their release; after their return, they may wind up reoffending and in prison yet again.[43] Some studies have found that as many as 2% of particular communities' residents were sent to prison in just one year; obviously, over a period of several years, such communities house an extraordinarily high concentration of current and ex-offenders in their midst.

Consequently, a key principle of community justice is that the cycle of locking people up and releasing them back into communities with no proffered services serves only to further deteriorate the quality of life in such neighborhoods. Additionally, this philosophy's working assumption is that community residents have both a personal and a collective stake in helping break the cycle. Everyone is affected by the social disorganization that results from sending so many residents to jail and prison, and by the difficulties this poses for large numbers of these residents' families and friends. Therefore, community justice approaches suggest that neighborhood residents themselves assist in deciding the kinds of sanctions (including, in the most serious cases, prison) that are appropriate for different kinds of offending. In many cases, the community may wish to offer preventive or proactive and restorative programs that can benefit both the community and the offender.

A well-known example of community management of offenders is the Vermont Restorative Sentencing Boards. These boards are made up of private citizens who tailor punishments for nonviolent crimes that will assist simultaneously an offender, his or her victim, and the community. Depending on the crime that has been committed, these punishments may take the form of community service and/or restitution to the victim; victim and offender mediation panels are also a mainstay of restorative justice measures.

While questions remain about which crimes are appropriate for communities to deal with themselves (as opposed to the criminal justice system), and how to pay for preventive and restorative programs, the community justice approach poses another important alternative to current punitive trends. This is especially so in communities where the quality of life for many residents has been lessened by high rates of crime.

PRISON EXPANSION'S ONLY "MODEST" RELATIONSHIP TO CRIME REDUCTIONS

Finally, critiques of the present climate have focused on the lack of an impressively large, well-demonstrated relationship between prison expansion and crime reductions. That the national recidivism rate is over 50% and the reconviction rate for people released over a three-year period is approximately 25% suggests to critics that prison in itself is not a long-term deterrent for a quarter to a half of those who have been incarcerated.[44]

Surprisingly little empirical research has been done on the deterrence and incapacitation effects of prison. In general, most writers have concluded that such effects, while existent, are small. In Tonry and Petersilia's words, these effects are "probably modest."[45] Other research on the contribution of prison expansion to national crime declines also finds relatively minor deterrence effects. For instance, in a rigorous and detailed review of the best empirical studies on the relationship between prison and crime conducted over the last decade or so, William Spelman recently concluded, "Given the similarities among the studies, it should not be surprising that (with one exception) the results are remarkably consistent. A one percent increase in prison population (or in one case, prison commitments per year) would reduce the aggregate Index Crime rate by between 0.16 and 0.31 percent."[46] Thus, according to Spelman, a 10 percent increase in prison populations nationally would cause crime to drop by between 1.6% and 3.1%.

While this might reflect the nationwide effect of prison expansion, this relationship would clearly not apply to all states. The fact that Idaho's prison population expanded by 175% from 2,256 in 1992 to 6,204 in 2002, and violent crime *increased* by 14%; that Tennessee's prisons grew by 111% and violent crime *rose* 11%; and that Mississippi's prison population increased by 132% and violent crime decreased by only 8% illustrates that any supposed national relationship between prison growth and crime does not necessarily apply at a state level.

A report on the connection between incarceration and crime done by Jenni Gainsborough and Marc Mauer likewise found that states that increased incarceration the most from 1991 to 1998 actually experienced, on average, smaller declines than other states that had smaller increases in incarceration.[47]

In terms of whether further prison expansion is warranted on a national scale, on the basis of a cost-benefit analysis that weighs the financial savings of prevented crime with the costs of incarceration, Spelman says that with regard to further prison expansion, the evidence is lacking: "What the studies do not tell us is whether the reduction is large enough to warrant continued expansion."[48] He concludes his literature review and analysis with the following:

> Finally, it is critical that we stop considering prison expansion decisions in a vacuum. Even if we could be certain that prison construction was cost-effective, it may still be true that some other program or policy was more cost-effective. Certainly many primary prevention programs at least appear to be worth their salt: family intervention, Head Start, self paced education, and job apprenticeship programs are all examples. Many secondary prevention programs, including environmental design initiatives, community organizing, victim training and even some offender rehabilitation programs, have shown tremendous promise when applied to the offenders, victims, and environments they fit best. It is easily conceivable that initiatives such as those will yield benefit-cost ratios much greater than the 1.50 to 2.00 that is the best we can expect from continued prison expansion.[49]

Though there is a literature that touts incarceration by contending it is cost-effective when compared with monetary losses sustained through crimes themselves (including the pain and suffering caused victims and their families),[50] this work has been severely criticized for methodological flaws.[51] In fact, in a review of Edwin Zedlewski's work on the cost-effectiveness of prisons,[52] Franklin Zimring and Gordon Hawkins demonstrate that by using Zedlewski's assumptions about how much crime is prevented per incarcerated person, all crime should have been eliminated in the United States.[53]

Perhaps the central question to ask about prison growth, then, is to what extent this policy has succeeded in preventing and reducing crime. Clearly, one of the primary goals of incarceration is to prevent crime through incapacitation and deterrence. However if this worked, critics say, the quadrupling of the prison population over the last two decades should have had significant rather than only modest demonstrable effects. Moreover, given that we spend $60 billion annually to maintain the country's corrections systems, and that (as just discussed) promising and successful alternative programs and approaches exist, is this huge expenditure and recent expansion in the use of prison justified by its contribution to crime reductions? Based on the research done to date, the answer seems to be no.

While the points discussed above are the ones most often lodged against the rising incarceration phenomenon, analysts have recently posed another important question: Has the trend in prison growth begun to reverse on its own? It is to this counterargument that I turn before proceeding, in this chapter's remaining sections, to discuss structural impediments that have made it difficult for these critiques, however valid, to reverse the incarcerative trend.

HAS PRISON GROWTH RECENTLY DECLINED?

If it is the case that prison populations have been declining dramatically on their own, with no policy intervention, the thrust of this book's argument deflates accordingly. Since I have been contending that intervention is needed, it may be useful to investigate two questions. First, have national prison growth rates actually stagnated, as recently reported? Second, even if growth rates have declined considerably, how does this affect states' budgetary expenditures on corrections?

In response to the first query, indeed, the rate of expansion of the U.S. prison population slowed during the 1990s. By 2001, the state prison population showed its first year-to-year no-growth rate, although the federal prison system grew by over 8%.[54] Figure 2.1 illustrates the year-to-year rate of growth at both the state and federal levels since 1980.

Clearly, growth rates in the total numbers of prisoners have slowed considerably. During the 1990s, growth rates peaked at 9% in 1994; they have since declined to the point where the 2001 growth rate was just 1%, though 2001–2002 showed a 2.6% rise. The recent growth from 2001 to 2002 is far lower than the average rate for the last half of the 1990s but is the largest increase in the past three years. Thus there is no question that the dynamics of growth have changed. From 1998 to 2001, the rate of growth slowed considerably. By 2002, however, the growth rate increased once again, though still less than the rates in the 1990s. In further analyzing these numbers, it makes sense to disaggregate them in order to see if and how the federal and state prison systems differ, and which states are responsible for driving down the rates of growth (as well as what these states' system projections appear to augur for the future).

In 2001, when the total number of prisoners grew by 1%, state sys-

Figure 2.1

Year to Year Rates of Growth and Numerical Increases in State and Federal Prisoners in the U.S., 1990–2002

Year	Number Increase (000)	% Increase over Prior Year
1991	51.6	6.7
1992	56.9	6.9
1993	64.9	7.4
1994	84.3	8.7
1995	71.2	6.7
1996	57.5	5.1
1997	58.8	5.0
1998	58.4	4.7
1999	43.8	3.4
2000	18.1	1.3
2001	14.8	1.1
2002	36.6	2.6

Source: Bureau of Justice Statistics, *Prisoners in 1996, Prisoners in 1998, Prisoners in 2000, Prisoners in 2001,* and *Prisoners in 2002,* www.ojp.usdoj.gov/bjs/prisons.htm.

tems actually grew by only 0.3% while the federal system grew by 8.0%. Since the federal system is so much smaller than state prison systems (there were almost 157,000 federal prisoners compared to 1.25 million state prisoners in 2001), the average turns out to be 1%, as shown in Figure 2.1. It should be noted, too, that the 8% year-to-year increase is the largest ever recorded for the federal prison system, while the state annual growth of just 0.3% was the smallest for state systems since 1972.[55] In 2002, the number of state prisoners increased by 2.4%, almost eight times the rate of growth from the prior year. This 2.4% increase in state prisoners is still a low rate of growth compared even to the latter half of the 1990s, when growth rates had already begun to slow, but it is still the highest rate of growth since 2000. The federal system grew at just about half the rate it did the prior year, 4.2%, but still at a far greater rate than the state systems.[56]

Thus there are now two different dynamics of growth for state and federal prisoners in the United States: the federal system is growing at its fastest rate ever, while the state systems are growing at a far lower rate during the 2000s than they did for the prior two decades. Though these significantly lowered rates of growth are certainly cause for some optimism in terms of the projected size of state prison systems (though the recent increase from 2001 to 2002 might suggest otherwise), two other factors must be considered. The first involves ascertaining which states are most responsible for the slowing of growth and what criminal justice policies they are planning to follow into the future. The second involves checking whether prison spending actually decreases with marginal decreases in prison populations.

Immediately evident upon looking at the growth rate for all states during 2000–2001 is that while the national rate of growth for state prison systems was 0.3%, most state systems—36, to be exact—exceeded that rate of growth. During this period, rates of growth of state prison systems ranged from 9.3% and 6.0% in West Virginia and Mississippi, respectively, to –5.5% for New Jersey.[57] In 2002, 33 states grew more than the national average, and Maine and Colorado grew by 11.5% and 7.9%, respectively.[58] The fact that most states grew in absolute numbers at a rate higher than the national average means that the slowing of the growth rate is being driven largely by a small number of states. Indeed, a closer examination of the state-by-state growth rates shows that three states accounting for almost a third of the country's state prisoners—California, Texas, and New York—showed population declines from 2000 to 2001.[59] More specifically, the Texas prison system declined by 2.8%, New York by 3.8%, and California by 2.2%.[60] From 2001 to 2002, the California prisons began to increase once more, by 1.8%; Texas ended its decline and stayed steady; and New York continued to decline, though by fewer than 500 prisoners, far less than its 2001 decrease.[61] By the first half of 2003, only New York continued to decrease its prison population. The state's prison population fell by another 1,150 beds, or 1.7%, from the end of 2002 to the middle of 2003. On the other hand, in the first half of 2003, Texas again began to increase its prison population with a growth of 2,200 prisoners; this represented an increase of 1.4%. Likewise, California continued to grow, increasing its prison population by 2,000, representing a rise of 1.2%.[62] Precisely because these states' experiences are thus likely to exert a strong influence on national trends over the next few years, their projections of expected growth are worth examining in closer detail.

Texas

The Texas prison population declined by just over 6,000 from June 2000 to December 2001, a 4% decrease in just 18 months.[63] This is a substantial decrease indeed—more than the entire size of the Idaho prison system—for a state that now ties California as having the largest state prison system, and which was one of the fastest-growing systems in the country over the past two decades. If this trend were to continue, it would certainly shrink one of the largest systems in the country. At the same time, the decrease might also spur debate about prison use in this "conservative" law-and-order state that leads the United States in the number of capital punishment casees[64] and has an incarceration rate more than one and a half times the nation's.[65] By the end of 2002, however, the decrease had leveled off, and recent population projections done by the Criminal Justice Policy Council (CJPC), the state's (now disbanded) criminal justice policy and analytical agency, show that Texas expects by 2008 to require 13,700 more beds in its system.[66]

California

Like Texas, California saw a large decline in its prison population from June 2000 until the end of 2002. During that time, the system shrank by over 5,000 beds, from 164,490 to 159,444—a decrease of 3%.[67] Though this may seem a small decrease, it has to be seen in the context of a state whose prison system grew by over 66,000 beds and over 70% from 1990 to 2000.[68] Though the recent decrease is small, any decrease is significant in the face of such massive growth. As in the case of Texas, if this decrease were to continue over the next several years, it would have significant implications for the total size of the nation's prison system. However, like Texas, California's prison population decline didn't continue, and by the end of 2002 it had risen again to 162,317, an increase of almost 2%.[69] By the middle of 2003, the prison population increased another 1.2%.[70]

The California Department of Corrections projects that its population will decrease by just over 6,000 by 2006 and hold steady at that level due to a number of proposed parole and reentry initiatives (further discussed in Chapter 5). Yet an unexpected increase of several thousand inmates in mid-2004 has already cast these optimistic projections very much in doubt.[71]

New York

Of the big states, New York has had the most sustained decrease in its prison population over a several-year period. From the end of 1999 until the end of 2001, the number of prisoners dropped from 72,899 to

67,534, a 7.4% drop.[72] Unlike both California and Texas, by 2002 the number of prisoners in New York continued to drop, albeit at far slower rate than in previous years. There were about 470 fewer prisoners in 2002 than in the prior year, a decrease of less than 1%.[73] By the middle of 2003, the prison population fell by another 2,000.[74] The decline in New York over this four-year period, however, represents one of the largest ongoing declines of any prison system in the country; for this and other reasons, Chapter 4 analyzes in more detail how and why this decrease in the prison population happened. Briefly, though, the New York State prison system contracted as a result of changed law enforcement policies in New York City that saw police making far more misdemeanor arrests and prosecutors and grand juries choosing to indict far fewer people for felony crimes. Also differentiating New York from Texas is the fact that New York does not currently project an increase in prison population over the next several years, assuming a stable population.

Thus, of the three largest states that had experienced declines in the early 2000s, one is projecting an increase, one is projecting a decrease, though it has already exceeded its projections, and one is assuming stable population. The last remaining "big four" state is Florida, where, unlike in the other three states, prison population has continued to increase. In addition to these recent increases, Florida officials project a steady increase of about 22% above its 2004 population by 2009, an increase of over 15,000 prisoners.[75] Since Texas also projects continued growth over the next several years, after a few years of decreasing population, California has experienced recent and unexpected growth, and New York expects to maintain its current population, there do not seem to be any large-scale decreases on the horizon, absent any new initiatives, for this group of states that comprise over one-third of the state prisoners in the country.

When these trends are combined with the fact that the great majority of state prison systems continue to grow at rates above the national average, it is difficult to see how any radical decline in state prison populations can occur short of policy changes specifically directed to this purpose. Thus, while the recent slowing in the rate of growth of state prison systems is good news that adds impetus to the task of reversing current trends, reported declines in state prison population growth rates will not substitute for consciously initiated efforts at reform. But this brings me to the second query raised above, by way of answering

Figure 2.2

Comparison of States with Two Successive Years of Declining Prison Population and Two Years of Prison Budgets, 1999–2001

	Change in Prison Population		% Change in Budget (All Funds)	
	1999–2000	2000–2001	1999–2000	2000–2001
Massachusetts	−5.6	−1.1	1.6	22
Kansas	−2.6	−2.7	7.7	4.7
Ohio	−2.2	−1.2	11.6	−0.6
Texas	−3.2	−2.8	6.3	4.6
California	0.0	−2.2	4.5	15
New York	−3.7	−3.8	1.1	−9.5
New Jersey	−5.4	−5.5	8.3	2.5
All States	0.7	0.3	6.1	4.9

Source: Bureau of Justice Statistics, *Prisoners in 2000* and *Prisoners in 2001*; 2000 and 2001 *State Expenditures Report*, National Association of State Budget Officers.

this potential counterargument. Even if prison growth rates did continue to decline, how, if at all, would this affect most states' projected corrections expenditures?

One reason it is essential to achieve large-scale reductions in the use of prison is to realize significant fiscal savings. In this regard, though, marginal declines in prison populations rarely result in commensurate budgetary decreases. The reasons for this are common knowledge to fiscal and policy experts. One is that staff, equipment, rent, power, and food all tend to cost more each year. Employees get raises; landlords raise their rents; utility companies charge more for power (especially in California); and food growers and distributors raise their prices. Consequently, a corrections system with absolutely no growth from one year to the next will still show an increase in its budget for the same period. In fact, even systems that have shown marginal decreases in population from one year to the next often end up requesting, and receiving, more funding. Some savings might result if states planned for, and in fact budgeted, an increase of 10% in corrections costs from one year to the next, only to find that it ended up having to pay just 7%. But most states do not budget for more than one year at a time, and it is difficult to quantify and reallocate savings based on lower-than-expected growth rather than absolute savings.

Figure 2.2 juxtaposes changes in state prison population over the two-year period 1999–2001 and changes in correctional budgets. The table lists every state that had two successive years of prison population .

reductions from 1999 to 2001 and their corrections budgets. What is striking is that no budget reductions of more than 1% resulted from marginal declines in prison populations except for a one-year period in New York. Moreover, most of the year-to-year budget increases are substantial, even where shrinking prison population figures apply. When the growth rates for all states are examined, state prison populations grew by just over 1% from 1999 to 2001, but state corrections budgets increased by over 11 times that rate of growth.

Therefore, again, my point is that while marginal decreases constitute an important development, they are not in and of themselves sufficient to drive significant change. Purposeful and substantial reforms are still needed before prison systems and prison costs can be brought under control. But why haven't such reforms occurred despite the set of critiques—from incarceration's racial and class inequities, to its unintended consequences, to the underfunding and underuse of promising and/or proved alternatives to incarceration, to insufficient deterrence results—that so many writers have thoroughly and thoughtfully raised? I proceed now to delineate a set of cultural, political, and economic factors that strike me as the major reasons these criticisms have not succeeded in reversing the tide of increasing incarceration. These factors need to be taken into account before I begin, from Chapter 3 onward, to show how other recent developments (as surveyed in Chapter 1) may at this point allow an alternative outcome to emerge.

SIX STRUCTURAL IMPEDIMENTS TO PRISON REFORMS

I. The Politics of Punishment

For most of the 1980s and 1990s until the present, politicians and law makers have perceived "tough on crime" rhetoric to be in their interest. As Elliot Currie summarizes the prevailing sentiment among politicians:

> Why is there such a wide gap between what criminologists know and what policy makers do? One reason is the failure of nerve, honesty and seriousness among too many of our political leaders, which has ensured that there has been little serious debate in recent presidential or congressional campaigns about the roots of violent crime or the state

of the criminal-justice system. Neither presidential candidate in 1996 spoke to the issues raised by the mushrooming of America's prisons or offered an articulate response to the crisis of violence among American youth. Instead, the candidates reached for the most symbolic and least consequential issues: both Clinton and Dole, for example, supported the extension of the death penalty, along with a vague call for "victims rights," boot camps, and school uniforms. That none of these has ever been shown to make a difference in the rate of violent crime didn't detract from their apparent political appeal. The political debate, such as it is, has become increasingly primitive and detached from what we know about the roots of crime and the uses and limitations of punishment.[76]

Not only did neither candidate in 1996 address these issues, but the lines between the presidential candidates in the 2000 election, George Bush and Al Gore, were even more blurred. Both were and are strong supporters of the death penalty and of continued prison expansion. In effect, during the 2000 presidential election, no debate about crime and criminal justice issues occurred.

Ever since the Reagan-Bush years, federal bills that are tough on crime have been a recurring part of criminal justice policy, working in tandem with much of the discourse on crime. In 1986, the first Anti-Drug Abuse Act passed Congress and was signed into law by President Reagan. This law imposed 29 new mandatory minimum sentences for drug offenses; the bill also created the five-year minimum sentence that equated the crimes of selling 500 grams of cocaine and 5 grams of crack. Several years later, two other notable events emerged on the national landscape. The first was the passage of another Anti–Drug Abuse Act that created the office of the federal Drug Czar and simultaneously promulgated a host of new mandatory minimum penalties.

The second was the case of Willie Horton, who committed a vicious rape while on a furlough program in Massachusetts. The case received tremendous national attention when George Bush Sr., then running for president against Michael Dukakis, the Massachusetts governor at the time, made unending use of the event by attacking Dukakis as the "furlough king"[77] who allowed this crime to happen. The political ads showing pictures of the disheveled African-American Horton who had raped a white woman in her house touched a nerve in the American public about fear of crime and, more specifically, white fears of crime.

There is little question that the Horton commercials were designed, in the words of *Lockdown America* author Christian Parenti, "to invoke the tried and trusted specter of the Black rapist, a threat to white womanhood, white supremacy, and white society."[78] The incident not only helped elect Bush but also dovetailed nicely with the already prevailing national conservative mood about crime and fear of crime; doubtless it also influenced a variety of tough-on-crime legislative measures.

Six years later, under a democratic and more "liberal" president, Bill Clinton signed into law the Violent Crime Control and Law Enforcement Act of 1994, better known as the 1994 Crime Bill. The Crime Bill provided $8.8 billion for hiring 100,000 new police officers and almost $8 billion for new state prison construction, as well as expanding capital punishment to 16 new crimes and eliminating the Pell Grants that paid for college education for prisoners. The ramifications this legislation has had on the size of the U.S. prison system are huge.

Because the Crime Bill required that a state make progress toward ensuring that Part I violent offenders[79] serve at least 85% of their sentences in order for that state to receive the maximum prison grants, many governors and legislatures felt they had to change their laws to meet this truth-in-sentencing requirement. To meet the federal requirement, state after state began to revise its criminal sentencing laws by eliminating indeterminate sentences and replacing them with determinate sentencing schemes. Though indeterminate sentencing involves ranges such as 5–10 years, if parole boards were granting early release after 6.5 years, then only 65% of the maximum sentence was being served, and the state could not receive the maximum truth-in-sentencing funding. Therefore, state legislatures quickly began to replace indeterminate sentencing systems with determinate fixed sentences, where 85% of the sentence became the minimum time served. In many cases this led, in effect, to the abolition of discretionary early release by parole boards, since everyone now had to serve at least 85% of his or her sentence.

One year after the Crime Bill passed, 11 states adopted truth-in-sentencing laws. By 1998, 27 states had adopted these laws, with another 13 requiring truth in sentencing for particular offenses. Only five states had truth-in-sentencing laws prior to the 1994 Crime Bill.[80] By 1997, just three years after the Crime Bill took effect, prisoners convicted of Part I crimes were serving an average of 49 months, compared to 43 months in 1993.[81] This 14% length-of-stay increase in just

four years was one of the primary reasons for prison expansion during this period.

Thus, continuing tough-on-crime rhetoric has given rise to a national cycle of punitively oriented crime bills every few years, spurring
even greater growth in prisons and enforcement in turn. Moreover, the
sociological and political purposes apparently served by prisons make
large-scale decreases even more difficult, at present, to imagine. As Garland notes:

> Why has prison moved from being a discredited institution destined
> for abolition, to become an expanded and seemingly indispensable
> pillar of late modern social life? Not because it was the centerpiece of
> any penal programme that argued the need for mass imprisonment.
> There was no such programme. Imprisonment has emerged in its re-
> vived, reinvented form because it is able to serve a newly necessary
> function in the workings of late modern, neo-liberal societies: the need
> for a "civilized" and "constitutional" means of segregating the prob-
> lem populations created by today's economic and social arrange-
> ments. The prison is located precisely at the junction point of two of
> the most important social and penal dynamics of our time: risk and
> retribution.[82]

Garland's theory is not the only one that attempts to explain how
larger political and social forces in the United States have created our
current system of harsh punishment. Ted Caplow and Jonathan Simon
also place politicians' recent concerns about fear of crime and punishment within the larger context of changing culture and criticisms of the
U.S. "welfare state" over the last several decades. Thus political elites
found the issue of crime control attractive: punishment "invokes a pri-
mordial understanding of state power that remains highly credible."[83]
Moreover, the recent War on Drugs has provided an almost endless
number of new prisoners. Taken together, according to Caplow and
Simon, these political trends, as well as organizational incentives for
growth and expansion that persist in the criminal justice system, explain the massive U.S. incarceration growth.[84]

Michael Tonry's theory about the rise of mass imprisonment in the
United States centers on the role of different policy cycles, changing
sensibilities (he defines these as "the ethos or zeitgeist of a moment that
influences but does not determine what most people think and believe

about a particular subject"),[85] and moral panics that have occurred in America over the last fifty years. Tonry writes:

> In our time, cycles, sensibilities, and moral panics coincided in ways that produced current crime control and penal policies. Crime rates rose, and steeply, for an extended period. The world changed with globalization, economic restructuring, fundamental social changes, and increased population diversity. All these things raised fears and anxieties that were in part displaced to people (criminals) and things (crime and disorder) that were ready objects of hatred and derision.[86]

Overall, then, the political and social "location" of prisons in American society has contributed to a multilayered politics of punishment that remains structurally pervasive, posing a potentially quite intimidating barrier to reform at all levels of government.

2. The Role of Private Prisons

From 1987, just three years after the Corrections Corporation of America (CCA) secured a contract in Tennessee to run one prison, until 1998, the number of prison and jail beds operated by the private prison industry increased from 3,100 to 116,626, an increase of more than 35-fold.[87] While the private prison industry houses less than 6% of the nation's prison and jail beds, a recent government report predicted that the industry will continue to grow but will have difficulty reaching 10% of the total market.[88] Despite the industry's relatively small share of the total prison pie, its annual revenues are in the neighborhood of $1 billion[89] and growing, and the two largest companies, CCA and Wackenhut, now run private prisons in Great Britain, Scotland, and Australia.

Debate has emerged over whether private prisons save money or operate more efficiently than public prisons. Certainly one *raison d'être* for private prisons, and a large selling point to financially strapped governments, is that private prisons are cheaper than public prisons; private prison proponents contend that private prisons are anywhere from 5% to 15% less expensive to run than public prisons. To date, however, no reliable research validates this claim. In the most recent federal report on private prisons, the authors found, "In summary, the cost benefits of privatization have not materialized to the extent promised by the private sector. Although there are examples of cost savings, there are other examples in which such benefits have not been realized. Moreover, it is probably too early to determine if the initial cost savings can be sustained over a long time period. It only takes one riot or a series of escapes for such costs to greatly accelerate."[90]

Likewise, in terms of day-to-day operations, no compelling research shows that private prisons are better run than public prisons, though they can conceivably be built faster by private companies than by government. Moreover, there is reason to believe that levels of violence in private prisons are higher than in public ones.[91] James Austin and Garry Coventry sum up these comparisons between public and private prisons by saying:

> For these reasons it may be concluded that there are no data to support the contention that privately operated facilities offer cost savings over publicly managed facilities. Similarly, no definitive research evidence would lead to the conclusion that inmate services and the quality of confinement are significantly improved in privately operated facilities. It is clear that private prisons can function as well as public-sector prisons for certain types of inmates (such as minimum security) and that they are aggressively pursuing a share of the multibillion-dollar prison and jail industrial complex.[92]

The introduction of private capital in the form of the private prison industry into an area that has long been run and controlled by government has the effect of even further discouraging attempts to shrink the size of the prison system. When private business enters the public sector, it is to make money—to profit. Therefore the prison industry has a structural self-interest in continuing to expand the market (prisoners) in order to capture a greater market share; this is an elemental rule of capitalism and a maxim subscribed to by all businesses. In this instance, a billion-dollar industry bequeaths a desire for more prisoners, more detainees, in order to sustain and expand business opportunities.

Moreover, private prison industry representatives are quite sophisticated in their dealings with state and federal legislatures to lobby for more business and a greater market share. Despite recent declines in the value of stock in the major private correction companies, a result of several high-profile escapes and disturbances (CCA stock peaked at $141 a share in 1999, hit a low of $1.88 in 2000 and has steadily climbed back to $38 in 2004),[93] these companies remain a potent political force. The cofounder of CCA, Tom Beasely, was the chairman of the Tennessee Republican Party, and its longtime chief operating officer (now replaced), Michael Quinlan, was a former director of the Federal Bureau of Prisons.

Nationally, these companies are very active in their financial support of the conservative American Legislative Exchange Council (ALEC), a public policy organization that actively advances the causes of privatization and mandatory and three strikes legislation. Representing over 40% of all state legislators, this organization is very active in state legislatures across the country.[94] In terms of their overall political influence, these companies are, according to Parenti, "a government-backed juggernaut of mutually reinforcing corporate interests. These companies are led by people—powerfully connected men—with sophisticated political agendas and who are positioning for long-term growth and political influence."[95] These connections were probably of no small consequence when the Federal Bureau of Prisons awarded CCA a contract for over 3,300 beds in 2000.

There is another way in which the presence of the private prison industry helps fuel incarceration. As noted above, private prison companies have proved themselves remarkably adept at building prisons quickly; they often build prisons "on spec" (i.e., on speculation).[96] This means a private company may initially decide to build a prison without a contract or request from a governmental entity. The theory is that, once completed, an existing and available private prison will prove extremely attractive to state prison systems that are overcrowded or under court order to relieve crowding. Indeed, in his survey of private prisons Douglas McDonald found that the major reason given by corrections administrators for contracting with private prison companies was the speed with which prisoners could be housed once that decision was made.[97] This was said to be even more important than cost. Consequently, the ability to quickly add prison capacity through already available or rapidly built new construction is another way that the private prison industry manages to sustain and increase incarceration.

With new private prison beds as a seductive and virtually immediate option to handle the flow of new prisoners, states are also spared the far more difficult and politically onerous task of confronting other ways to control increasing prison populations. In the absence of available building options, states would have to reexamine sentencing policy, create alternatives to incarceration, or change their enforcement policies. While any of these might be far more effective and less costly over the long term, such choices are also politically difficult to make. In contrast, the decision to contract with a private company for additional prison beds to handle expanding numbers of prisoners does not raise a specter of potential political controversy, as would sentencing or parole reforms, which take more time to realize in any case. Thus policy makers are confronted with a choice of immediate, expensive, and politically popular relief from overcrowded prisons or the more arduous, less popular route: making basic changes in the practices of punishment and sanctioning that can lead to "soft on crime" accusations leveled by one's next political opponent. In this context, the choice of private prisons as a temporary, albeit simplistic, solution is difficult to resist. Why do hard when you can do easy?

The power and economic self-interest of the private prison industry is clear; more ambiguous is precisely what this industry's growth means for the growth of incarceration itself. That the prison industry is a potent force to be reckoned with seems obvious. That it creates attractive political incentives for corrections administrators and governors who have immediate overcrowding problems has been amply demonstrated. Consequently, any attempt at large-scale correction reform must also take into account the role that this industry now plays in the formation of correctional policy by providing rapid, if temporary, solutions for dealing with increased numbers of prisoners.

3. The Role of Correction Unions

Like the private prison industry, public corrections unions have risen alongside prisons to become exceedingly powerful and politically influential forces in the field of corrections. From 1982 to 2001, the number of employees in corrections at all levels of government increased from 299,000 to 747,000, an increase of 150%. This rate of increase is far larger than that for police, which grew by 46% (724,000 to 1,060,000). It is also higher than the figure for all legal and judicial employees, whose numbers grew by 97% (248,000 to 488,000) over the same time period.[98] This extraordinary growth has led to the creation and establishment of public-sector corrections unions that exert influence through political contributions and their power to provide valuable assistance at election times.

Nowhere is the power of public corrections officers more obvious than in California. The California Correctional Peace Officers Association (CCPOA) is now one of the most potent political forces in the state. As Todd Clear observes:

> In California, for instance, where the number of officers has increased by 500% since 1980, their union has become a potent political force lobbying not only for better wages and working conditions but also for expansion of prison facilities. This union has become a major contributor to political campaigns, helped pass the "three strikes" legislation, has lobbied against private prisons, supported victims rights and pushed for hiring more correction officers.[99]

Bob Stern from the Center for Governmental Studies in Los Angeles also says of the CCPOA, "They're one of the most powerful interest groups in California, if not the most powerful group."[100] In the 1998 California governor's race, the CCPOA contributed $1.5 million directly to Grey Davis's campaign, and the union spent over $5.3 million in all campaigns in that year, including legislative races, initiatives, and the governor's race—the largest single contribution from any organization.[101] The exceptional power of the CCPOA can also be seen in then-Governor Davis's decision to close four private prisons; he planned to close all nine private prisons in the state as their contracts expire as part of his effort to deal with the state's huge $23 billion budget deficit.[102] The fact that the public prison system has survived with only minimal reductions (until Governor Schwarzenegger imposed significant budget reductions in 2004, discussed more fully in Chapter 6) while the private prisons were closed is testimony to the clout of the CCPOA. According to the *Los Angeles Times*, the CCPOA donated $251,000 to Davis's reelection campaign after he finally proposed eliminating five of the nine private prisons and approved a 34% pay hike for corrections officers over the next five years.[103]

On the other side of the country, corrections unions also wield significant political influence in New York. The New York City union of corrections officers, the Correction Officers Benevolent Association (COBA), was a key supporter of Rudy Giuliani in his successful races for Mayor. Interestingly enough, COBA was also the only large union to support Michael Bloomberg through his surprise mayoral victory in November 2001. In addition, COBA and the state corrections officers union have strongly supported Governor George Pataki and endorsed him in his successful third try at reelection. They have been major contributors to the governor's campaigns, and Norman Seabrook, the long-time COBA president, was a visible presence on the stage when Governor Pataki made his victory speech in his 1999 win for a second term as New York's governor. Perhaps not surprising, Governor Pataki signed off on legislation at the end of 1999 that increased the size of New York City corrections officer pensions. The City of New York was forced to fund this new legislation, and then-Mayor Rudy Giuliani called it "a major sell out of the City in terms of money."[104]

Another illustration of the power of corrections unions can be drawn from the proportion of private prisons housed in nonunion states. Private prisons are anathema to public prison unions. They threaten the number of prison jobs held by their members and pose a significant potential threat to their long-term viability should they gain too much of a foothold in a particular state. Therefore, it can be reliably predicted that any political capital accumulated by public corrections unions will be used to ward off prison privatization. Interestingly enough, then, of the 158 private prisons in the United States, 43, or approximately 23%, are found in Texas alone[105]—a state with nonunionized corrections officers.

While public corrections unions regard the private prison industry with scorn, these two organized groups have one interest in common: in different ways they both seek, in effect, to enlarge the prison system; both would fight efforts at shrinking this system. For public corrections unions strive to protect and increase their membership, while private prisons strive to increase their market share of beds. This commonality of interest may coalesce in legislatures and governors' offices around the country, posing yet another formidable obstacle to downsizing-oriented reforms.

4. Prisons as Economic Development

Rural America was not a beneficiary of the economic boon of the 1990s. A long migration of manufacturing jobs to the South and overseas, the consolidation of agriculture into huge agribusiness, and the closing of military bases all over the country left many rural areas in severe economic straits. With national rural economic development efforts barely making a dent in the economic misfortune suffered by these areas, the prison boom of the 1990s offered one kind of immediate financial relief. The amount of money spent to build and operate prisons during the 1990s alone proved an irresistible lure for rural communities. For example, in 1996, all states collectively spent $1.3 billion on constructing prisons, almost double what they spent in 1990.[106] By 2000, states were spending $2 billion on prison construction, three times what they were spending a decade earlier.[107]

Moreover, every region of the country is engaged in prison building projects. For instance, in the years 1999 and 2000, New York State alone spent $716 million on prison construction projects, Florida spent $190 million, South Carolina spent $42 million, and Washington spent $260 million. In 1999 alone, Colorado spent $143 million on prison construction.[108] While urban residents have historically viewed prisons and jails as entirely undesirable buildings to find placed in their communities, rural residents have felt just the opposite as construction dollars poured into economically depressed regions. Then, too, from governments' point of view, building costs in rural areas tend to be cheaper; construction is also easier and faster, since prisons are usually built on open, vacant land, as opposed to being squeezed into already-crowded urban areas.

In addition, the annual operating costs of new prisons provide ongoing employment to communities in the form of corrections officers and civilian support staff. Since unemployment rates are high in many rural areas, corrections jobs offer a readily available workforce secure, high-paying positions with good benefits in the form of pensions and health care. But local economies benefit in other ways as well, since prisoners are big business. From 1984 to 1996, annual operating expenses for corrections increased more than threefold, from $7 billion to $22 billion;[109] by 2002, these expenses rose to $37.6 billion,[110] an increase of 71% in just six years. Given the magnitude of this increase, it is not surprising that prisons tend to create secondary and tertiary support systems that also create jobs and sustain development. Once prisons are operating, they require, for instance, outside health care systems to provide medical care to inmates and transportation businesses and hotels to bring and house people visiting prisoners. Food-service businesses are likely to spring up to provide food for inmates, staff, and visitors. Finally, as a result of hundreds of residents holding relatively high-paid and secure jobs with benefits, a wide array of businesses with which these residents deal—from insurance to hardware—also reap financial benefits.

Not surprising, then, communities such as Rome, New York; Crescent City, California; and Fort Stockton, Texas, have all lobbied for and received prisons in the last decade. One of the most well known examples of prisons as economic development is in Fremont County, Colorado, where, according to Todd Clear, 18% of the county's 40,000 residents are "involuntary guests" at the four federal and nine state prisons. Clear writes, "Already a home for state prisons Freemont residents bought 600 acres and donated the site to the U.S. government to lure the prisons. The 13 prisons employ 3,100 workers, with an average salary of $30,000."[111]

In Virginia, where the Department of Correction has historically made money by leasing out excess beds to other states, a declining number of out-of-state inmates has resulted in a revenue loss of $48 million. In trying to compensate for this loss of revenue, the Correction Department is planning to close two facilities in Southampton and Brunswick Counties that would cost 639 jobs. Elected officials from those communities, as well as the state corrections union, are strenuously fighting these cuts. "These people have house payments to make, car payments to make, health care payments to make," Tommy Wright Jr, a Republican legislator from the area, told the Corrections Facility Task Force. "This should be measured in human suffering, not just dollars and cents." The Mayor of one of the towns in the affected counties told legislators that "we get all the prisons and all the garbage and I'm proud of it."[112] Clearly, in areas that are already depressed, the specter of prison closings and the loss of jobs that go with them can quickly become an emotional bread-and-butter issue for many local residents.

The total economic impact from new prison construction is not clear. Certainly, prison construction cannot make up for significant losses of manufacturing and agriculture jobs in suburban and rural communities. Indeed, some communities are lately discovering that with states in an economic tailspin and correctional populations leveling off, existing prisons or planned prison projects are being closed or canceled. In this respect, then, prison is not the recession-proof industry that many had hoped. In fact, a recent report done by the Sentencing Project on the economic impact of prison building on rural communities stated, "Overall, over the course of 25 years, we find no significant difference or discernible pattern of economic trends between the seven rural counties in New York that hosted a prison and the seven rural counties that did not host a prison. While prisons clearly create new jobs, these benefits do not aid the host county to any substantial degree since local residents are not necessarily in a position to be hired for these jobs."[113] The economic benefits, then, may be far lower than is perceived by rural counties, though it is also still true that many rural communities see prisons as an economic boon.

It is also arguable that whatever the economic effects of prison building, this job-providing "function" takes place at the expense of predominantly urban minority residents who have been shipped to rural prisons. The result is rural prisons staffed overwhelmingly by white men who guard mostly urban minority men, a social mix that under some circumstances may be a recipe for disaster.

Despite these issues about the long-term viability of using prisons as economic development, and the even more ethically questionable problem of transferring urban minorities to rural prisons to relieve local distress, the desire for continued prison building in rural areas should not be underestimated. Rural legislators and their communities will fight strongly for prisons and put up significant political resistance to any attempts to close prisons in their areas.

Consequently, any strategy to downsize prisons must contend with this structural impediment too. As Marc Mauer writes, prisons have become "vital to the development strategy of many small rural communities that have lost jobs in recent years but hold the lure of cheap land and a ready workforce. Communities that once organized against the siting of new prisons now beg state officials to construct new institutions in their backyards."[114]

5. Returning Prisoners as a Barrier to Reform

Of all inmates who left prison in 1994, more than half, or 51.8%, were back within three years.[115] This astoundingly high rate of recidivism raises a number of important theoretical and practical questions about the effectiveness of prison. For instance, does this return-to-prison rate illustrate the overwhelming failure of the prison experience either to deter future criminal behavior or to rehabilitate prisoners? Does it signify that the criminal justice system is, in fact, effective at locking up, monitoring, rearresting, and then reconvicting the most serious law breakers? These are important questions, and the remainder of the book will address them. However, for the purely practical goal of shrinking the size of the prison system, the simple fact of this return rate is daunting.

The national rate of 51.8% also masks the tremendous variations around the country in return-to-prison rates. For instance, Washington State's return-to-prison rate after three years is 25.8%;[116] California's rate is more than double this, 56%, after only two years;[117] Pennsylvania's rate is 42.3% after three years.[118] While Washington's return-to-prison rate is less than half the national average, California's rate exceeds the national average in just two-thirds of the time. Clearly, in a state like California, the extraordinarily high rate of recidivism is a primary reason behind the continuing size of the its prison system.

Looking at what happens prior to someone being returned to prison helps illustrate the incredible cycle of arrest, conviction, and re-arrest. Of the people who left prison in 1994, 67.5% were rearrested. Property and drug offenders had the highest rearrest rates, at 73.8% and 66.7%, respectively. Violent offenders had the lowest rearrest rate, at 61.7%. Almost half those arrested, or 46.9%, were convicted for a new offense.[119] These rearrest and reconviction rates have remained remarkably level over the last decade. The last time the Bureau of Justice Statistics examined recidivism in 1983, a slightly lower percentage of people were rearrested, 62.5%, and an almost identical percentage, 46.8%, were reconvicted. The stability and the scope of the rearrest and reconviction rates therefore present a significant hurdle in any strategy to lower prison populations.

High reconviction rates are not unique to the U.S. prisons. Great Britain, which has also massively expanded its prison system over the last decade, has reconviction rates that even exceed those of the United States. In 1997, of those released from a British prison, 58% were reconvicted within only two years. As high as the U.S. reconviction rates have remained, Great Britain's are far worse—11% higher after two years than the U.S. rate in three years.[120] Perhaps these rearrest and reconviction rates are predictable accompaniments to hugely expanding criminal justice systems that emphasize high levels of incarceration and control. In any case, given the relative stability of the rates in the United States over the last ten years and similar problems in the European system closest to ours, these rates pose yet another structural impediment to change.

Further complicating this picture is that, according to a 2002 Department of Justice study on recidivism, of the 51.8% who return to prison, more than half (or 26.4%) are sent back not for a new criminal conviction but for violating one or more of the many conditions of parole or postrelease supervision.[121] Parole agencies are now returning more ex-prisoners to prison than the police and the courts are returning ex-prisoners who commit new offenses. In California, of the 134,821 people on parole in 2000, parole agents technically violated and sent back to prison 73,340. This represents well over half, or 57%, of California's total prison admissions in 2000. Since each of these technical parole violators spends, on average, 156 days in prison, the group occupy over 31,300 prison beds on any given day, or 19% of the entire California prison system.[122] Although no state has the huge absolute numbers of California, it is not unusual for technical parole violators to constitute a majority of prison admissions and take up anywhere from 10% to 20% of an entire prison system. For example, in Kansas, technical parole, probation, and postrelease supervision violators make up fully two-thirds, 66.6%, of all yearly prison admissions.[123]

Because parole agencies are hugely underfunded, parole officers have unmanageable caseloads and few, if any, programs to deal with parolees who start to violate the rules of parole by using drugs or reporting irregularly. Hence a technical violation becomes an attractive option, even more so because it allows parole officers not to assume more risk than necessary in an already politically charged environment. Technical violations have undergone geometric increases in very short time frames. In 1983, California technically violated 5,275 parolees; in 2003 this number rose to 62,377, an almost twelvefold increase.[124] In the four-year period from 1997 to 2001, Kansas saw a 57% increase in the number of technical parole violators.[125] Obviously, the number of technical parole violators entering prison is rising, thereby contributing to the maintenance and size of many systems and posing yet another substantial obstacle to the task of shrinking state prison populations.

6. The "Realities" of the Budget Process

One of the most common requests made to budget offices by government officials and advocates is to "invest now" in a program that promises to save huge sums of money "later." Such requests may be as nebulous as greatly increasing spending on education today so that, in the future, better-educated and more productive young people will commit less crime and thus will save the juvenile and criminal justice systems millions of dollars (while bringing in further revenue, as these people pay taxes).

In the case of prisons, the fiscal reality of no available funds in an era of tight budgets, combined with the current politics of punishment, makes funding programs that in the long run might lower prison populations extremely difficult. This too, then, poses what could be called a sixth, and this chapter's last identified, structural impediment. It may well be the case that huge funding increases in a combination of early childhood education, after-school programs, prison rehabilitation programs, and postrelease programs can, over time, reduce prison populations and save money. However, this strategy requires two terribly difficult decisions. The first is that law makers must come out strongly and publicly for prevention and rehabilitation programs in a perceived tough-on-crime political environment; the second is that they must make substantial cuts in existing government programs or raise new revenue to fund these programs.

Confronted with both problems, most law makers, even ones who might be personally sympathetic to this strategy, will shy away from actually pursuing it. Even without the political problem of funding alternatives to prison or prevention programs, the competition for scarce resources is so intense during tough economic times that coming up with "new" money to fund new programs is next to impossible. In the pursuit of any strategy to reduce prison populations, requests for significant monetary investments up front must contend with and somehow overcome this budget reality.

Moreover, even when claims about future savings from investing now are not particularly nebulous, policy makers are hesitant about pursuing a course that cannot, by definition, yield any immediate fiscal benefits. In 1996, the Rand Corporation did a well-known and quite concrete study suggesting that investment in childhood education today would eventually produce significant savings down the road in prison and human service costs.[126] But this up-front investment never materialized. Why not? The Rand Corporation has a solid reputation for excellent research; certainly, Rand cannot easily be labeled, and thereafter dismissed, a liberal think tank with a leftist agenda. One explanation is that the politics of making large-scale investments in social programs to prevent crime is always difficult at times when tough-on-crime policies hold powerful sway. But another reason is that even if the politics of the issue could be overcome, budget officials and legislators typically reply to advocates that there is "no money now to invest in programs that won't save us money until a decade from now."

Especially in lean budget times this sentiment, while perhaps foolhardy in the long term, does pose a practical dilemma in the short run. Where is the money to come from for programs that require a large investment with no payback for years? Do you raise taxes, or do you cut essential or popular programs? Either course could create a further political problem in its own right, while potentially showing results long after current legislators are no longer in office. Why risk it? Most legislators don't. Given such reasoning, the decision to ignore Rand's advice seems to make a pragmatic, if troubling, kind of sense.

SUMMARIZING CRITICISMS AND IMPEDIMENTS: WHERE DO WE GO FROM HERE?

In conclusion, would-be reformers of the U.S. corrections system face a paradox. On the one hand, research and experience with issues ranging from rehabilitation to diversion programs and alternatives to prison offer evidence and hope that punishment can take forms different from the current incarceration boom. Knowledge and evidence also exist about the current system resulting in significant harm to families, to communities where prisoners resided, and to prisoners themselves (as, after prison, high rates of reoffending frequently ensue). We know that hugely disproportionate numbers of minorities are incarcerated, especially for drug-related crimes, and that recent increases in incarceration have contributed relatively little to public safety. (In this regard, we also know that current three-strikes and mandatory sentencing schemes are keeping many people imprisoned well beyond their typical crime-committing years.) Finally, we know that funding for prison expansion ultimately comes at the cost of other services, such as education and health.

All this comprises one side of the paradox. On the other side is a host of factors, structural in their ability to exert institutional weight that serves to impede large-scale efforts at reform. The strength of tough law-and-order rhetoric, and politicians' evident fear of going against the tide, has prevented much genuine debate from surfacing in American political discourse from the 1980s through the present. The power of the private prison industry and public corrections officers' unions, along with current policies that use prisons as a mode of economic development in rural areas, also pose daunting structural obstacles. Moreover, arguments reflecting the common self-interests of the prison industry, corrections unions, and some rural communities in maintaining an expanded prison system have been reinforced by skyrocketing return-to-prison rates—especially among parolees sent back for technical violations. Last but not least, budget shortages and difficulties in finding new money to fund a different set of policies constitute yet a further thorny barrier to reform.

The trick to overcoming this paradox is to take advantage of what we know about prisons and their alternatives to make a case for change. Law and policy makers need other powerful political and economic incentives for reform, to counter arguments and forces against it. They need to see and use the political and substantive advantages of shrinking prison budgets to increase funds for (or prevent cuts in) other, more popular services, such as education and health care. They need a political strategy to deal with the volatile public issues of correctional and sentencing policy and practical ways to fund efforts to turn around 30 years of prison growth. The following chapters aim at shaping and suggesting such a strategy, beginning with a more detailed analysis of state economies and public opinion.

3

A New Reality for Prison Systems

THE BEGINNING OF the twenty-first century was not kind to states. After the boom years of the 1990s, state economies rapidly deteriorated as, by 2001, a national recession became apparent. Compounded by the attacks on September 11 and the financial aftermath of increased unemployment and reduced travel, as well as by large stock market drops in mid-2002, states faced shortfalls for the first time after a decade of substantial revenue growth. Something else changed around this time, too. While the national crime rate began to decline in 1993, and continued to fall through the end of the century, it took until 2001 for the number of Americans who said crime was falling to exceed the number who perceived it as still rising. Public opinion polls indicate that crime's perceived importance has lessened dramatically to the point where it is now far behind health, education, the economy, and even Social Security as issues citizens want government to address. This is down considerably, for crime was the number-one concern of Americans in the mid-1990s; by the early 2000s, at least twice as many people thought confronting problems in education was more important than tackling crime.

These two changes—deteriorating state economies and alterations in public opinions—are part of a different context within which would-be reformers of the criminal justice system now find themselves operating. Legislators and governors have exhibited a new willingness, born of financial desperation, to target prison systems for cuts. I suggest that some of these cuts, such as prison closings without concomitant reductions in prison population, may bring short-run budgetary gains at serious long-term social costs. Other state reactions, though, demonstrate a trend toward more thoughtful long-term means of addressing fiscal problems by revising sentencing laws adopted during the 1980s and 1990s as part of the "tough on crime" and "truth in sentencing" movements. Changing sentencing laws has been seen as necessary by some state legislators to stem a growth in prison systems they can no longer afford.

While these short- and longer-term state reactions to budgetary changes were happening, public opinion also shifted. As the public gradually started to perceive that crime rates were declining, and became relatively more concerned about other social problems, prison and sentencing policies were affected in turn. Among other developments auguring change were two voter referendums that evidenced altered attitudes already making their way into new policies. Two voter initiatives enacted in the last few years, in California and Arizona, amended these states' criminal codes to mandate treatment in lieu of prison for nonviolent drug offenders. Though both initiatives happened prior to the national economy's visible deterioration around 2001, they manifest a changing mood about the enforcement of drug-related crimes, especially in states reputed to be conservative on law-and-order issues (but which have also recently experienced huge increases in prison costs). These large-scale "prison diversion" initiatives were accomplished by public referendum and suggest one way by which newly evolving public opinion is affecting policy—and maybe, eventually, policy makers as well.

Thus budget declines and changes in sentencing and public opinion, along with large-scale prison diversion programs implemented in the last two to three years, offer a window of opportunity for arguing that this may be an excellent moment indeed for states to further reduce their prison spending. Many of the budget cuts to prison systems that have been implemented thus far have been relatively small; others have not. Many have been cuts that make little sense from either a long-term public safety or a financial perspective (here I would include prison closings without population reductions that result in forced overcrowding, eliminating meals, and many reductions in prison programming). Even many of the sentencing changes enacted thus far will not achieve large reductions in prison populations. However, the moves to cut prison spending and to change sentencing laws bode well for the future; both may engender further measures to implement far-reaching reforms that can significantly reduce the size of and spending on prison systems.

STATES' BUDGET CRISES AND THEIR EFFECTS
ON CORRECTIONS

States that for years had the ability to expand prisons, increase spending on selected services, and enact regular tax cuts have recently encountered a financial situation that requires tough and politically treacherous decisions. State capitols have resounded with debates over whether to rescind tax cuts, increase taxes, or cut particular services. Thereafter, state corrections system administrators, too, have encountered an unfamiliar situation: after years of increased funding, suddenly their systems were targeted recipients of budget cuts. Though most proposed reductions involved only marginal reductions in programs or services, others mandated prison closings and layoffs. Life for prison directors, staff, and in many cases prisoners themselves had changed.

Let me document the extent to which states in general experienced recent financial pressures before proceeding to discuss how states' corrections budgets were thereafter affected. A July 2002 National Conference of State Legislators (NCSL) report on state budgets begins by stating that fiscal year 2002

> was tumultuous in nearly every state in the nation. The fiscal boom of the late 1990s that had begun to sputter in early 2001 came to a screeching halt by the end of the year. National economic woes, exacerbated by the Sept. 11 terrorist attacks, made their way to the state level. Initially, the problems were on the revenue side of the ledger. But as the fiscal year wore on, an increasing number of states reported spending overruns as well.[1]

In another 2002 fiscal survey of states, the National Governors Association (NGA) and the National Association of Budget Officers (NASBO) pronounced, "The recent economic data suggest that the economy is recovering but states are still experiencing dismal budget situations. Revenue growth is anemic, spending pressures continue to rise and states are facing massive budget shortfalls."[2] This rather dismal statement was followed by another, equally depressing: "A national recession underscored by the economic fallout of the September 11th tragedy pushed state budgets to their lowest point ever."[3] The report concludes, "Although national economic indicators may be brightening, the prospects for state budgets will remain cloudy for the near future."[4]

By 2003, the NGA and NASBO were saying, "As the economy struggles to find footing, state fiscal conditions remain uncertain. With two years of budget imbalance behind them, the state fiscal story is much the same; revenues have fallen dramatically while spending pressures have grown, particularly in Medicaid."[5]

NCSL, NGA, and NASBO are the three major national-level associations that represent state legislators, governors, and budget directors. To understand why their assessments of states' current economic prospects have been so pessimistic, it is necessary to delve into budget-related problems encountered by states in just the last two years. By the end of fiscal year 2002, 43 states had a total of over $58 billion in gaps between spending and revenue, with California's massive $23.7 billion gap accounting for 40% of the states' revenue shortfalls.[6] Twelve states had budget gaps in excess of 10% of their state budgets. Twenty-six states collected less revenue in fiscal year 2002 than the year before, at the same time that their spending increased by 1.8%.[7]

This fiscal state of affairs resulted in almost every state cutting its budget or taking measures to bring its revenues and expenses into line. Included in these actions were 29 states making across-the-board budget reductions; 11 states resorting to layoffs of government employees; and 22 states using "rainy day" funds, or revenue accounts created for the express purpose of making it through tough economic times.[8] In a significant break with the past, one of the most common targets of state budget cutters was corrections: 25 states reduced funding allocated to prisons. In addition, 12 states cut optional Medicaid programs; 16 states reduced spending on higher education; 12 cut K–12 education spending; and 6 cut aid to cities and counties.[9] Perhaps most striking was another exception to preceding practices: a total of 16 states increased taxes to help make it through their troubled fiscal times. For instance Indiana, New Jersey, and Pennsylvania each raised state taxes in excess of $1 billion; Tennessee raised its taxes by more than $900 million. This meant that after seven years of tax cutting, a net state tax increase occurred in 2002.[10]

In 2003, the fiscal conditions of states continued to deteriorate. Thirty-nine states faced budget gaps, and in 20 of those states the gaps were over 10% of the general fund budget. The combined budget gaps for states early in 2003 were almost $30 billion, a huge deficit that followed the massive deficits of the prior year.[11] During 2003, 28 states cut services across the board, 17 states laid off employees, and 22 states continued to dip into their reserve rainy-day funds.[12] By the end of 2003, 37 states had cut their budgets by a combined $14.5 billion. This compares to total state budget cuts of $4.5 billion during the last national recession in 1992.[13]

Going into 2004, 31 states were still cutting services, including 15 states that cut corrections and 13 states that reduced spending on higher education. Eleven states laid off state employees.[14]

The reason for these state budget cuts, of course, was that revenue collections had quickly fallen below expenditures. According to the National Conference of State Legislatures July 2002 report, "for many states, the fiscal challenges were just beginning. Most were concerned about faltering revenues, especially from personal income tax collections. Forty-one states levy a broad-based personal income tax and, nationally, personal income taxes account for about 36 percent of state tax revenues."[15] Indeed, in the first four months of 2002 alone, state income tax collections brought in 14%, or $15 billion, less than they had in 2001.[16] This revenue decline resulted in 16 states actually showing negative growth during fiscal year 2003.[17] By 2003, the revenue picture in states had gotten no better. In its analysis of state revenues in 2003, the NGA and NASBO wrote, "Like the year before it, fiscal 2003 was a grueling one for state coffers. Revenue collections fell far short of the projections states made when they passed their fiscal 2003 budgets. Faced with large gaps between planned spending and the revenue that supports it—both in fiscal 2003 and as they begin fiscal 2004—states have cut spending, drawn on reserve funds, and increased taxes."[18] In total, in fiscal 2003, 30 states had lower-than-expected revenue collections, and in 29 states, governors recommended tax and fee increases totaling $17.5 billion.[19]

One criterion of a state's fiscal health is whether unspent surplus funds remain at the end of a fiscal year. The larger a state surplus in the form of rainy-day funds or cash reserves, the easier for that state to cover essential needs or deal with budget deficits. In fiscal year 2000, states ended the year with a combined $48.8 billion year-end surplus fund balance; by fiscal year 2002, those fund balances had shrunk to $14.8 billion. One year later, by 2003, those year-end balances had further shrunk to just $6.4 billion, an astounding 88% decrease in year-end fund balances from just three short years earlier.[20]

Even further aggravating this precipitous decline in revenue and year-end surplus funds, states are under pressure to continue funding programs that eat up significant amounts of their budgets. The largest of these budget "stresses" is Medicaid. Medicaid is a means-tested entitlement program, financed by both federal and state government, that provides health care to approximately 40 million Americans. Medicaid represents 20% of all state spending and is by far the highest cost in state budgets;[21] moreover, Medicaid has been the fastest-growing state expenditure over the last 20 years. In 1980 states spent a total of $11 billion on Medicaid; this figure rose to $88 billion in 2000, a staggering 700% increase.[22] The increases can be explained by the overall rise in the use and cost of health care generally, a greater enrollment of children in Medicaid, and hefty increases in the use and cost of long-term care and prescription drugs.

Moreover, Medicaid continues to grow at a faster-than-expected rate in almost every state. From 2000 to 2002, Medicaid expenses rose nearly 25%, compared to an overall state revenue growth of just 5% during the same period.[23] In states where the percentage of state budgets spent on Medicaid is well above the national average of 20%, resultant budget pressures are especially intense. These states include New York, Tennessee, and Pennsylvania, wherein the proportion of state budgets devoted to Medicaid funding are 33%, 30%, and 28%, respectively.[24] In 2003, Medicaid expenditures grew an additional 8%, and 28 states had Medicaid shortfalls in their state budgets, compared to 25 states in 2002.[25]

Further adding to recent budget pressures is the growth in many states of the numbers of families who are receiving Temporary Assistance to Needy Families (TANF). This is the cash assistance program that replaced Aid to Families with Dependent Children (AFDC) after the Welfare Reform Act of 1996 was enacted. From the time that welfare reform was enacted in 1996 until 2000, the number of welfare recipients fell by 55%; this represented a decline from 12.8 million to 5.8 million people. Every state saw a diminution in its welfare rolls, and 38 states had declines of more than 50%.[26] This allowed states to use the block-grant funding received from the federal government (which pays for about 50% of these expenditures) for a variety of other purposes.

However, in just a two-year period, the weakened economy has increased TANF caseloads in 20 states; as unemployment continues to rise even when recessions end, caseloads increased through 2003.[27] This means states will have to devote a greater amount of their existing

TANF funds to direct public assistance and will be constrained to continue funding other programs, such as job training and placement, that surplus TANF funds previously paid for.

The overall fiscal dynamic in states, then, is ominous and multi-faceted. Revenues are substantially down, and spending pressures, especially on Medicaid and to a lesser extent on public assistance, are extreme. The combination of declining revenues and rising Medicaid expenditures forces governors and state legislatures into an exceedingly problematic fiscal and political situation. It means that they have to intently reexamine non-Medicaid state spending in the corrections, education, and transportation areas; simultaneously, they must consider the possibility of raising additional revenue in the form of new taxes or fees. Since the usual political rule of thumb is that budgets must get cut before taxes or fees are raised, and since tax increases are regarded as anathema by politicians, states have tended to opt for cutting their budgets by reducing expenditures. This suggests that state fiscal problems are not likely to end in the very near future.

In a 2004 report on the outlook for state budgets, NASBO wrote, "In fiscal 2003, states faced budget shortfalls that neared $80 billion; in fiscal 2004 they continue to face difficult budgetary challenges. As states fight to balance their budgets, the choices available to them are increasingly difficult, and some of the most difficult fiscal decisions have yet to be made."[28]

Also in 2004, the Center on Budget and Policy Priorities reported, "State government fiscal conditions remain weak, despite recent improvement, according to three of the leading bipartisan or academic organizations that track state taxes and budgets. As states write their budgets for the 2005 fiscal year that begins in most states on July 1, 2004, their revenues are still well below pre-recession levels. States that borrowed money, used reserves, or shifted funds to balance their budgets in prior years have a budget 'hole' from which to dig out. And the spending cuts and reduced balances of the last several years have given states little cushion with which to work in enacting balanced budgets."[29]

For fiscal year 2005, states now face aggregate budget deficits of $36–40 billion.[30] The good news here is that, compared to 2004, this means that combined state deficits have been cut down by half. The bad news is that, clearly, states still need to make difficult fiscal choices for at least the short term.

Summing up the near term fiscal outlook for states, Ray Scheppach, the Executive Director of the National Governors Association, said "I think we've bottomed out and its going to get better, but not a lot better."[31]

It is in this recent period of fiscal crisis that prison expenditures have come under tremendous scrutiny and states have begun to systematically reduce their funding. Even as national economic conditions slowly rebound, the combined pressures of Medicaid growth, public clamoring for improved primary and secondary education, and ongoing desires for tax cuts will subject corrections agencies to far greater budget pressures than they encountered at any other time in the last thirty years.

HOW HAVE STATES REACTED? SHORT- AND LONGER-TERM MEASURES

In 2002, in different ways, 25 states reduced their correction budgets.[32] Thirteen states closed prisons or otherwise reduced capacity. Nine states, including Florida and Arizona, cut prison programs offering drug treatment and education.[33] Among the states that closed prisons, every region of the country was represented; these states included California, Ohio, Illinois, Michigan, Massachusetts, and Mississippi. Iowa, Illinois, and Michigan in combination laid off a total of nearly 500 correction officers. In perhaps the most publicized case of a prison program reduction, Illinois eliminated all college education in prisons and laid off hundreds of college instructors. Illinois's then-Governor Ryan even vetoed legislation requiring longer sentences for drug crimes, saying, "It is difficult to spend more money on drug traffickers at the same time funds are being cut at the federal and state level."[34] It is almost unimaginable that any governor would have vetoed such tough-on-crime legislation only a year or two earlier.

Classifying these reductions overall: again, 13 states closed prisons or otherwise reduced capacity; 12 states delayed or eliminated planned new prisons; 11 states reduced their staffs, including through the use of layoffs; 18 states instituted hiring freezes; and 9 states cut some of their programs. In three states—Massachusetts, Michigan, and Ohio—reductions of all five kinds ensued.[35] In 2003, prison-spending reductions continued. Seventeen states either closed facilities, delayed prison openings, or otherwise reduced prison beds; 25 states reduced prison staff or instituted hiring freezes; and 7 states eliminated programs or renegotiated contracts. Included in these last 7 states was Kentucky, which ended funding for educational programming, and Texas and North Carolina, which took the extreme measure of actually reducing the number of meals served to prisoners.[36]

Let us look more specifically, though, at the ramifications of one of the ways of reducing corrections budgets: prison closings. In fact, closing prisons is an eminently desirable way to reduce spending in corrections systems, as long as there are reductions in the prison population. Closing prisons as population declines makes financial sense and allows prisons to save money without reducing programs or making ill-advised staff cuts. However, closing prisons when the population is not declining, and in fact might even be rising, is different altogether.

While some prison closings around the country are the result of declining prison populations, many others simply compound problems of overcrowding by moving the same (or an increasing) number of prisoners into a smaller number of beds. In the short run, such overcrowding may conceivably save money; in the longer term, though, additional spending may ensue from increased prison violence and class-action "condition of confinement" lawsuits. Ultimately, prisons that are severely overcrowded cause harm to both prisoners and staff. According to the Vera Institute of Justice, then, while prison closings for budgetary reasons "may save money in the short term, it is difficult to predict their effect on long term costs and the ability of corrections systems to maintain public safety. According to critics, they are reflexive responses to an acute situation and do not necessarily enhance a state's ability to spend corrections dollars effectively or wisely."[37]

While the scope and severity of all these prison reductions break sharply with trends over the last several decades of corrections policy —and clearly indicate law makers' willingness to do so—it is difficult to see how some of these actions intelligently reconfigure or restructure state systems. This is especially true of systems that eliminate education programs or the number of meals served to prisoners. The good news is that a fiscal crisis has forced states seriously to reconsider prison funding, and that many have taken dramatic steps to reduce prison expenditures. The bad news is that many of these short-term cuts, even if they result in immediate budget savings, have the potential to cost more money over time and, perhaps most significantly, to undermine the integrity of corrections systems' ability to provide a safe and secure environment. More promising than these cuts, though, are efforts that many states have made instead of—or in addition to—budget reductions. For a number of states have eliminated or revised sentences or have otherwise instituted more fundamental changes in their sentencing and corrections policies.

No one could have possibly predicted in the 1990s that by 2001 two of the country's toughest law-and-order states would be the first to revise "tough on crime" laws they had enacted only a few years earlier. But this is exactly what has happened in Louisiana and Mississippi. Louisiana, the state with the highest per capita incarceration rate in the country and one that is almost twice as large as the average for all states,[38] had "lost control of the prison population,"[39] according to State Senator Charles Jones, the primary architect of the sentencing reforms. Facing two years of budget gaps and skyrocketing Medicaid costs, the state removed mandatory sentences for certain nonviolent crimes and cut many of these sentences in half. For example, the penalty for possessing 28 grams of cocaine was reduced from 10–60 years to 5–30 years. These sentencing changes also required that the first "two strikes" of the state's three strikes law be violent felony convictions, as opposed to *any* felony conviction.[40]

Evidently, then, Louisiana's deteriorating budgetary situation created an opportunity for sentencing reform that would otherwise not have happened in a state that makes more use of prisons, per capita, than any other in the country. State legislator Danny Martiny made this point clearly: "The people expect us to be tough on crime and they expect us to lock everybody up and throw away the key. And that's great as long as you've got a jail and you've got the finances. But we've come to a point where we just can't afford to keep doing it."[41] The state's precarious finances were also an issue for State Senator Donald R. Cravins, who said of Louisiana's sentencing reform, "This is an attempt to bring under control a system that was bankrupting the state and was not reducing crime . . . we had half the population in prison and the other half watching them."[42] Even Louisiana's then conservative Republican governor, Mike Foster, encouraged the legislative changes in the face of budget deficits, saying, "We have locked up a lot of people who are redeemable—a whole bunch of them."[43]

In the case of Mississippi, the state with the second-highest incarceration rate in the country,[44] truth-in-sentencing legislation was amended. This legislation had first passed in 1995, only six years prior to this change, abolishing all discretionary release on parole. Now the state restored the possibility of parole for all nonviolent first offenders who served one-quarter of their sentences; under the new law, over 2,000 prisoners became eligible for parole by 2002.[45] Not everyone is happy with these rapid alterations in Mississippi's sentencing code. Stephen Malloy, a former Deputy Director of the Mississippi Bureau of Narcotics and now a professor at the University of Southern Mississippi, called the sentencing changes "a joke" because "anyone in law enforcement knows these are not first time offenders. There is a strong likelihood that they've committed 30 or 40 crimes before they finally get caught."[46] Despite such criticisms, probably in no short supply in street-level law enforcement circles, in 2002, Mississippi also closed one of its prisons in a further cost-cutting move, despite the fact that its prison population was continuing to increase.

That these two particularly conservative states were the first to significantly change their sentencing laws has not gone unnoticed in political and correctional circles. Nor were these the only states to make sentencing or other changes to their criminal justice systems that would almost certainly not have occurred but for the immediacy of a budget crisis. In Connecticut, Indiana, and North Dakota, mandatory minimum sentences for nonviolent crimes have been repealed. According to Michael Lawlor, the Chairman of the Connecticut House Judiciary Committee, this state's new legislation ending mandatory prison sentences for nonviolent drug offenders will be "the most significant change in criminal justice policy we have made in more than 10 years."[47]

In addition, like Mississippi, Virginia and Texas have recently expanded eligibility for early release on parole or community supervision. Iowa has granted judges more discretion over some offenses, and Alabama and New Mexico have eased habitual or predicate felon laws. West Virginia has enacted legislation allowing the state to give money to counties to create alternatives to incarceration, thereby saving money on prisons. And Montana has passed new legislation allowing those convicted of driving under the influence to serve their time in community-based programs.[48]

By 2003, more states joined the ranks of those trying to squeeze out budget savings from their corrections systems through both legislative and policy changes. In a 2003 report summarizing policy and legislative changes in corrections policy in states around the country, Judith Greene found:

- Eighteen states had rolled back some minimum mandatory sentences or other harsh penalties.
- The Michigan legislature, with broad bipartisan support, repealed all the state's mandatory-minimum drug sentences, long regarded as some of the country's toughest, and replaced them with sentences giving judges broad judicial discretion.
- Texas had replaced mandatory-minimum prison sentences with mandatory drug treatment for possession cases involving less than 1 gram of narcotics.
- Kansas had amended its drug laws to divert nonviolent drug offenders convicted of drug possession into mandatory drug treatment and eliminated mandatory-minimum sentences for repeat drug offenders.
- Mississippi restored parole for first-time violent offenders.
- Fifteen states had adopted a variety of policies designed to shorten prison stays, including increasing parole approval rates and providing alternatives to prison for technical parole and probation violators.[49]

In a *New York Times* article on state policy and legislative changes in sentencing and corrections policy, Fox Butterfield confirmed the same trend toward sentencing and policy reform:

After two decades of passing ever tougher sentencing laws and prompting a prison building boom, state legislatures facing budget crises are beginning to rethink their costly approaches to crime.

In the past year, about 25 states have passed laws eliminating some of the lengthy mandatory minimum sentences so popular in the 1980's and 1990's, restoring early release for parole and offering treatment instead of incarceration for some drug offenders. In the process, politicians across the political spectrum say they are discovering a new motto. Instead of being tough on crime, it is more effective to be smart on crime.[50]

Passed in New York State in 1973, the harsh and eventually no-torious Rockefeller Drug Laws had mandated extremely long prison sentences even for drug possession; some of these sentences were longer than people served for committing several violent offenses. But even in New York, where efforts to change the Rockefeller Drug Laws have been stymied for years—despite general legislative agreement that reform is needed—policy changes have been implemented that could significantly affect prison populations. Prisoners convicted of nonviolent crimes can earn a certificate of good behavior that can get them presumptive early release without having to go to the parole board, and inmates convicted of serious drug crimes can earn a one-third reduction of their sentence through good behavior and participation in prison programs.[51]

In a summary of all legislation passed by state legislatures in 2003 alone, the Vera Institute of Justice found that 29 states passed a variety of laws designed to address rising prison populations and costs. The report found that 5 states repealed mandatory-minimum sentences or reduced sentence lengths, 12 states mandated drug treatment in lieu of incarceration or increased alternatives to prison programs, 11 states created sentencing or study commissions to grapple with rising prison populations, 6 states altered parole or probation technical violation policies, and 11 states expanded early or emergency release from prison programs.[52]

All told, in just a two- to three-year period, more than 30 states have undertaken a range of fairly serious efforts involving sentencing or pol-icy reform. Some of these states' recent changes, such as those enacted in Kansas, Michigan, New York, Texas, and Mississippi, are likely to have a large impact on the numbers of people entering prison, since the scope of the legislation passed is quite broad. Other states, such as Mon-tana and Iowa, have passed laws that will have less significant reper-cussions. Yet the most striking aspect of all these state actions is that they exist at all. To a greater or lesser extent, each of these state initia-tives flies in the face of the overall trend toward tougher and longer sentences that has characterized U.S. corrections policy over the last two decades.

At present, the value of many of these legislative changes is partly symbolic; they suggest that, at least for now, law makers are willing and obviously able to implement prison reforms that run counter to the prevailing tide. This gives a powerful signal to other states and to the U.S. public generally that prison reform is in fact possible, and in an era of fiscal crisis even desirable. As Fox Butterfield has written, the changes "reflect a political climate that has changed markedly as crime has fallen, the cost of running prisons has exploded and the economy has slowed."[53]

THE ROLE OF PUBLIC OPINION IN FURTHER SIGNALING CHANGE

As suggested above, state legislative initiatives aimed at revising their sentencing policies may seep into public awareness, slowly but surely signaling a new political context within which criminal justice policy will be made. However, even more important to show is that public opinion had been shifting even before and through the years when states, for their own, largely budgetary reasons, started revising their tough-on-crime policies.

Let me begin this discussion with a few general comments, and caveats, about polling. Gauging public opinion is a tricky business. However, it is a business that has subsisted for decades as the number and types of polling organizations, and the sophistication of polling techniques, have expanded. Not only political campaigns but government in its day-to-day operations now incorporate polling as a matter of course. A pitfall of polling, though, is that opinions gathered represent only a snapshot in time; in response to unusual high-profile events, opinions can change virtually instantly. Reactions to the terrorist attacks of September 11, 2001, present a case study in this phenomenon. Prior to 2001, the Gallup Poll, a national polling organization that has been surveying Americans for decades about a wide variety of issues, did not ask a single question about domestic terrorism. When, in 2002, its poll did understandably incorporate a new terrorism-related question, respondents overwhelmingly ranked this issue as their number-one concern. Thus terrorism surged ahead of other social problems, including crime, the economy, education, and health care, that had comprised Americans' chief worries for the previous decade.[54] While this may be an extreme example, there is little doubt that in the area of crime high-profile incidents—for example, the rape committed by Willie Horton or the murder of Polly Klaas—can also rapidly reshape public opinions and fears about crime.[55]

Moreover, the strong influence of high-profile incidents on public opinion may explain why, at least in the area of criminal justice, the public has seemed less than perfectly informed.[56] Although the national crime rate started to decrease in 1993, continuing to do so steadily until 2001, it was not until the latter year that more Americans said crime had declined than reported crime had increased. Figure 3.1 shows Americans' beliefs about crime from 1989 to 2003. Note that it took almost seven years, and crime having declined by 27%, for Americans to register that crime was declining (or even just staying the same in comparison with the prior year). Again, while crime actually began to decrease in 1993, the table makes clear that it was not until 2000 that more people thought crime rates were either the same or lower than the year before, compared to those who thought they had gone up. Interestingly, beginning in 2002, Americans once again believe there is more crime than the year before by large margins. One assumes that the issue of terrorism might play a role in this reversal.

However, even keeping these caveats about polling in mind—their temporary character, the ability of singular events to suddenly sway opinions, and time lags during which the public remains poorly informed—there seems little doubt that Americans' opinions about crime have changed dramatically in the past decade. Perhaps the best way to demonstrate the dramatic character of this shift is to cull a variety of sources that, taken together, point consistently to the same conclusions. These conclusions are, first, that most Americans now rank crime well below other social issues that they now believe more pressing in importance, and second, that most Americans no longer believe "get tough" criminal justice policies can be justified in the same way as they were in the recent past. I will elaborate on each of these common conclusions that emerge from myriad public polling sources.

In comparison to other social problems, crime has gone from the number-one issue of Americans' concern to far down the list in the space of several years. As Figure 3.2 concretizes, issues such as the economy, education, health care, unemployment, and (at least temporarily) terrorism now far surpass crime in terms of perceived urgency. More specifically, crime, which had dominated polls as the issue of most concern to Americans during the 1990s, has now slipped behind terrorism, the economy, unemployment, education, and health care. While the

Figure 3.1

Percent of Americans Who Believe There Was More,
Less, or Same Amount of Crime Compared to
One Year Ago, Selected Years, 1989–2003

	More Crime	Less Crime	Same Amount
1989	84	5	5
1990	84	3	7
1992	89	3	4
1993	87	4	5
1996	71	15	8
1997	64	25	6
1998	52	35	8
2000	47	41	7
2001	41	43	10
2002	62	21	11
2003	60	25	11

Source: Sourcebook of Criminal Justice Statistics Online, The Gallup
Poll, "Attitudes toward Level of Crime in the U.S.," Table 2.31.
Available at www.albany.edu/sourcebook/1995/pdf/t231.pdf.

Figure 3.2

Percent of Americans Who Believe the Following Issues
Are the Most Important Facing Government,
Selected Years, 1994–2003

	1994	1998	2003
Crime	37	20	2
Economy	14	6	34
Education	5	11	4
Health Care	20	6	5
Terrorism	n/a	n/a	10
Unemployment	18	5	10

Source: Sourcebook of Criminal Justice Statistics Online, The Gallup
Poll, "Attitudes toward the Most Important Problems Facing the
Country," Table 2.1. Available at www.albany.edu/sourcebook/
1995/pdf/t21.pdf.

September 11, 2001, terrorist attacks no doubt played a role in these re-
assessments, crime has declined so significantly that its new relative
unimportance cannot simply be explained away by the events of 9/11.
This is reinforced by Figure 3.3, which shows crime declining in perceived importance well before the terrorist attacks ever happened, and
remaining a lowered priority even thereafter.

Figure 3.3

Percent of Americans Ranking the Two Most Important
Problems for the Government to Address,
Selected Years, 1994–2003

	1994	1998	2001	2002	2003
Crime	36	13	5	5	>.5
The War	n/a	n/a	n/a	n/a	38
The Economy	12	9	12	15	37
Terrorism	n/a	n/a	n/a	23	16
Iraq/Saddam Hussein	n/a	n/a	n/a	n/a	15
Health	45	11	10	8	8
Education	6	14	30	12	5
Taxes	6	16	23	8	4
Social Security	n/a	6	12	5	1

Source: *Sourcebook of Criminal Justice Statistics Online,* The Gallup Poll, "What Are the
Two Most Important Issues for Government to Address?" Table 2.2. Available at
www.albany.edu/sourcebook/1995/pdf/t22.pdf.

Figures 3.2 and 3.3 clearly show that crime is now far less important
than it used to be to Americans, and that education, health care, and
various aspects of the economy have become of relatively greater concern. As also noted when introducing this chapter, crime went from its
number-one spot in the mid-1990s to being tied with Social Security for
fifth place in 2002. And, by 2003, the issue of crime as one of the most
important problems for government to deal with scored less than 1%,
lower than 24 issues raised by the poll. Again, as with crime, the quick
rise of the war and terrorism's importance probably somewhat deflated
the prioritizing of education and health (and perhaps some of the other
issues). On the other hand, just as the decline in crime's perceived importance has been a steady one, so Figure 3.3 illustrates that public concerns about other issues have been steadily greater than crime from the
early 2000s onward.

Important to underscore here is that a social problem dropping in
perceived significance from number 1 to (say) number 6 does not necessarily indicate that the public is less concerned about that problem.
But it may mean that the public feels relatively stronger about other issues. Yet for political purposes, that is, when it comes to the amount of
pressure politicians feel about individual issues, these rankings are
likely to be meaningful indeed.

Crime's diminished relative importance to Americans is not sur-

Figure 3.4
Percent of Americans Who Fear Walking Alone at
Night Anywhere within a Mile of Where They
Live, Selected Years, 1965–2003

Year	Percent
1965	34
1975	45
1982	48
1992	44
1996	39
2000	34
2001	30
2002	35
2003	36

Source: *Sourcebook of Criminal Justice Statistics Online*, The
Gallup Poll, Table 2.35. Available at www.albany.edu/
sourcebook/1995/pdf/t235.pdf.

prising given that crime has decreased sharply at the national level.
Moreover, as Figure 3.4 illustrates through answers to a question about
walking alone in one's neighborhood, Americans' fear of crime has also
been dissipating. Far fewer people were afraid to walk alone in 2000
than in 1982, when almost half (48%) of Americans feared venturing
out alone within a mile of their residences. By 2003, this percentage decreased to just more than a third of all Americans, or 36%. Interestingly,
there has been a recent increase in fear of walking alone at night despite
crime continuing to drop. However, the general decline of this particular manifestation of fear of crime suggests that reductions in crime since
1992, and media attention to this decrease, have indeed started to affect
public perceptions.

Along with the decline in the crime's perceived importance and in
fear of crime, the public appears to have slowly but significantly moved
away from believing that prisons ought to be the main criminal justice
method for dealing with offenders. On this topic, Americans seem to
have far more progressive and "nuanced" views than one would think
from listening to politicians talk about crime. For example, in 2002, the
Open Society Institute commissioned Peter D. Hart Research Associates
to conduct a national poll on public opinion and criminal justice.[57] This
poll found that public views of crime noticeably changed over the last
decade, and concluded that

Americans have a fundamentally different view on addressing the nation's crime problem today than in 1994, the heyday of tough anti-crime political rhetoric. The public is no longer seeking a purely punitive approach to crime. Rather, they support a balanced approach that includes not just punishment, but a renewed commitment to the prevention of crime. In addition, with a majority of states facing severe budget deficits, focusing on a "lock-'em-up" approach is too costly.[58]

Indicative of sharp change, too, was the response given to the question of whether America needed a tougher approach to crime (using stricter sentencing, more capital punishment, and less parole) or a tougher approach to the "causes of crime" (emphasizing job training, family counseling, and more activities for young people). Figure 3.5 shows the difference from 1994 to 2001 in the public's relative evaluation of these two approaches.

By 2001, more than twice as many Americans thought it made more sense to deal with the causes of crime than to increase penalties for crime. Somewhat surprising, even in 1994, more Americans thought the same thing, albeit by a much smaller margin. This suggests that public opinion on crime issues has long been more complex than the politic rhetoric surrounding it.[59] When these figures are broken down further, the study also shows that those whose attitudes have changed most since 1994 are people traditionally thought to favor punitive approaches: even among white Republican men, a more progressive approach to crime was preferred.[60]

Strengthening these results' credibility is that they are mirrored by Gallup Poll results that found, in 1994, that 57% of Americans thought that "attacking" social problems made sense, as opposed to 39% who wanted more law enforcement. By 2003, the poll found that 68% of Americans favored attacking social problems, as opposed to 29% who favored more law enforcement.[61] While the percentages are somewhat different in this second poll, both polls register a shift in public preferences away from more law enforcement and toward confronting social causes of crime.

In addition, the Hart Poll found a reversal of opinions about mandatory sentencing as opposed to judges having discretion over sentencing. In 1995, 55% percent of Americans thought that mandatory sentencing was a good idea, as opposed to 38% who believed that judges should have greater discretion. By 2001, only 38% of Americans

Figure 3.5
Percent of Americans Who Prefer Tougher Approach to
Crime or Tougher Approach to the Causes of Crime,
1994 and 2001

	1994	2001
Tougher Approach to Crime	42%	32%
Tougher Approach to Causes of Crime	48%	65%

Source: Peter D. Hart Research Associates, Inc. (2002) *The New Politics of Criminal Justice*, Washington, D.C.

thought that mandatory sentencing made sense, as opposed to 45% who thought judges should have discretion.[62] This shift stands in almost complete contrast to the overall direction of American criminal justice policy over the past decade.

Americans also took a dim view of the country's War on Drugs. In what the pollsters called "a resounding condemnation of America's war on drugs," 70% of Americans thought that the War on Drugs was "more of a failure," as opposed to only 18% who said it was "more of a success."[63] Moreover, by a margin of two to one (63% to 31%), the public said that drug use should be handled mainly through counseling and treatment, rather than as a serious crime to be processed through the courts and prisons.[64] These polling results accord with other indicators of change, such as the overwhelming public support received by the California and Arizona ballot propositions to divert nonviolent drug users from prison. The poll also found that 74% of respondents favored mandatory treatment, as opposed to prison, for those convicted of drug possession; that 75% of respondents favored supervised community service/probation for nonviolent offenders; and that 70% of respondents favored prisoners obtaining an education so they could find jobs upon release.[65]

Finally, the poll asked where cuts should be made to help balance state budgets. Prisons topped the list, tied with transportation (28% each), of areas where the public would most like to see reductions enacted. This was followed by child care for working families (10%), security against terrorism (10%), education and job training (5%), and health care (2%).[66]

Again, the significance of these national findings is fortified by their broad general agreement with other polling results. In 2001, a statewide

poll found that 35% of California residents would target energy contracts (a very specific California issue) and 34% would target prisons
to help close the state's massive budget deficit.[67] In 2002, the Hart poll
presented two hypothetical campaign positions on crime, one supposedly put forth by a conservative candidate and another supposedly put
forth by a progressive candidate. The two arguments were phrased as
follows:

> Conservative Argument: The best way to fight crime and protect law-
> abiding citizens is to make sure that criminals face punishment that is
> swift and certain. Young people need to know that if you break the
> law, you go to prison. We need truth in sentencing that eliminates
> early parole and ensures that criminals serve their full sentence. And
> prison should mean hard labor—not watching TV or working out in a
> gym—so that it is an effective deterrent. By getting tough on crime
> with such laws as three-strikes-and-you're-out, we are bringing crime
> rates down and protecting law-abiding Americans.

> Progressive Argument: It's time for a balanced, commonsense ap-
> proach to crime. We need tough laws to hold people accountable for
> their actions, and we must prevent crime by dealing with the causes.
> Let's require offenders to work and take basic education classes, so
> they can get jobs and become law-abiding citizens when they're re-
> leased. We should place nonviolent drug offenders in mandatory
> treatment programs, and use prisons to keep violent criminals off the
> streets. And let's invest in after-school programs, and teach personal
> responsibility and moral values to young people, to prevent crime be-
> fore it occurs.[68]

Surprising given the current direction of criminal justice policies, more
Americans supported the progressive position (54%) than the conservative one (39%).[69]

One reason the progressive candidate's hypothetical position was
chosen by more respondents may have been that the phraseology used
—including terms such as "balanced," "require offenders" to work, and
"personal responsibility and moral values"—do not entirely jettison the
political rhetoric with which people are familiar. Obviously, in this case,
the pollsters presented neatly wrapped positions that do not reflect

distortions that take place when, especially over crime, candidates exchange charges and countercharges in actual campaign settings. Yet the relatively liberal position most people selected unambiguously advocated prevention and alternatives to incarceration, suggesting that more people—including apparent conservatives—are, and can be, receptive to arguments running counter to the past two decades of criminal justice policy.

This seemingly surprising result, that a balanced and more liberal position trumped a purely punitive one, can also be understood given the findings of a recent review of decades of public opinion research and polling data. In a 2000 article analyzing American public opinion on punishment and corrections, Francis Cullen et al. concluded that Americans hold fairly complex views on punishment and do not simply have a one-dimensional, purely retributive opinion. Their study, which reviewed almost 200 articles, polls, and books on public opinion and also included original public opinion research, concluded that there was substantial room for a variety of non–purely punitive correction policies, especially with regard to nonviolent offenders. The study's conclusion is worth quoting at length:

First, consistent with the claims of commentators such as Johnson and DiIulio, the public is punitive toward crime. Get-tough attitudes are real and not simply a methodological artifact. Second, this punitiveness is not fixed on a single point but is "mushy." Even when expressing punitive opinions, people tend to be flexible enough to consider a range of sentencing options, including sanctions that are less harsh than those they may have favored either at first thought or when provided with only minimal information on which to base their views. Third, members of the public must be given a good reason not to be punitive. They moderate their punitiveness when less stringent interventions have utility for victims, the community, and offenders. Fourth, violent crime is the great divide between punitiveness and nonpunitiveness. Citizens are reluctant to take chances with physically dangerous offenders; they generally want them behind bars. For nonviolent offenders, however, a range of correctional options will be entertained. Fifth, despite the sustained attack leveled against the concept of offender treatment, the public continues to believe that rehabilitation should be an integral goal of the correctional system. Sixth,

people strongly support "child saving," encouraging both the rehabilitation of youthful offenders and the use of early intervention programs that seek to direct children at risk for future criminality into a
conventional life course. In fact, compared to imprisonment, early prevention is favored by a wide margin as a solution to crime. Seventh,
the central tendency in public opinion is to be punitive and progressive—to endorse the use of a balanced response to lawbreakers, which
includes an effort to do justice, protect society, and reform offenders.
When the full body of survey data are taken into account, it thus appears that with regard to punishment and corrections, the public is
more rational than irrational in the policy agenda it embraces.[70]

Their conclusion, while recognizing the continuing punitive nature
of public opinion concerning violent crime (somewhat more so than the
Hart poll), clearly shows that the complexity of public opinion about
nonviolent crime creates an opportunity for a political candidate to put
forth a balanced approach that is seen as fair and having utility in terms
of benefiting offenders, victims, and the community.

To summarize this section on polling, Americans' views on issues
of corrections and punishment are obviously more complicated than
can be discerned from the simplistic character of recent political discourse. Moreover, Americans' views are clearly in the process of changing. Recent polling suggests far more public support than previously
exhibited, both for alternatives to prison for nonviolent offenders, including low-level drug dealers, and for mandatory treatment and community supervision for nonviolent drug users. In addition, Americans
overwhelmingly describe the War on Drugs as a failure and favor dealing with the causes of crime or tackling underlying social problems
over more law enforcement. Even the use of mandatory sentences has
fallen out of favor, most Americans now believing that judges should
have more discretion. These conclusions appear to reflect long-term
trends rather than "blips" in public opinion potentially attributable to
single high-profile incidents and their repercussions.

But the existence and significance of a long-term, patterned shift in
American public opinion on crime is evidenced in another way as well.
In the next and final section of this chapter, I turn to analyzing two voter
referenda that put into practice the sentiments Americans expressed
only on paper when answering the questions posed by various polling
organizations.

MANIFESTING ALTERED PUBLIC OPINION THROUGH VOTER REFERENDA

On November 7, 2000, Californians voted overwhelmingly for a public referendum called the Substance Abuse and Crime Prevention Act of 2000, or Proposition 36, as it was more popularly called. This referendum proposed that individuals convicted of nonviolent drug possession offenses receive probation and court-ordered drug treatment in lieu of prison. In addition, parolees with no serious or violent prior convictions could be diverted into treatment if they had drug-related violations of the conditions of their parole. Once the parole is diverted into treatment, Proposition 36 permits up to three drug-related violations of the conditions of treatment (including arrests for drug possession) before anyone sentenced under the law can be reincarcerated. Simultaneously, the proposition appropriated $120 million of funding for drug treatment of the estimated 37,000 drug offenders to be served under the new system.[71]

Obvious from the margin of victory by which the proposition passed—61% in favor, compared to 39% opposed—was that the citizens of California were ready to move away from incarcerating nonviolent drug offenders and toward providing treatment instead. Thus, paradoxically enough, the same state that had passed the toughest three strikes laws in the country only several years earlier now became the state with the largest single program aimed at diverting an entire class of offenders from serving prison time.

The campaign to put the referendum on the ballot in California was the brainchild of three wealthy businessmen: insurance magnate Peter Lewis; financier and philanthropist George Soros; and John Sperling, the founder of the University of Phoenix. Initially Lewis, Soros, and Sperling commissioned a poll that found—not surprising, given the polling results surveyed above—that only 11% of Californians considered the drug war a success and that 65% of the states' residents preferred treatment over prison for nonviolent drug offenders.[72] Based on this seemingly strong public support for alternatives to prison for drug offenders, the three created an organization that collected enough signatures to place the initiative on the ballot. They then ran a well-financed professional campaign to get the ballot passed. Public support for the initiative was exemplified in the words of 73-year-old Santa Monica resident Rita Lowenthal, as quoted in the *Los Angeles Times*, when she declared, "Locking people up for drugs—for an illness many of them can't control—is just primitive. What are we going to do, lock everybody up? All our sons and daughters? Where is it going to stop?"[73] Many in the medical community also strongly supported the proposition, believing that drug addiction and use were more kindred to disease than to rational criminal activity. For instance, as the head of the California Society of Addiction Medicine said in support of the proposition, "It makes as much sense to put [addicts] in prison as it did to lock up schizophrenics 100 years ago."[74]

Not only did the proposition pass overwhelmingly in general, but in particular, it did remarkably well in one of California's most conservative areas: Orange County.[75] What allowed the proposition to win, despite vigorous opposition by almost every California law enforcement agency and by many judges who saw their discretionary power over drug-related cases about to be eliminated? For one thing, the proposition had been generously financed; its proponents spent nearly $3 million campaigning for its passage. In addition, advocates successfully made the case that current policies of incarcerating drug users, who made up 12% of the California system's prison population, were far more expensive and inefficient than other alternatives. Whereas it cost over $23,000 annually to incarcerate such users, the annual cost of treatment was only $4,300 per person in need.[76] Joining these arguments were the findings of an analysis undertaken by the nonpartisan California Legislative Analysts Office (LAO). According to the LAO, Proposition 36 would save approximately $200 to $250 million annually and would yield a whopping one-time savings of $475 to $525 million as a result of diverting up to 37,000 drug offenders from prisons that otherwise needed to be built.[77] Such fiscal arguments, combined with a widespread sense that current law enforcement policies were ineffective, led Californians to pass decisively what is now the largest state prison diversion program in the country. That this occurred amid united law enforcement opposition, and in the state with the largest prison system and the toughest three strikes legislation, shows further that Americans are open to changing corrections policies, at least for the largest class of people admitted to prison nationally each year: drug offenders.

A few years before this referendum, but sufficiently well known that it also may have influenced California voters, the even more conservative state of Arizona passed another proposition mandating fundamental changes in drug policy. In 1996, Proposition 200, or the Drug Medicalization, Prevention and Control Act, was put on the Arizona ballot. It passed by an even wider margin than did Proposition 36 in California; in Arizona, the vote was 65% to 35%. The Arizona act had two major provisions. First, it allowed for the medical use of marijuana with a prescription from two doctors; second, it diverted nonviolent drug users from prison. The second feature differs in the Arizona and California propositions, in that the former state requires a finding or plea of guilty on a felony for an individual to be diverted into treatment, whereas in California, Proposition 36 called for diverting people into prison prior to sentencing and for no conviction at all if the conditions of probation and treatment were met. Despite this difference, the two propositions are similar in their overall goal of diverting nonviolent drug offenders from prison into treatment.

As also later happened in California, law enforcement agencies vigorously opposed Arizona's Proposition 200. The Arizona legislature blocked the initiative's implementation for a full year before finally, in 1998, putting the referendum on the ballot again. Once more, the referendum passed strongly, with 57% of Arizona's voters in favor compared to 43% opposed.[78] In the face of such strong opposition, what enabled a reform proposition to succeed in Arizona too? Again, according to Norm Helber, then-Director of Adult Probation in Maricopa County, cost arguments helped to shift public opinion and to persuade normally conservative Arizona voters to favor the proposition.[79] As in California, the proposition's proponents claimed huge cost savings based on the difference between treatment and prison costs; in 1999, a report from the Arizona Supreme Court estimated that Proposition 200 would save almost $7 million annually by diverting drug offenders from prisons.[80] In the end, as Arizona's Court of Appeals Judge Rudy Gerber told the *New York Times*, "It was like a turnstile. Many of us came to the conclusion that we were parading them through the courts and prisons without out solving the root problem."[81]

All told, the actual results of these propositions are not yet certain; they have not been in effect long enough for their hoped-for cost savings and public safety benefits to be ascertained. What is clear, though, is that two otherwise conservative states, especially on issues of law and order, decisively passed laws that divert an entire class of offenders from prison. This, too, evidences a shift in public opinion that is hard to ignore. The California and Arizona experiences suggest that major changes in criminal justice policy may be possible to achieve in other states, both conservative and more liberal ones.

This trend toward changing public opinion and diverting significant numbers of drug offenders from prison has been further evidenced, most recently by sentencing reforms in Texas, Kansas, and Michigan. In 2003, Kansas and Texas, through the legislative process (and not, like California and Arizona, through public referendum), passed laws requiring treatment in lieu of prison for nonviolent drug offenders. In both states, the laws passed with bipartisan support, and both states are considered conservative and tough on issues of crime and punishment. In Michigan, the legislature repealed most of the state's mandatory minimum sentences for drug crimes. There is little doubt, given the recent diversion of drug offenders from prison in Michigan and the reforms in the four generally conservative law-and-order states mentioned above (Texas, Kansas, California, and Arizona), that other states are in a political position to begin to consider and adopt similar diversion programs.

IN SUM

Clearly, deteriorating state economies have driven state law makers to the point where they are willing to reduce corrections budgets, the fastest-growing state expenditure other than Medicaid in many parts of the country. Simultaneously, by 2003, polls showed that the American public was more concerned about education, employment, the economy, and health care than about crime. Together these trends create a new political landscape that, for the first time in over 25 years, raises genuine hope that the size and cost of state prisons can be substantially reduced. Given budget pressures and shifting public opinion combined, an opportunity now exists to alter correctional policy and to make long-term changes in how the United States devotes resources to preventing and punishing crime.

Even with a national economic recovery, many of the budget pressures now felt by states are likely to persist for many years. While states may again one day be able to deliver (if so desired) massive tax cuts, more prisons, and adequately funded education and health care, the almost geometric growth of Medicaid and the future impact of prior tax cuts make this an unlikely scenario in the near term.

Consequently, law makers may well wish to seize this present opportunity, this "alignment of the stars," to promote policies that reduce the size of prisons, protect public safety, and assist in funding other pressing social needs such as education and health care. As this chapter has shown, public support exists. But the two developments surveyed in this chapter—budget crises that states have recently encountered and a state budget outlook that remains constrained, even with an improved national economy—could be called external factors. These developments can be used to argue for shifts in criminal justice policy, but they originate and are in a sense outside the control of the criminal justice system per se. In contrast, the next two developments to be discussed, in Chapters 4 and 5, involve reasons for downsizing the prison system that are rooted in recent experiences with the criminal justice system itself. These developments are internal and relatively controllable, to the extent they involve two lessons—one about the lack of any clearly demonstrated relationship between prison expansion and crime reduction, and the other about the pitfalls of sending hundreds of thousands of technical parole violators back to prison—that have immediate practical implications.

4

Why Prison Growth Does Not Substantially Reduce Crime

PERHAPS NO OTHER city in the world has received the kind of attention showered over the last decade on New York City after its recent and highly publicized reductions in crime. Law makers, policy makers, and journalists from other states and nations have visited in large numbers to investigate how New York City accomplished this reduction. Rudy Giuliani, the city's well-known two-term mayor, successfully made this issue the centerpiece of his tenure as statistics catapulted him to national visibility as probably the country's most famous crime-fighter. The other prominent figure most often associated with the crime reduction is William Bratton, New York City's Police Commissioner from 1994 to 1996 (and the current Police Chief in Los Angeles). Both men were extremely active in publicizing the decrease in crime, each sometimes claiming the lion's share of credit for the city's progress.

Scrutinizing the city's declines closely, it is easy to understand why New York garnered a national and international reputation for big-city crime reductions. From 1993 to 2003 the number of reported violent crimes in New York City declined by 64%; homicides fell by 69% while robberies and assaults dropped by 70% and 55% respectively.[1] In 2001, New York ranked tenth of the ten largest cities in total per capita index crime and eighth per capita for violent crime. From 1993 to 2001, apart from San Diego, no other city in the United States experienced reductions in crime comparable to New York in such a short time period. In fact, of the 25% drop in violent crime reported nationally by the FBI from 1993 to 2001, New York City's contribution was responsible for about one-sixth of the decline.[2] Finally, at 52%, New York's decrease in violent crime from 1993 to 2001 is more than twice as large as the 25% national reduction rate. Thus New York's crime decline is both hugely significant in its own right and a major factor that has driven down national numbers.

A host of explanations have been offered as to how and why the "New York City miracle" happened. Indeed, investigating possible reasons for New York City's striking 52% decline in violent crime from 1993 to 2001, and its equally if not more striking 63% homicide reduction during the same period,[3] became a virtual cottage industry in New York City criminal justice and criminology circles. Theories abound. They range from the reengineering of the City Police Department by William Bratton and the success of the department's "zero tolerance" approach in fighting street crime,[4] to the evolving nature of the city's drug markets.[5] Some people suggest that the city's impressive crime reduction rates resulted from demographic changes;[6] others attribute the drop simply to the city riding the crest of a national trend touching large cities in general.[7]

I do not aim to assess these myriad explanations' validity; I leave it to others to analyze the reasons for New York City's striking declines, as well as where and to whom credit belongs. Instead, I will focus specifically on the role that increased incarceration—in the form of prison and, to a lesser extent, jail—did or did not play in the city's well-known accomplishment. Investigating the part played by incarceration in realizing the largest and most well known case of crime reduction in recent U.S. history seems especially relevant in light of one of this book's central tenets: that public safety can be maintained and even enhanced while prison populations are reduced through various alternative policy and criminal justice means.

To make this argument, I survey the increasing use of incarceration in the United States over the past decade, also looking at rates of violent crime during this same period. Second, I present a case study of New York City from 1993 to 2001 and detail dramatic shifts in how the city's policing and criminal justice system operated. Here special attention is paid to the impact of one shift in particular on the city and state correction systems. Between 1993 and 2001, many more people arrested for committing low-level offenses were given short-term pretrial jail stays, and many fewer were given posttrial long-term prison sentences. Analyzing the implications of this trend in depth, I contend that while exactly what caused New York City's famous crime decline is hard to know, one factor that did *not* cause the decline is much easier to ascertain: increased use of prisons.

In this regard, San Diego's experience is also relevant: after New York, this is the city that has achieved the largest crime decrease in the country, albeit through the use of quite different law enforcement strategies. However, as in New York City, San Diego realized significant crime reductions without sending more people to prison. Last but not least, I return to the larger picture to explore both how states reduced their crime rates with far lower than average prison increases and also how the converse occurred—i.e., how states with hugely increased prison systems experienced very low, if any, crime declines.

Thus the success of both New York and other states in reducing crime while funding much lower than average prison increases offers yet a third way to argue against the "tough on crime" rhetoric that has dominated the American political landscape for the last several decades. Whereas the previous chapters concentrated on how deteriorating state budgets and changing public opinion have altered that landscape, this one presents an argument against rising incarceration that stems from reevaluating state and localities' own recent criminal justice policies from within.

This discussion of crime reduction in relation to prison expansion or reduction is also important since tough criminal justice measures are still viewed by law makers, and often by the public, as the most effective way to fight violent crime. Such a premise was the rationale of the 1994 Federal Crime Bill that provided states and cities with billions of additional dollars for hiring more police officers and building new prisons. Clearly, ongoing increases in the number of prison and jail beds have been a central component of this country's crime control strategy for the last two decades. Yet the New York City case study discussed here, along with other states' and localities' experiences, calls this presumed relationship between prison expansion and public safety into question. In New York City's case, "toughness" in the form of greatly expanded prison use cannot account for the city's 52% decline in violent crime rates: quite simply, this is not what happened.

The case study of New York City to follow is quite detailed, requiring explanation of precisely how the city's criminal justice system has changed over the past decade. While this analysis contains some implicit and explicit criticisms of some of these systemic changes, it also recognizes the efficacy of many of the reforms New York City has instituted. Nevertheless, I do not offer this example to convince other cities' policy makers to follow New York's model in particular. My goal is a more broadly criminological one. If no clear-cut relationship can be shown to exist between expanded prison use and decreased crime in New York City, this conclusion—and the analysis on which it is based —may well apply to other city and state contexts too, including ones that run their criminal justice systems quite differently. On a more general level, this case study also suggests that prison reductions can come from changes in law enforcement—precisely what happened in New York City—as their unintended consequence.

On the other hand, though, it seems simplistic to conclude that many states are not interested in the special character of New York City's criminal justice experiences, having historically regarded (or disregarded) the Big Apple as too liberal and socially permissive. For, as just discussed, New York's crime reductions gained the city tremendous respect, as well as visits from many states and countries. Before returning to New York, though, let me begin this chapter with the national context within which that miracle became possible.

THE NATIONAL PICTURE: HOW DO PRISON EXPANSION AND CRIME REDUCTIONS RELATE?

Rich and often caustic academic and policy debates have emerged over the question of how crime and expanded U.S. incarceration rates interrelate. The simple fact of our national experience with incarceration seems itself to stimulate controversy. The United States incarcerates a larger proportion of its population than any other country in the world. In the United States, 702 per 100,000 people are currently incarcerated in both prison and jail, whereas Russia, previously the world leader in prison rates, locks up 628 per 100,000.[8] In addition, as noted earlier, those imprisoned in the United States are disproportionately African-American and Latino. In 2002, the U.S. incarceration rate for males was 450 per 100,000 for whites; 1,176 per 100,000 for Hispanics; and 3,437 per 100,000 for African-Americans.[9] On the national level, the nation's combined jail and prison populations quadrupled, from 500,000 to over 2,000,000, since 1980.[10] Again, expenditures for prisons and jails have correspondingly skyrocketed. In 1982, the United States spent $9.57 billion on its state and federal prisons and local jails. By 2001, that figure rose to $60.4 billion. This represented an astounding 531% increase, which was far greater than had occurred in any other part of the criminal justice system.[11]

The massive use of incarceration, racial disparities among those incarcerated, and the huge drain on state resources thereby created are major themes in a burgeoning political and academic literature that has questioned this national policy's merits in terms of morality, public safety, and efficiency.[12] However, as I have noted elsewhere, incarceration rates have continued to raise, such debate notwithstanding; most state prison systems are still expanding even as their overall rate of expansion has leveled off. Total spending on corrections, too, has steadily gone up.

Interestingly enough, recent continuations in prison growth have occurred virtually alongside significant declines in the national violent crime rate. As previously noted, from 1993 to 2001, the amount of serious violent crime in the United States fell by 25%.[13] Some commentators have concluded from this that the 46% rise in prison populations during the same years must have been a major contributing factor to the falling crime rate.[14] Other conservative and empirically based appraisals of the effect of prison expansion over the last decade estimate that over 25% of the national crime decline can be attributed to increased incarceration.[15] In this vein Allen Beck, the chief of corrections statistics for the Justice Department, recently stated: "In the 90s, there was a much greater chance that violent offenders would be incarcerated, and would stay longer. But those reforms had their effect, and now we're finally starting to see the prison population stabilize."[16]

Thus, if one simply looks at the past decade of national crime reduction and incarceration figures and at some extant research, the policy of using prison expansion to bring down crime rates seems to have some rational basis. However, as Figure 4.1 illustrates, the relationship between rising prison populations and violent crime rates over time is less than clear.

Figure 4.1 shows that while rates of violent crime have been decreasing from 1993 onward as the prison population increases, violent crime rates have increased along with prison population rates during other time periods. For instance according to the *Uniform Crime Reports,* from 1988 to 1992, violent crime rates increased by 24%[17] although the prison population increased by 40% during the same period.[18] If the growth in the prison population was really a major influence on crime reduction from 1993 to 2001, why would this correlation between violent crime and prison growth not hold from 1988 to 1992 as well? What this suggests is that the relationship between incarceration and crime is not particularly amenable to simplistic explanation. Yet it is easy to see why policy makers find it tempting—especially in a "get tough" environment—to relate violent crime to prison growth anyway. At a national level, this connection is almost irresistibly appealing. Given that

Figure 4.1
Serious Violent Crime, Crimes Recorded by the Police and
Correctional Population, U.S., 1980–2002

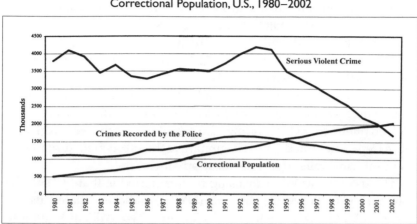

Source: Bureau of Justice Statistics, Key Crime and Justice Facts at a Glance, www.ojp.usdoj.gov/bjs/glance/tables/4meastab.htm and www.ojp.usdoj.gov/bjs/glance/tables/corr2tab.htm. *Serious Violent Crime* figures from the *National Crime Victimization Survey, Crimes Recorded by the Police*, from *FBI Uniform Crime Reports*.

the central anti-crime features of the federal government's recent crime bill necessitate granting billions of dollars for new police officers and new prison construction,[19] showing crime decline and prison growth as positively correlated may seem like political manna from heaven.

Much of the national research to date has found that, all told, prison has played some—though a relatively small—role in the U.S. crime decrease of the last decade. Yet a simple graph of prison growth and national crime rates over the last twenty years (Figure 4.1) raises more questions than it can answer. Perhaps, though, investigating more concrete local examples—such as the New York City and smaller San Diego cases to which I now turn—can yield more specific insight into whether prison and crime are necessarily related, a question that on the national level seems only inconclusively resolved.

NEW YORK CITY AND SAN DIEGO: REDUCING CRIME WITHOUT EXPANDING PRISON

When investigating New York City crime declines and their relationship to prison expansion, it makes sense to focus on the eight-year period from 1993 to 2001, for two reasons. The first is that, even though violent crime rates began declining in 1991, their rate of decrease became proportionately greater in 1993. More specifically, violent crime decreased by approximately 9% during 1992 and 1993, the last two years of Mayor David Dinkins's tenure in office.[20] However, from 1993 to 1994, violent crime decreased by 11.1% in one year alone;[21] between 1993 and 2001, it declined by 52%. Nonetheless, many people do not realize that crime began to decline under then-Mayor Dinkins. This no doubt remains a source of frustration for the former Mayor, who barely received public credit for funding a huge build-up of the New York City Police Department, and for the beginning of the subsequent turnaround of violent crime rates after years of steady increases.

The second reason for focusing on this period is that in 1994, the New York City Police Department (NYPD) radically altered its approach to law enforcement. Mayor Giuliani hired William Bratton to head the NYPD with a clear understanding that "zero tolerance" or "quality of life" policing would be his governing orientation. The hallmark of this policing approach is that low-level crimes such as street-level drug dealing and use, aggressive panhandling, and public drinking needed to be strictly enforced. Bratton believed in a theory he intended to prove true in practice: that more serious crimes would decrease once an environment had been created where even the smallest crimes were punished. By arresting, searching, and performing warrant checks on low-level offenders, so this theory went, police were also likely to find people who had or would have committed more serious crimes.

Thus, focusing this analysis on the years 1993–2001 captures both the period of greatest crime reductions in New York City over the past several decades and the point at which the city's huge and complicated criminal justice system began implementing an altered policing strategy. This focus also allows me to examine whether the city jail system and the state prison system expanded as a result of this dramatically changed enforcement strategy, and whether expanding incarceration was an essential reason for New York City's drastic crime reductions.

Just as these two factors explain why I have focused on the years 1993 to 2001, other reasons exist for studying New York City in particular, where, indeed, something unusual appeared to be happening. For one thing, the New York State prison system grew by 5% between 1993 and 2001. While it was therefore obviously expanding, its rate of growth was far lower than the national rate of growth (45%) during the same years.[22] New York City prisoners constituted 66%[23] of all state prison admissions, yet from 1993 to 2001 the number of people sentenced to prison from New York City declined by 42%.[24] This tremendous decline in the number of prisoners sent from New York City to the state prison system was responsible for the state prison system's low rate of growth in these years. However, if it were true that the more people who are imprisoned, the more crime declines—as the conventional wisdom has held—then the rest of the country should have evidenced far greater crime decreases than New York City. But this was not the case: instead, New York City's crime decrease was over twice as large as the rest of the country's, while its prison system growth was a fraction of the nation's (as the number of people sentenced to prison from New York City declined significantly).

This was one way in which the New York City experience was different from that of the rest of the country. But New York was defying larger national trends in a second way. On the whole, the jail population in the United States increased by 39% from 1993 to 2001.[25] In contrast, New York City's jail system steadily declined in size from 1993 to 2001, dropping from 19,345 to 14,494,[26] a decrease of 25%.[27]

What accounts for these distinctively different criminal justice trends? To answer this question, the three subsections below detail how, from 1993 to 2001, New York City's system of punishment drastically changed its character. Fascinatingly, an unintended consequence of these changes was that they led to New York City exemplifying (somewhat ironically, since the philosophies of then-Mayor Giuliani and then–Police Commissioner Bratton were intended as part and parcel of a larger tough-on-crime approach) how dramatic crime reductions could be achieved without resorting more punitively to increased prison use. In the first of these subsections I look at precisely what the New York Police Department began to do differently. Here I elaborate on how, while the numbers of people sent to prison between 1993 and 2001 systematically declined, the numbers of those who were arrested, put into the system, and went to jail for short periods increased. The intense police effort to enforce quality of life through high-volume misdemeanor arrests and the virtual elimination of summonses also contributed to another unintended by-product of these policies: rates of felony indictment also fell during this period due to the "poor quality" of many cases. Taken together, these factors resulted in the city's jail population declining and in a prison system with one of the smallest growth rates in the country.

After explaining these changes, the second subsection below looks at how they affected the city's jail system, and the third at how they affected the state's prison systems in turn.

The Role of the NYPD in Reducing the Use of Prison

It is police enforcement policies that are ultimately responsible for a city's statistics on how many people have been prosecuted, indicted, and sent to jail or prison in a given time period. In the case of New York City, where police strategy changed drastically between 1993 and 2001, close attention to these policies is particularly important. Moreover, it was then that New York developed its now national and international reputation as the city best able to hugely reduce crime through effective crime-fighting strategies (even as, over these same years, high-profile crime incidents involving Abner Louima, Amadou Diallo, and Patrick Dorismond also earned New York a reputation within the city's minority communities for overly aggressive enforcement). Specifically, then, what did the police begin to do differently that resulted both in its shining reputation and, as these policies' unintended consequence, in decreasing the number of people New York City sent to prisons upstate?

Probably the most publicized feature of the police strategy enacted by then–Police Commissioner William Bratton was the CompStat program (abbreviated from "computerized statistics"), known for its systemic ability to immediately identify crime hot spots and to hold precinct commanders accountable for lowering crime in their neighborhoods.[28] This system takes the electronic crime reports filed by officers each day at their precinct houses, quickly identifies their exact geographic location, and uses a geographic information system and statistical software to analyze and display their patterns. CompStat also gives top NYPD staff real-time data on crime trends and reinforces their knowledge of the status of ongoing criminal investigations in particular precincts. Twice weekly, the top managers of the NYPD meet with the executives of each precinct and the managers of specialized squads operating in the precinct. At these meetings, the Chief of the Department as well as a number of deputy commissioners and deputy chiefs display maps and graphs of crime trends and grill the precinct commanders about what strategies they have developed to respond to

Figure 4.2
Arrests by Category, New York City, 1980–2002, in Thousands

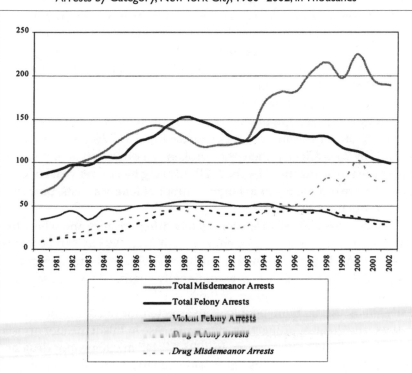

Source: New York State Division of Criminal Justice Services, Criminal Justice Indicators.

them. The pressure on precinct commanders to reduce crime was and remains palpable.

In addition to the advent of CompStat, the ranks of the NYPD began to increase significantly in 1993 as a result of a major initiative by Mayor Dinkins to add thousands of officers to the force.[29] From 1993 to 2001 the number of police officers in New York climbed from 34,600 to 40,045, an increase of 16%.[30] Thus a swelling police force, the implementation of the CompStat program, and an aggressive zero-tolerance policing strategy all occurred at about the same time that the city's crime rate began rapidly to decline. Moreover, this combination of increased police officers and aggressive public-order policing started to change historical arrest patterns. Exactly how these arrest patterns changed is illustrated in Figure 4.2.

Figure 4.2 shows a steady increase in felony arrests in New York City from 1980 to 1989; rising from 86,846 to 153,059, such arrests nearly doubled. The main factor accounting for this rise was the number of new drug arrests made in the city following the introduction of crack cocaine. However, beginning in 1989, felony arrests began steadily to decline as, under Dinkins, the NYPD shifted to a community policing model that emphasized crime prevention and visible police presence over arrests. Although felony arrests rose again slightly from 1993 to 1994, they continued gradually to decline afterward: overall, from 1993 to 2001, felony arrests in New York City declined by 17% and, from 1994 to 2001, by 25%. Clearly, then, the "broken windows" style of policing that started to be practiced by the NYPD during these later years of Giuliani's tenure did not result in larger number of felony arrests. But what about misdemeanor arrests?

Misdemeanor arrests are a completely different story and where the real impact of changes in police enforcement from 1993 to 2001 becomes apparent. As Figure 4.2 shows, misdemeanor arrests mushroomed, from 129,404 to 194,485.[31] This exceptionally sharp, 50% increase is the most telling workload measure of the NYPD's zero-tolerance policy. By 2001, almost 70,000 more people were arrested for misdemeanors than in 1993. The greatest proportion of this increase in misdemeanor arrests was for drug sale or possession. In 1993, 27,447 misdemeanor drug arrests were made; by 2001 this figure had risen to 79,901, representing an eight-year increase of 191%. Of the rise in misdemeanor arrests in New York City from 1993 to 2001, drug arrests accounted for 81% of the total increase.[32]

Not only did the number of misdemeanor arrests increase but, beginning in 1996, the NYPD began phasing out summonses. For years, summonses had been used to process low-level misdemeanor arrests. "Desk Appearance Tickets" (DATs) had been issued to people arrested for misdemeanors once they arrived at the police precinct, as long as they had identification and background checks did not show a serious criminal record or outstanding warrants. The standard practice had been that, within a few hours after their arrest, most people arrested for misdemeanors were given DATs.

This started to change in 1995 when the NYPD decided that issuing summonses was not consistent with its new zero-tolerance approach. In addition, eliminating summonses addressed city prosecutors' long-

Figure 4.3
Percentage of Misdemeanor Arrests Issued DATs* in New York City, 1993–2002

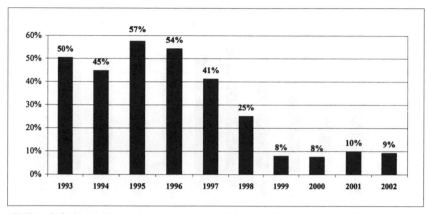

* DATs include those making it to arraignment as well as those which are voided or those prosecutors decline to prosecute.

Source: New York City Criminal Justice Agency and New York State Division of Criminal Justice Services, Criminal Justice Indicators.

standing concern about the failure of people given DATs to appear in court; in the second half of 1990, for instance, the nonappearance rate for persons given DATs was 43%.[33] The old DAT policy ended unofficially in 1995 and in most cases officially in 1997, when the NYPD issued more stringent regulations. As Figure 4.3 shows, since 1993, the increasing number of misdemeanor arrests, coupled with the virtual elimination of DATs by 1999, has resulted in tens of thousands more people locked up every year while they await criminal court arraignment. In 1993, 50% of all misdemeanor arrests were issued DATs. This figure increased to 57% in 1995 and then spiraled downward to 10% by 2001. Though on its face a seemingly mundane change, the drastic reduction in the use of DATs has significantly altered the experience of people who are arrested for misdemeanors. In police parlance, they are "put into the system"—locked in a cell at a police precinct, handcuffed, and transferred to a holding cell in a court, all before finally being arraigned. For the past several years this confinement has lasted an average of 24 hours. In 1993, a little more than 64,000 people arrested for misdemeanors went through this process. By 2002, over 100,000 more people, or about 172,000, were put through the system.

Figure 4.4

Number of Misdemeanor Arrests Admitted to Jail after Arraignment, 1993–2003

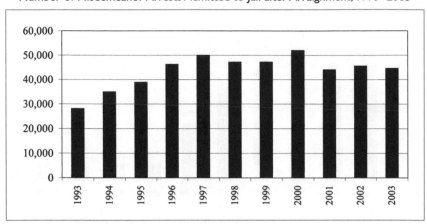

Source: New York City Department of Correction Population Research Unit.

Not only have those charged with misdemeanors spent one and sometimes two days in a cell before arraignment; in addition, after arraignment, more people have been remanded to the city's jails. This trend is documented in Figure 4.4.

As Figure 4.4 shows, the number of people admitted to the jail system for misdemeanors increased by 56% from 1993 to 2001, or from 28,175 to 44,079 people. Misdemeanor admissions have stayed at this high level for most of the last decade. Since the average detainee charged with a misdemeanor stays in jail 19 days postarraignment, this means 16,000 more people were spending almost three weeks in jail in 2001 than in 1993. The cumulative result of essentially eliminating DATs and increasing misdemeanor arrests was that in 1993, 64,294 people spent an average of one day in prearraignment detention. By 2001, that number jumped to 175,360, an increase of more than 100,000 people in pretrial detention.

If increasing misdemeanor arrests and numbers of people detained pretrial were therefore a prominent aspect of the changing New York City criminal justice system, felony arrests and indictments comprised another. After initially increasing 10% from 1993 to 1994, felony arrests have slowly declined through 2001 (see Figure 4.2). In 1994, 138,029 felony arrests were made in New York City; by 2001, the number of felony arrests had come down to 104,105, a 17% decrease from 1993 and a 25% drop since 1994. Everything else being equal, we should expect to see a parallel proportionate trend in the reduction of felony indictments and convictions.[34] This has not been the case. Instead, the number of felony indictments fell by 46% from 1993 to 2001, or from 47,364 to 25,801, more than two and half times the rate of decrease for felony arrests during this same period. Figure 4.5 shows the rate at which the city's felony arrests were indicted since 1980 and how that indictment rate has declined over the past decade. Figure 4.5 shows that the percent of felony arrests resulting in indictment in New York City steadily rose from 23% in 1980 to a high of 39% in 1992. Again, this rise can be explained by the appearance of crack cocaine in the early 1980s. The increase also grew from a proliferation of police undercover "buy and bust" narcotics operations, which resulted in huge numbers of felony arrests where the undercover officer was both the complainant and the witness, producing strong and easily indictable cases. Finally, the rise related to the city budget office having showered financial resources on the city's district attorneys' (DAs) offices through the 1980s, allowing DAs to assign more prosecutors to assist the police in pursuing felony indictments and convictions.

Figure 4.5
Percent of Felony Arrests Resulting in Indictment, New York City, 1980–2002

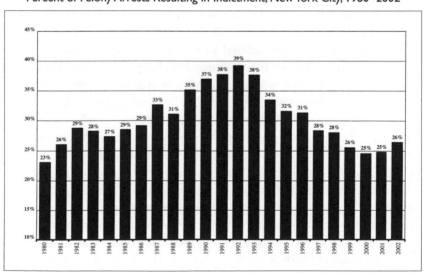

Source: New York State Division of Criminal Justice Services, Criminal Justice Indicators, New York City, 1980–2002.

It was in 1993, though, that the percentage of felony arrests result-ing in indictments began to fall; by 2001, this figure had fallen to 25%, compared to 39% eight years earlier. Why? As criminal justice experts know, whether an arrest ultimately results in an indictment depends on the quality of the felony case itself. Felony arrests that do not result in indictment—and Figure 4.5 shows that in New York City these were the great majority of such arrests over the past 20 years—suggest that either a prosecutor or a grand jury has decided that a felony charge is based on weak evidence. By this standard, the quality of the city's felony ar-rests had deteriorated from 1993 to 2001. Perhaps even more surprising than the steady decline in the overall felony indictment rate is that the decline was substantial for both violent and nonviolent felony arrests. By 2001, only 24% of violent felony arrests were indicted, compared to 35% in 1993; during the same period, the indictment rate for felony drug arrests declined from 57% to only 40%.

Thus a possible explanation of the decline in the percentage of fel-ony arrests resulting in indictments is that, for a number of reasons, the felony cases presented to prosecutors and grand juries had weakened. One aspect behind this, as previously discussed, is that the total num-ber of reported violent felonies declined by 52% from 1993 to 2001. This meant that the pool of cases for which an arrest could conceivably be made shrank correspondingly. But if the police were determined to maintain a high number of felony arrests, the quality of the arrests was likely to decline; keeping arrests at about the same level would proba-bly dilute their strength. Related to this, police officers may have felt significant pressure from their managers to keep felony arrest numbers up. Officers may have worried that others would interpret declining felony arrest numbers as a sign of police ineffectiveness or inefficiency; consequently, through this period, they may have pushed up to the felony level arrests that should have been made as misdemeanors. As a result, while felony arrests would increase in this scenario, they would be less likely to result in indictments since, upon review, prosecutors might well reduce the felonies to misdemeanors. Finally, prosecutors and grand juries may have received relatively weaker felony drug cases from police because of a curtailing of open-air drug dealing that also oc-curred in these years. One effect of all the drug enforcement efforts and the huge number of drug arrests in New York City over the last several years is that open drug dealing is now much more likely to result in

arrest; as a result, many drug dealers may have moved their operations indoors. This change likely reduced police opportunities to make
strong felony cases vis-à-vis relatively easy—albeit often dangerous—
high-volume "buy and bust" operations, thereby also resulting in far
fewer arrests.

A competing theory is that the dramatic decline in the number of
felony arrests resulting in indictments stemmed from a change in how
the city's prosecutors and grand juries were typically handling such
cases. Again, from 1993 to 2001, the indictment rate for drug felony arrests declined from 59% to 40%, and the rate for violent felony arrests
decreased from 36% to 24%; perhaps, then, prosecutors and grand juries
were treating such cases more leniently? Yet there is no evidence that
the city's prosecutors had relaxed their policies for indicting felonies
and especially violent felonies; far more probable is that they continued
to accord high priority to this serious category of arrests. Consequently,
the first possibility—that weaker police cases were presented to prosecutors and grand juries in the 1993–2001 period—seems to offer a more
convincing explanation for the city's decline in felony indictment rates
during these years.

Regardless of why felony indictment rates declined, though, this
trend poses a problem for alleged felons who may or may not find
themselves treated fairly by the criminal justice system. Cases that start
out as felonies only to be reduced to misdemeanors or dismissed by
prosecutors drain enormous resources from the criminal justice system.
Though 7 of 10 felony arrests are presently not indicted, many of these
cases are still presented as felonies at arraignment. Alleged felons have
a greater chance of being remanded to jail based on the seriousness of
the felony charge. And obviously, before reducing felony charges to misdemeanors or dismissing them altogether, prosecutors will have spent
vast amounts of time reviewing such cases. This raises important questions about the current level of police "overcharging" in New York and
the appropriateness of making so many felony arrests, given the small,
and declining, proportion of cases that are resulting in indictments.

Having reviewed these dramatic changes in how New York City
administers punishment—including huge increases in misdemeanor
arrests and declines in felony indictment rates—I proceed now to delineate how such alterations affected, in turn, the city's jail and the
state's prison systems.

The Effect on City Jails

As total arrests increased by 17% from 1993 to 2001,[35] driven by huge increases in misdemeanor arrests, so did the number of admissions to the city's jail system. The New York City jail system deals largely with detainees. Almost two-thirds of the system's population is in custody awaiting trial, while the remaining one-third have been sentenced to a jail term of one year or less or are awaiting transfer to state prison.[36] This ratio of detainees to sentenced prisoners has remained relatively constant for the last decade. Since the overwhelming number of new admissions to the jails results from defendants being remanded to the jail system after their arrest, it is hardly surprising that increasing arrest rates have led directly to a rise in jail system admissions. Whereas 108,112 people were admitted to the city's jails in fiscal year 1993, by 1999 this number had increased by 23%, to 133,000, declining to 120,000 by 2001, an 11% increase since 1993.[37] On its face, there is nothing unexpected about jail admissions moving in the same direction as police arrests; after all, arrests drive jail admission numbers.

However, this is where the expected ends and the unexpected starts. From 1993 to 2001, despite an 11% increase in admissions, the population of the city jail system actually shrank by 22%, from 18,624 in 1993 to 14,490 in 2001.[38] In fact, the jail system—which had peaked in 1991 with an average daily population of 21,448—had, by 2001, experienced a 32% reduction.[39] Here, then, is the first indication of an exceedingly counterintuitive trend: increased arrests and increased jail admissions were accompanied by a decline, not a rise, in the city's jail population. How was this possible?

By way of explaining the apparent paradox, let us return to the changing nature of New York City's felony and misdemeanor arrests; for the key to why jail population dropped during this period lies in the differences between misdemeanor lengths of stay and felony admission lengths of stay. In the case of misdemeanors, a detainee's average length of stay is 19 days; for a felony admission, this average rises to 63 days (and 125 days for felony admissions subsequently indicted).[40] Judges tend to set generally low bail amounts for less serious misdemeanor cases and the highest bails for indicted felony cases. Those with the highest bails tend to stay in jail the longest awaiting trial, since many cannot afford to pay the amounts set.

As the above analysis also shows, many fewer accused felons are entering jail, since felony arrests are down. In addition, those accused felons who are entering are less likely to be indicted. These factors, combined with misdemeanants spending approximately one-third of the time in jail as felons, means that the city's jail population has actually declined despite a striking rise in new jail admissions.[41] Consequently, in spite of rising misdemeanor arrests, the virtual elimination of summonses, and increasing jail admissions, the New York City jail system population is at its lowest level in 10 years, and there are a number of mothballed jails.

The Effect on Prison

These changing patterns—declining numbers of felony arrests, felony indictment rates, and, as an obvious result, felony convictions—have also had notable consequences for the state's prison system. The major effect is that the number of people sentenced and sent to New York State prisons from New York City has significantly declined between 1993 and 2001. Specifically, from 1993 to 2001, the Supreme Court handed down 47% fewer prison sentences.[42] The number of prison sentences stayed relatively constant at about 20,000 a year from 1989 to 1993. However, from 1990, when 20,500 people were sentenced to prison, the number of prison sentences underwent a steady decrease to 10,960 by 2001.

This trend toward decreased prison use is the exact reverse of what happened in New York City in the prior seven-year period. From 1985 to 1992, the number of prison sentences increased by 75%. This period also saw an increase of 18% in reported violent crime.[43] In contrast, from 1993 to 2001, New York City's use of state prison declined by 47%, and violent crime rates decreased by 52%. Therefore, New York City made significantly less use of state prison for newly convicted felons during the period of an absolutely staggering crime decline.

This analysis helps explain why, during the period from 1992 to 2002, the New York State prison system had one of the slowest growth rates in the country; only one other state (Massachusetts) had a lower rate of growth. New York's prison system grew by 9% during this period, compared to the national average of 63%.[44] Since New York City prisoners make up almost 75% of the state prison population, the decreased number of people sentenced to the state's prisons primarily accounts for this slow growth rate. The growth that the prison system has experienced is due to an increase of felony convictions from outside

New York City of 16% from 1993 to 2000[45] as well as to an overall increase of eight months in the average length of stay for all prisoners from 1993 to 2000.[46]

Summarizing the New York Case Study: Behind the Numbers

Given the preceding analysis, it seems difficult to attribute any of New York City's crime declines to increased use of prison. Before reaching this conclusion, though, it makes sense to investigate whether other significant changes in the use of prison occurred that might explain the huge decrease in crime between 1993 and 2001. Indeed, in 1995, an important legislative change took place in New York when Governor George Pataki proposed, and the state legislature passed, a law eliminating parole for repeat violent offenders. This law also replaced discretionary parole release with a determinate sentencing structure for all repeat violent offenders. Additionally, in 1998, Governor Pataki proposed and the legislature again adopted a law eliminating parole for all first-time violent offenders; here, too, discretionary parole release was replaced by a system of determinate sentences. However, no changes could possibly have been felt as a result of these laws until 1999, since all the prisoners covered by these laws would still have been in prison, given the average length of stay for violent offenders (which, in 1995, was almost 47 months). Since crime in New York City had already declined by 44% from 1993 to 1998, neither of these tough-on-crime changes can help explain the city's crime decrease.

Another theoretical possibility is that in the years 1991 and 1992, before the city's large crime decrease began, the city so effectively improved its targeting of felony offenders that it managed to convict and imprison precisely those offenders who would otherwise have committed new crimes during the years 1993 to 1995. Since those offenders would have been incapacitated, a critic might say, perhaps this explains some of the city's crime decline. However, there is absolutely no evidence—nor could there easily be—that the above hypothetical scenario actually happened. Obviously, violent felons were also incarcerated in the prior decade, when crime significantly increased in New York City. Unless there was something extremely different or higher-risk about more recent felons in comparison—and there is no evidence that supports this proposition—why would crime have decreased during one group's incarceration but increased during the other's?

Finally, another possibly relevant change that occurred during this period was that the average length of stay for all prisoners increased steadily, from 31.4 months in 1993 to 35.5 months in 1998.[47] It is hard to imagine that increasing the average age of parolees by roughly one month each year from 1993 to 1998 is somehow responsible for any large part of the New York's crime decline. However, within this overall number, the average length of stay for those convicted of violent felony offenses increased from 45.2 months in 1993 to 57.7 months in 1998. This increase, attributed to the Parole Board becoming far more stringent about discretionary release for violent felony offenders, is more significant than the rise for the total prison population. Even here, though, it is important to query carefully how this increase took place. From 1993 to 1996, the length of stay for violent offenders increased from 45.2 months to 48.7 months. This increase of 3.5 months in the average age of a released parolee who committed a violent crime coincided with a 36% decrease in reported violent crime and a 50% drop in homicides in New York City during this period.[48] Though it is theoretically possible that those additional 3.5 months in prison represented some tipping point at which the great majority of these offenders would no longer commit crimes, again it is difficult to imagine this is the case.

In sum, when all the evidence is examined and these varied counterarguments have been considered, it is difficult to come to any conclusion other than that increased use of prison was not significantly related to New York City's renowned crime decline. Buttressing further the argument that expanded prison use and crime reductions are not demonstrably related is that it can be generalized in other local contexts as well. To illustrate this, I now turn to a much less detailed discussion of San Diego, a city that achieved large crime reductions by using very different law enforcement strategies from those used in New York. This suggests that, whether or not other cities follow the particular criminal justice model New York used between 1993 and 2001, crime reductions can be realized without expanded usage of prisons.

A SHORT SAN DIEGO DISCUSSION

Though the fact is not as well known as the case of New York City, San Diego also experienced remarkable crime declines over the past decade. From 1993 to 2001, violent crime in San Diego decreased by 45% and homicides dropped by 62%;[49] these percentages represent reductions of a magnitude similar to those recorded in New York City. The San Diego Police Department utilized strategies different from those employed in New York City to combat crime, as is reflected in numbers of police officers hired and types of arrests that were made. For instance, more than New York's, the San Diego experience has been closely associated with community policing. As Jerry Sanders, San Diego's retired Police Chief, told Fox Butterfield in a *New York Times* report, "Our basic premise was, we didn't have enough police officers to do it all, so we needed participation by the community."[50] In the same article, Sanders said that in addition to working with the community and using a group of 1,200 volunteers to watch over neighborhoods, he measured his department's success with annual surveys of department satisfaction, the most recent of which showed an 89% approval rating.[51]

In statistical terms, these differences can be summarized as follows. Whereas New York City increased its police force by 16% from 1993 to 2001, San Diego increased its number of officers by 9%; whereas New York increased the number of misdemeanor arrests by 50%, San Diego decreased its misdemeanor arrests by 1%. Unlike New York City, which nearly eliminated its use of summonses for misdemeanors by 2001 (a decline from 64% to 10%), San Diego's use of summonses for misdemeanors increased from 64% to 72% from 1993 to 2001. In New York, felony arrests declined by 17%; in San Diego, they fell by a similar amount, 16%.[52] As in New York, significantly fewer people in San Diego went to prison during this period. Comparing the number of San Diego prison sentences with the experience in the rest of California and nationally is useful here. (Data are available from the county of San Diego, not the city of San Diego, and are the basis of the figures used here. However, since the majority of arrests and prosecutions in the county occurred in the city, these figures are likely a reliable measure for both the city and the county. It should also be noted that since national sentencing data are not available for 1993, and the latest year available as of this writing is 2000, comparisons made here span the period 1994 to 2000.)

From 1994 to 2000, San Diego County saw the number of prison sentences reduced by 25%. California also reduced its number of prison sentences but by less, 14%.[53] Nationally, 6% fewer people were sentenced to prison in state courts during this period.[54] During this same period, San Diego had a 43% reduction in violent crime compared to 34% for California and 23% for the United States.[55]

What this analysis suggests is that while the two cities obviously used different styles of policing, in terms of growth in the number of police officers and the large differences in the growth and kinds of arrests they made, both managed to achieve substantial crime decreases far larger than the national averages while making less use of prison. Criminologists may argue about how effective either style is for crime-fighting and community-empowerment purposes: common to both styles, though, is that they were able to bring about the largest decreases in crime of U.S. cities while making relatively less use of prisons.

POLICY AND POLITICAL IMPLICATIONS

The significance of the New York City and San Diego case studies is the strength with which they suggest that increasing prison use was not responsible for striking crime declines. In turn, this finding has ramifications for state policy makers, as these are real world examples that can be "put on the table" when arguing concretely for reducing prison populations. Perhaps most important of all, though, these major cities' experiences mean that crime reduction and reducing the use of incarceration are not incompatible: making the case for downsizing prisons does not mean compromising public safety. For both in and outside New York, many policy makers and members of the public alike have feared that prison reduction strategies would lead, as though by law of nature, to a resurgence in violent crime. The examples of New York City and San Diego put the lie to this fear.

Moreover, in addition to these recent experiences of a large and relatively small U.S. city, respectively, the argument for reducing prison systems is bolstered by looking at the recent experiences of states. Let us look at how different states fared in the 1990s and early 2000s as crime rates in the nation as a whole declined by 26%. Figure 4.6 is fascinating in that it shows no relationship between crime reduction and the states that made the largest expansions in their prison systems. Note from Figure 4.6 that of the 10 states with the highest increases in their incarceration rates (in fact, each more than doubled their prison populations) during these years of decline in the national crime rate, none had a crime decline above the national average. Five of the 10 states— Idaho, Montana, Utah, Tennessee, and West Virginia—actually had a crime increase through this period. Conversely, of the 10 states with the

Figure 4.6

Percent of Increase in Prison Population and Percent
Change in Violent Crime, 1992–2002, States with the
Highest/Lowest Percent Increase in Prison Population

	Percent of Increase in Prisoners in Custody of State Correctional Authorities	Percent Change in Violent Crime
Total States	59	−26
States with the highest percent increase in prisoners		
Idaho	175	14
West Virginia	171	10
Wisconsin	170	−11
Texas	168	−11
Mississippi	155	−8
North Dakota	133	−6
Montana	113	128
Tennessee	111	11
Colorado	109	−21
Utah	106	4
States with the lowest percent increase in prisoners		
Illinois	35	−31
Michigan	29	−25
South Carolina	27	−1
Rhode Island	27	−23
Maine	36	−14
New Jersey	23	−34
Maryland	21	−14
Ohio	19	−31
New York	9	−53
Massachusetts	3	−33

Source: Bureau of Justice Statistics, 1992 numbers for prisoners from
Table 5.1 from *Correctional Populations in the United States, 1993*; 2002
numbers for prisoners from Table 3 of Prisoners in 2002. Numbers for
violent crimes are from bjsdata.ojp.usdoj.gov/dataonline/Search/
Crime/State/StateCrime.cfm.

smallest increases in incarceration, four had crime declines above the
national average: New Jersey, Ohio, New York, and Massachusetts. Not
one of these states had an increase in reported violent crime rates. New
York's decrease in violent crime was twice the national average and
New York's and Massachusetts's crime declines were 6 and 11 times
greater than their prison growth. No other states in the country were
able to match what could therefore be termed New York's and Massa-

chusetts's "efficiency." In other words, if the goal of expanding prisons is to increase public safety, then this payoff should be easy to demonstrate through clear-cut crime declines gained while prison sizes were increasing. Yet the states of New York and Massachusetts realized far greater public safety gains than can be explained by their quite modest incarceration expansions; moreover, New York led the nation in crime decline generally.

It is instructive to delve even further into statistics this table presents on other states' situations. For states such as Idaho, Montana, Tennessee, and West Virginia all demonstrated negative relationships between prison expansion and crime. With huge prison expansion in these states came huge crime increases, not exactly the sort of readily demonstrable efficiency rates of which law makers could be proud. For instance, Wisconsin, which increased its prison population by 170% and saw a violent crime decrease of only 11%, has lately encountered serious fiscal problems. In 2002, Wisconsin legislators had to pass a budget that included layoffs, across-the-board service reductions, hiring freezes, and fee increases. In 2003, the state ended the year with a budget deficit.[56] Had these legislators reexamined the cost and efficiency of their correctional policy, they might have avoided these dra conian and surely also politically unpopular measures.

Moreover, Wisconsin legislators would have been helped in undertaking this reexamination were they able to cite far greater crime decreases, like those realized in the many other states that have used less prison expansion while achieving this gain. As a matter of public safety and fiscal policy, then, Wisconsin taxpayers received relatively little from the massive investment in prison expansion they have made over the last decade. Taxpayers in other states as well—say, in West Virginia, Mississippi, Tennessee, and Montana—might also, if informed on this topic, question the wisdom of their state government allocating so much money to prisons when so little comes back in the way of demonstrable reductions in violent crime.

In a 2000 study done on the relationship between state prison increases and crime reductions, Gainsborough and Mauer similarly found that states with the largest increases in incarceration had the smallest decreases in crime, and that the crime decreases in the 1990s were the result of not increased incarceration but a growing economy, changes in the drug market, and better policing.[57] These state-based analyses of the relationship between increased incarceration and crime are consistent with the Spelman's findings (discussed in more detail in Chapter 2) that a 1% increase in the use of incarceration would result in only the marginal benefit of a crime reduction between 0.16% and 0.31%.[58]

In conclusion, the New York State, San Diego, and other state examples to which I have just alluded, along with the extant national and state-based research on incarceration and crime, constitute a specific criminal justice development that legislators can use to advocate often politically difficult policy changes involving the downsizing of prisons. These clear state examples along with the national research may be especially helpful for politicians who fear that they will be accused of being soft on crime if they attempt to make substantial policy changes. Because such examples are wonderfully concrete, they can stimulate more persuasive arguments than those made simply by citing academic research. Where simplifying the results of meta-analyses and sophisticated empirical studies of prison effectiveness may be next to impossible, citing cases showing that "more prisons do not equal more public safety" is relatively easy. It may also be simplistic, glossing over the fact that in any state or city there are probably 100 or so variables that contribute to more or less crime in addition to the use of prison. Yet the plain and understandable cases discussed here, exemplifying cities and states where no apparent connection exists between prison expansion and crime reduction, happen to jibe with much of the academic research that has been done on prison and crime rates over the last decade. This seems a hopeful connection indeed. For if cities such as New York and San Diego, as well as several states, have managed to preserve and even enhance public safety while expanding prisons at only a fraction of the average national growth rate, why wouldn't other states and localities wish to follow suit?

In the next chapter, I review yet a fourth development germane to my larger argument about the need to downsize prisons. This development also occurred inside the criminal justice system and involves an observation little known to interested parties outside: namely, that during the 1990s, a huge number of parolees were being technically violated and sent back to prison. Once more, this trend brought significant social and economic costs and needs to be addressed within a larger political strategy aimed at decreasing unnecessarily high U.S. incarceration rates.

5

Why Parole and Probation Policies Need to Change

ALMOST EVERYONE WHO goes to prison comes out of prison. In fact, except for the 5% who are sentenced to life without parole, executed, or die of natural causes, 95% of all prison admissions are released, and 80% are released to parole or some kind of after-prison supervision.[1] Yet the parole system is one of the most misunderstood components of the criminal justice system. This government function has garnered an almost pejorative connotation in the public's eyes through high-profile crime cases centering on parolees and the national movement to abolish discretionary release on parole that captured media attention over the last decade.

Ironically, though, a large segment of the public (and likely many journalists as well) do not know the distinction between probation and parole: that probation involves a sentence in lieu of prison, whereas parole involves community supervision once a portion of a prison sentence has been served. Exactly what parole officers do on a day-to-day basis, and how they decide to send well over a hundred thousand parolees back to prison each year for rule violations, tends to be a mundane "inside baseball" process that is sometimes misunderstood even by those within the criminal justice system.

Nonetheless, this often overlooked part of the criminal justice system and the esoteric bureaucratic processes it employs can entail hundreds of millions, and probably billions, of dollars of expenditures on prison expansion. Especially in an era of fiscal crisis or restraint, these expenses force budget reductions in other parts of government, such as education, that have nothing to do with parole. Consequently, it is crucial to evaluate how parole has come to play this enormous role in maintaining a swollen U.S. prison system. Shining light on the "under the radar" operations of parole may assist in spurring the creation of alternative parole or community supervision policies that can meaningfully reduce prison spending while protecting public safety.

Virtually no one in government can spend money like a parole officer. While agency heads and commissioners have control over very large budgets, these budgets are tightly constrained by labor contracts, mandated expenses, support services, and by numbers and type of personnel. Should a commissioner wish to spend money on something discretionary over and above an agency's budget, this almost always involves a nightmarish process of review by the executive branch and, often, legislative approval as well. Not so for the parole officer, who has no budget to control and may work in a cramped and overcrowded office in a rundown building in a rundown part of town. He or she may have little or no access to programs or treatment for parolees and may earn much less than a correction or police officer. Adding insult to injury, the parole officer has no control over who or how many people have been put on that officer's caseload.

However, without any executive or legislative oversight or public understanding of how this happened, the decisions of a single parole officer can mean that a given state has to spend over a million dollars per year on prisons. In contrast, parole officers have no ability to compel parole agencies to spend additional funds on less expensive parole services such as drug treatment, job training programs, or additional officers to lower caseloads. Thus, taken together, parole officers' decisions have had the effect of fueling the U.S. incarceration boom by sending many parolees back to prison who have not been convicted of any new crime but have broken one or more of the rules of conditions of parole.

How did this situation that impacts so greatly on the U.S. prison system come to exist? Even more important, what can be done about it? To answer these questions, one needs to look at how the parole system has grown and changed over the last two decades, eventually becoming quite varied in its operations from state to state. Indeed, states have strikingly different cultural and political environments that affect their parole practices and, in turn, their respective rates of prison expansion. To argue for changing the parole system, too, requires explaining to law makers—many of whom are struggling with ongoing increases in public spending—precisely how political, fiscal, and even public safety benefits can accrue from using parole to quickly and effectively reduce the size and cost of the U.S. prison system on a state-by-state basis.

RECENT CHANGES IN PAROLE: HOW DID WE GET HERE?

The concept of indeterminate sentencing was a bedrock of sentencing and corrections policy in the United States for most of the twentieth century. Judges had the authority to sentence people to a minimum and maximum length of time to be served in prison; as executive agencies, parole boards determined when a prisoner could actually be released. In fact, the power of parole boards to reduce lengths of sentences was a cornerstone of theories of rehabilitation through the mid-1970s; at that time, the primary goal of the correction system began to shift from rehabilitation to punishment. Parole boards were predicated on the notion that people could and would have incentives to rehabilitate themselves once in prison. Thus, parole was a key part of the goals of rehabilitation. According to Zimring and Hawkins, rehabilitation was "the law's stated objective in the criminal sentencing system and remained the dominant ideology in the architecture of the model penal code reforms of the 1960's. Correctional administrators were no less uniformly enthusiastic about reform as a penal purpose."[2] It was hoped that the possibility of early release would be the "carrot" convincing a prisoner to rehabilitate himself (or herself) to the point that a parole board no longer viewed him as a threat to public safety.

Several works have focused on the history and problems of the U.S. parole system. For instance, both David Rothman and Jonathan Simon have identified several theoretical and practical deficiencies of the parole system's operations over the last century, including the system's inability to prevent recidivism and predict risk.[3] In *Crime and Punishment in American History*, Lawrence Friedman also discussed parole's past problems, noting, "Parole, like the indeterminate sentence, was part of the process of making criminal justice better suited to the *individual* case. And this was, in theory, profoundly humanizing. In practice, the results were somewhat checkered."[4] However, notwithstanding all parole's shortcomings, many of which are reviewed later in this chapter, parole owes its evolution to the notion of rehabilitation.

Therefore, it should not be surprising that as American criminal justice policy has become more retributive through longer, determinate, and mandatory sentencing, parole boards' role in determining early discretionary release has been severely curtailed. Sixteen states have eliminated discretionary release on parole entirely; another four states have done away with discretionary release for selected crimes. To explain these terms, which by now sound technical indeed, it is worth a moment to quickly review them.

KEY DEFINITIONS

Parole is a period of supervised release that follows a prison term. Prisoners may be released to parole either by a parole board (discretionary parole) or by law or statute (mandatory parole).

Discretionary parole is when parole boards use discretionary authority to release prisoners based on a legal or administrative determination of eligibility. In 2002, 39% of everyone entering parole was released from prison by this method, down from 50% in 1995.[5]

Nondiscretionary or mandatory parole usually occurs in states that have determinate sentencing statutes. By law, prisoners are released after serving all or a portion of their original sentences minus any good time earned. In 2002, 52% of everyone entering parole was released from prison by this method, up from 45% in 1995.[6]

In cases of discretionary and nondiscretionary or mandatory parole, prisoners are released *conditionally*. In other words, they are subject to all the conditions and terms of parole or community supervision for the entire period that their community supervision lasts.

Maxing-out refers to prisoners who have served their entire sentence and who have accumulated no "good-time" credit. They are released from prison *unconditionally*. Once such prisoners have left prison, they are not under parole or community supervision at all. In 2000, about 112,000 prisoners were released back to their communities with no supervision, up from 51,000 in 1990.[7]

Parole violators are those who have committed one of two kinds of parole violations. The first is a violation that ensues because of a *new criminal conviction* while on parole. Here, parolees are sent back to prison because of a new sentence related to a new criminal case. These new sentences can tend to be fairly long since such parolees have at least one prior felony conviction for which they were already sent to prison and released on parole. The other type of violation is a *technical violation* of the rules or conditions of parole. These violations do not involve new convictions (though they can involve a new arrest for which there is no conviction) but, rather, rule-breaking behavior. The general conditions of parole almost always include being drug free, reporting on schedule, being employed, and attending any required treatment programs. If a parolee is found to break any one of these rules through, for example, drug use, irregular reporting or nonreporting, being un-employed or not actively seeking employment, the parole officer can begin an administrative violation process. This process may result in the parole board (or, in some cases, a judge or hearing officer) send-ing the parolee back to prison for all of part of his or her remaining sentence.

Indeed, parole officers have the power to immediately incarcerate parolees who are accused of a technical violation. The administrative process to determine whether the violation actually occurred, and the penalty to ensue, takes place while a parolee is locked up in a county jail or state prison. The reason parole officers have this extraordinary power is because people on parole are still considered prisoners; while they have the right to representation by an attorney during their tech-nical violation hearing, they can be immediately reincarcerated.

Important to underscore about the present system's evolution is that al-most every state retains a community supervision function once some-one has been granted a conditional release from prison. Consequently, the movement to "abolish parole" is really a movement to abolish pa-role boards that have the power to release prisoners prior to the end of their sentence. This movement has spurred new laws that specify exact sentence lengths and how much "good time" can be earned and applied to shortening the sentence. As a result of these new determinate sen-tencing laws, the numbers of prisoners released by parole boards as a percentage of everyone released from prison steadily declined, from 67% in 1977 to 55% in 1980, 39% in 1990, and, finally, just 24% in 1999.[8]

This dramatic and fairly rapid decline in parole boards' decision-making powers provides empirically observable evidence of how much the very concept of rehabilitation has also declined. By now, parole boards seem increasingly irrelevant, insofar as these boards possess only discretionary early release powers in a small proportion of all re-leases nationally. However, in examining prison populations, it is also important to look beyond national numbers to examine enormous state-by-state variations. For instance, in 1997 a host of states, including Pennsylvania, Florida, Mississippi, Iowa, New Jersey, Washington, and

North Carolina, continued to release over 90% of their prisoners through discretionary release. Other states, such as California, Illinois, Oregon, and Minnesota, released fewer than 10% of all prisoners through discretionary release.[9]

At the same time, though, the number of people under parole supervision over the past two decades has, like prisons themselves, expanded considerably. In 1980, 196,700 people were on state and federal parole in the United States; by 2002, that number increased to 670,169, a more than threefold increase. Most of this growth occurred in the 1980s. From 1990 to 2002, these numbers grew more modestly, increasing from 502,000 to 670,169; this represented an increase of 33%.[10] Interestingly, the relatively small rate of growth of parole from 1990 to 2002 was far less than the 84% growth in prison systems through the same period, primarily because of changes in sentencing and declining rates of discretionary release on parole. As parole release rates slowed, people were slower to leave prisons, thus increasing lengths of stay that drove up the size of prison populations.

Again, these national numbers mask important state-by-state variations that illuminate differences in parole use over the last decade. Figure 5.1 shows the percentage changes in numbers of people on parole by state in the United States from 1990 to 2002. Note the wide variation in the growth rates of parolees, from Idaho's 517% increase to Washington State's 99% decrease. While 15 states experienced declines in their parole population, the remaining 35 had increases, and 13 states more than doubled their parole populations. Overall, the total number of people on state parole increased 42% from 1990 to 2002. Strikingly, too, three states—California, New York, and Pennsylvania—were responsible for more than half of all parole growth during this decade. California alone was responsible for about 27% of the growth and, in absolute numbers, contains almost a quarter of all the people on parole in the United States. Because of its sheer numbers, many of the aggregate national numbers on parole are skewed when California is included. Thus, any discussion of parole trends and practices nationally should make clear how such changes "look" with and without California. For, regardless of absolute numbers, there are few states where the size of the parole or postprison supervision system does not contribute significantly to the growth of that state's prison system.

Perhaps the most important measure with respect to parole is the proportion of people who complete their terms successfully. The plu-

Figure 5.1
Percentage Change in Adults on Parole, 1990–2002

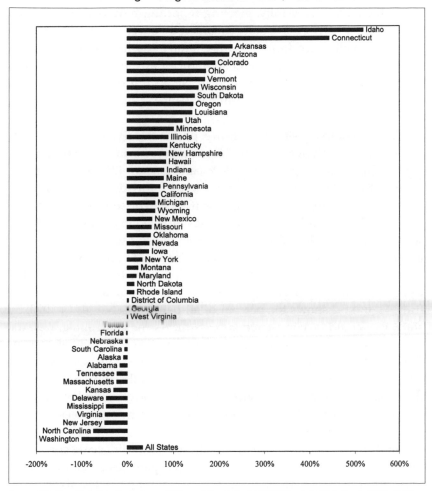

Source: Hughes, Timothy, Doris James Wilson, Allen J. Beck (2001) *Trends in State Parole, 1990–2000*. Washington, D.C.: U.S. Department of Justice, Office of Justice Programs, Bureau of Justice Statistics; and Glaze, Lauren E. (2003) *Probation and Parole in the United States, 2002*. Washington, D.C.: U.S. Department of Justice, Office of Justice Programs, Bureau of Justice Statistics.

perfect measure of success on parole may well be the attainment of a well-paying job with benefits, remaining drug free, reconnecting with community and family, and, of course, the complete abandonment of crime commission. However, while this is certainly the goal that corrections officials ought to seek, more common measures of success involve simply whether or not someone on parole permanently absconds or winds up back in prison. Someone who is on parole and completes the term successfully, meeting reporting requirements and not ending back in prison, is usually considered a success story. This person may remain alienated from his or her family and have untreated mental illness or drug addiction and sporadic, if any, employment. But as long as this person has not wound up again in prison, especially for committing a new crime, the criminal justice system views the result positively.

By this relatively simple measure, parole supervision has been unsuccessful. In 2002, over half, or 55%, of everyone on state parole in the United States failed parole.[11] This meant that of 420,000 people discharged from state parole, 45% stayed in their jurisdictions, reported to their parole officers, and did not get sent back to prison (successes); 41% were sent back to prison for new crimes or rule violations; and 9% absconded from parole.[12] These are certainly not statistics that can inspire much confidence in the efficacy of our prison and parole system.

As always, state-level data reveal some startling differences between states in the percentages of people who complete parole successfully. Figure 5.2 shows the percent of all parole discharges in 1999, by state, that could be considered successful. As the chart illustrates, the range of successful completion of parole statistics by state is tremendous. Utah and California occupied one end of the scale, with only 19% and 21%, respectively, of their parolees successfully completing parole. (Utah has since improved its success rate.) On the other end of the scale, Massachusetts and Mississippi both had 83% of their parolees successfully completing parole.

In theory, three explanations for these extraordinary discrepancies in success rates are conceivable. One is that parolees in California are very different than in Mississippi. The former might be less likely to rehabilitate themselves than the latter, perhaps more entrenched in lives of crime in California than their counterparts in Mississippi. While this is a possibility, no evidence confirms that such differences exist. Another possibility is that the two parole supervision agencies in these states have hugely disproportionate resources. Perhaps Mississippi parole agents have at their disposal enormous resources in the form of drug treatment, job training, day center and subsidized employment programs, and richly funded enforcement and supervision efforts. But this hardly seems likely given that the per capita cost per parolee under

Figure 5.2
Percentage Successful among State Parole Discharges, 1999

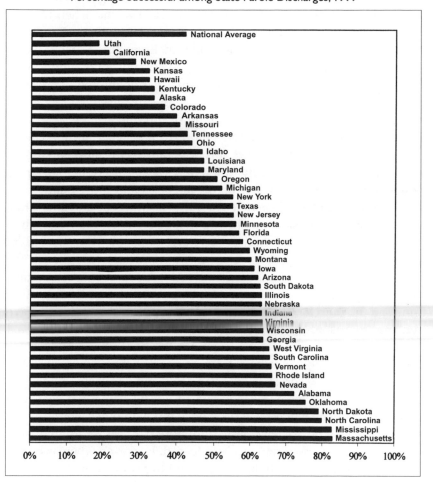

Source: Hughes, Timothy, Doris James Wilson, Allen J. Beck (2001) *Trends in State Parole, 1990–2000.* Washington, D.C.: U.S. Department of Justice, Office of Justice Programs, Bureau of Justice Statistics.

supervision by the California Department of Corrections is $3,364, about five times the $617 figure that Mississippi spends.[13] While these numbers are not, strictly speaking, comparable—unlike California's, Mississippi's aggregate numbers include probationers as well as parolees. Nonetheless, there is no question that California spends far more per parolee than does Mississippi.

A third possible explanation is that the two states' parole agencies have completely different policies, procedures, and organizational cultures with respect to decision making about how and when to send parolees back to prison for violating their paroles. Of these differences in success rates, a reported by the Urban Institute notes: "More likely, the policies and practices of the parole agencies contribute significantly to these discrepancies. They set the terms that define the parameters of success and failure—which conditions must be observed by the parolee, what qualifies as a violation of those conditions, how rigorously are those violations detected and enforced, and what are the consequences of a violation."[14] Indeed, this possibility is the most persuasive of the three, given enormously different success rates of parole supervision around the country. For parole agencies and individual parole agents have great latitude in determining who succeeds and fails while under parole supervision; nowhere is this discretion more visible than in state-to-state variations in the percentage of people who succeed on parole.

Scrutinizing parole failures more closely also reveals a sharp difference between the success rates of people released on parole for the first time and the rates for those who have been on parole once before, have returned to prison, and have been placed on parole again. The national success rate for those released to parole the first time is three times greater than for those who have been on parole before—63% and 21%, respectively.[15] Once someone fails on parole and has been sent back to prison for either a technical violation or a new crime, the chance is 80% that he or she will be sent back once more. In other words, as the total parole violation rate increases and more parolees return to prison, more people will also ultimately be released. However, whereas before chances of success (i.e., not being returned to prison) were 6 out of 10 cases, this rate now plummets to only 2 out of 10 cases (or an 80% failure rate).

The price of failure on parole (both in terms of technical violations and new convictions) can be seen most clearly in the number of parolees who return to prison. Figure 5.3 shows that, nationally, parole violators constituted 36% of all prison admissions in 2001, up from 29% in 1990. In four states, parole violators make up over half of everyone admitted to prison. Once again, states vary substantially in the proportion of their prison admissions who are parole violators. California, Louisiana, and Hawaii lead the pack: given these states' low rate of success on parole,

Figure 5.3
Percentage of Parole Violators among Admissions to State Prison

	1990	1999	2001
National Average	29	35	36
California	58	67	70
Louisiana	15	53	61
Hawaii	28	49	58
Utah	51	55	52
Alaska	14	44	48
Illinois	25	27	43
Arkansas	22	25	42
Maine	21	41	41
Missouri	26	39	41
Tennessee	33	36	38
Pennsylvania	26	36	38
New Jersey	21	36	35
New York	18	32	34
Delaware	6	25	34
Colorado	21	37	33
Michigan	23	37	32
New Hampshire	19	32	32
Kansas	35	38	31
Minnesota	23	32	31
Texas	37	21	29
Wisconsin	19	31	28
South Dakota	18	21	28
South Carolina	23	24	26
Kentucky	28	32	25
Oregon	48	25	24
Arizona	14	23	22
Ohio	13	18	22
Wyoming	6	35	20
Nevada	19	18	20
Maryland	14	33	18
Georgia	21	21	18
North Dakota	14	19	18
Massachusetts	31	23	17
Iowa	27	19	17
Connecticut	43	17	16
Vermont	15	17	16
West Virginia	13	10	13
Nebraska	16	16	12
Mississippi	14	10	12
Montana	20	53	11
Indiana	5	10	10
New Mexico	28	36	9
Oklahoma	3	14	8
Alabama	26	9	8
Idaho	20	32	6
North Carolina	13	13	6
Virginia	10	11	6
Washington	13	11	6
Florida	5	7	6
Rhode Island	25	19	3

Source: Hughes, Timothy, Doris James Wilson, Allen J. Beck (2001) *Trends in State Parole, 1990–2000*. Washington, D.C.: U.S. Department of Justice, Office of Justice Programs, Bureau of Justice Statistics; and Bureau of Justice Statistics, National Prisoner Statistics, unpublished data.

it is inevitable that they would lead the nation in the number of parole failures who return to prison. California's astounding rate of 70% of prison admissions who are parole violators is more than 2 times Texas's rate and almost 12 times Florida's rate. Thus, the states with the three largest prison populations in the country have exceptional differences in the numbers of parole violators who enter their prisons. Moreover, these differences greatly affect the size of each prison system. If the numbers changed appreciably in any of the states, their prison sizes would change in turn. For instance, if California had, in 2001, the same percentage of parole violators entering its system as Texas, 22,800 fewer prison beds would be needed in California prisons; this amounts to a decline of about 14% and an annual cost savings of about $684 million.[16]

Here again, it is important to show the effect of California alone on national numbers. In 2001, a total of 215,450 parole violators were admitted to state prisons nationally; California accounted for 41% of these admissions. Moreover, if the national rate of parole violators readmitted to prisons was recalculated, leaving California out of the numbers, this rate drops from 36% to 27%.[17]

From 1990 to 2001, 31 states experienced increases in the proportions of their prison admissions who were parole violators; in 4 states (California, Hawaii, Utah, and Louisiana), more than 50% of all prison admissions were parole violators. Several states saw the proportion of their prison admissions who were parole violators double from 1990 to 2001, including Louisiana, Hawaii, Alaska, and Wyoming, while only 18 states experienced declines in this figure. Among the states where proportions of parole violators readmitted to prison declined were Connecticut (where the number fell from 43% to 16%) and Texas (where the number fell from 37% to 29%). As discussed later in the chapter, both states had directly tackled the issue of increased parole violator readmissions. Other states, such as Illinois and Arkansas, had small increases from 1990 to 1999 but then saw large increases from 1999 to 2001.

Clearly, then, the number of parole violators who reenter the nation's prisons is a major driving force behind our prison systems' enormous size and ongoing expansion. From 1990 to 2001, the rate at which parole violators reentered prison (55%) grew at two and half times the rate of first-time sentenced offenders entering prison (22%).[18] Taking a slightly longer view of how parole violator readmissions to prison have changed over time, the number of parole violator prison admissions increased nationally from 21,177 to 215,450 from 1980 to 2001, amounting to a staggering increase of 917%.

However, as previously noted, not all parole violators are the same. Parole violators can be broken down into primarily two types: those who have violated their parole because of a new arrest and conviction, and those sent back to prison for rule, or technical, violations of the condition of their paroles.[19] These two kinds of violators pose very different issues for law enforcement, parole agencies, and prison systems.

First, those who are sent back to prison for a new arrest and conviction tend to be sentenced, on the new case, for a substantial period of time. These parolees are treated by the criminal justice system as new cases, separate and apart from their original crime and their initial parole conditions. However, prosecutors may sometimes decide that instead of pursuing a new arrest, they will drop a new charge and pursue only the technical violation of parole. This is possible because arrest itself is a technical violation of parole, allowing prosecutors to supersede uncertain court processes and send violators for sure back to prison (albeit for relatively short periods of time). Yet, while no national data exist on the frequency of this prosecutorial occurrence, state data strongly suggest that parolees arrested for new and serious violent crimes are almost always prosecuted on the new case. Consequently, when prosecutors decide to pursue a technical violation rather than a new charge, this means almost by definition that the latter cannot be proved or does not rise to the level of seriousness that a new case requires.

The second type of parolee is someone who has been sent back to prison for rule or technical violations. The most common kind of technical violations result from acts such as drug use, irregular reporting to parole officers or non-reporting, or failing to attend required programs, rather than from the commission of new crimes. These truly technical violations do not involve prosecutors, having been determined solely by a parole officer, whose decision is then confirmed by a parole board or judge.

The reason this distinction is so critical is that the two types involve very different enforcement mechanisms; even more important, each kind of parole failure points to different solutions. Different (though sometimes overlapping) policies and programs need to be forged depending on whether the goal is to prevent parolees from committing new crimes or to improve how parole officers respond to rule-breaking behavior. Yet, while it is extremely important to know for each state how many of each kind of parole readmission have occurred, it turns out that obtaining this information is extremely difficult.

The Bureau of Justice Statistics of the U.S. Department of Justice does collect national data on the number of parole violators, both technical and with new convictions, who enter state prisons each year. This data is quite useful for comparing one state with another or the same state over time in terms of aggregate trends. However, little national data, and almost no data at an individual state level, is kept on specific reasons for technical violations. This represents a huge gap in our knowledge about exactly why so many parolees are being returned to prison. Again, the range of possible technical violations is enormous, running the gamut from 1 to 10 positive drug tests, to missing 1 or 10 appointments, to not showing up 1 or 10 times at a treatment program. Thus, analyzing precisely why parolees are failing in any particular state is a hugely difficult if not impossible task. Moreover, the reason for failing to collect this data is fairly straightforward. Parole agencies are so structurally underfunded that almost none have sophisticated information technology systems that allow them to computerize their case files to include the specific reason(s) for a technical violation as well as any other alternative to violation that might have been tried. This dearth of data, in combination with a more general lack of understanding about how parole agencies operate, tends to keep legislators and other policy makers in the dark about the parole system and its operations—an ignorance that many parole agencies do not necessarily mind.

What we do know very reliably are the national recidivism rates for those who are released from prison. According to the largest study of national recidivism, 51.8% of everyone released from a state prison was back in prison within three years, and more than half of those, or 26.4%, were back for purely technical violations of parole.[20] These statistics highlight two startling facts about the U.S. prison system. The first is that, despite the system sending record numbers of people to prison for long periods of time and spending almost $40 billion annually on state prisons alone, more than half of all people released from prison return within 36 months. The second fact, more directly germane to this chapter, is that more than half of all parolees who return to prison are sent back for noncriminal behaviors.

Figure 5.4 shows that, for selected states around the country, the number of technical parole violators reentering prisons is a major force

Figure 5.4
Technical Violators as Percentage of Total Prison Admissions by State,
2001, Selected States

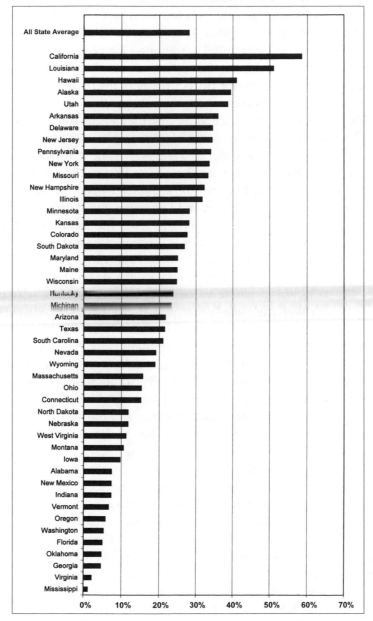

Source: Bureau of Justice Statistics, National Prisoner Statistics, unpublished data.

driving the size of their prison systems. What emerges clearly is that the proportion of prison admissions who are technical violators is 28% for state prisons nationally. While only 5% of the prison admissions in Georgia and Washington State were technical parole violators, percentages on the other end of the scale range from 33% in Missouri to 58% in California. These are substantial percentages for people who are reentering prison even though they have not been convicted of a new crime. Florida releases the majority of its prisoners unconditionally, which means that most cannot commit a technical violation.

Texas is an especially fascinating case that merits some discussion. Texas boasts a far lower percentage of prison admissions who are technical parole violators than California and New York. It also has reduced that percentage by more than one-third from 1994 to 2001.[21] On its face, this is surprising. Texas has the largest prison system in the country; moreover, except for Mississippi and Louisiana, the state has the highest incarceration rate in the country.[22] In 2002, Texas executed 33 prisoners, nearly four times the number of the next closest state.[23] Texas, in short, is a "tough on crime" state. However, the one area of its state correctional system that seems out of line with the state's political culture overall is its technical parole violation process. How and why does Texas, with an overwhelming bent to punish criminals severely, send so few people back to prison for technical parole violations?

Michael Eisenberg of the Texas Criminal Justice Policy Council offered one response, noting that "the technical parole violation process is an invisible fall-out of our toughness."[24] In other words, according to Eisenberg, a "progressive" system of diverting technical parole violators is possible because the overall toughness of the system is unquestionable; thus the policy of diverting parole violators from prison has not been a controversial issue either with the Texas legislature or with parole officers. Moreover, while Texas has a very tough criminal justice system, with very long prison sentences and more executions than any state in the country, the state also had one of the most sophisticated and respected criminal justice policy analysis and advisory agencies in the country. Headed by Dr. Tony Fabelo, the Texas Criminal Justice Policy Council had long been noted both for its analytic work on the Texas criminal justice system (such as detailed prison population projections) and for efforts to increase the system's efficiency. In this regard, the Council led a statewide effort to control the number of prison readmissions of parole violators by creating various alternatives to prison. Due in large part to these efforts, a consensus was created in Texas among the legislature, the judiciary, and the governor's office that most technical violators would not return to prison. Few if any states have devoted this kind of attention to the issue of how best to handle technical parole violators. Amazingly, Texas's Governor Rod Perry abolished the Criminal Justice Policy Council in 2003, purportedly for budgetary reasons. Overall, though, the Texas example is in stark contrast to California, where the absolute numbers and recent growth of technical parole violators have an almost immutable feel. In this particular area, California has much to learn from Texas.

Not only do states have wide variation in the number of technical violations admitted to prisons but also in the proportion of parole populations technically violated and sent to prison. Examining the percentage of parolees who are sent to prison each year gives us a good idea about disparities in how different state parole systems treat technical violations (see Figure 5.5). This analysis takes into account the different sizes of the state parole systems since the chart shows only the ratio of technical parole violations admitted to prison to the number of people on parole.

Again, California is the nation's leader, sending about three-quarters of its entire parole population back to prison each year for technical violations. Perhaps surprisingly, some of the smaller states with relatively few people on parole or conditional supervision return very high percentages of their parolees back to prison for technical violations. Tennessee and Arizona send back more than 6 of 10 parolees back to prison for technical violations. On the other end of the scale, Oregon and Pennsylvania return less than 1 in 10 parolees to prison for the same kinds of violations. Texas once again has a very low proportion of parolees returned to prison for technical violations, 16%.

This chart clearly indicates huge disparities in parole policies and goals among the states. But, regardless of the state in which parolees live, parole violations are very common. Consequently, these return-to-prison rates reflect states' conscious policy choices rather than some states having better-behaved parolees.

Several conclusions can be reached based on extant data on overall rates of recidivism, the percentage of successful parole completion, the percentages of prison admissions that are on parole, and the percentage of parolees returned to prison for technical violations. The most overwhelming conclusion, however, is that the rate of parole failure is

Figure 5.5

Total Parole and Conditional Release Violators Admitted to Prison as
Percentage of Adults on Parole, 2001, Selected States

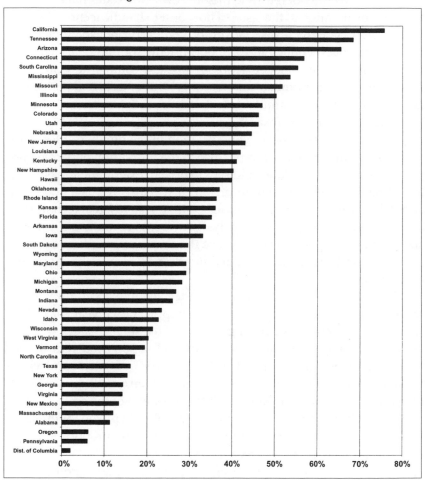

Source: Glaze, Lauren E. (2002) Probation and Parole in the United States, 2001. Washington, D.C.:
U.S. Department of Justice, Office of Justice Programs, Bureau of Justice Statistics; and Bureau of Justice Statistics, National Prisoner Statistics, unpublished data.

astounding. With more than half of people on parole returning to prison
after three years, and with more than one-third of all prison readmissions comprised of parole violators and most of them being technical violators, it seems unarguable that our postprison system needs a major
overhaul. If almost any one of the state parole systems were a Fortune

500 company, the CEO would take one look at it and shut it down. However, before examining alternatives that have the potential for far greater success at much less cost, let me turn to investigating the present parole system even more closely from within.

THE EFFECTS OF PAROLEES' PROBLEMS, DECLINING RESOURCES, AND RISK-AVOIDANCE STRATEGIES

In one respect, the depressing outcomes just described are not astonishing. Parole is at the "back end" of the criminal justice system, receiving people onto its caseload who have already had numerous contacts with the criminal justice system; often those contacts began in an individual's youth and continue after long periods of time spent in prison. Of all parolees expected to be released in 1999, 53% had been previously incarcerated and 54% had already been on probation or parole as an adult.[25]

In addition to these often long criminal histories, many parolees also have daunting mental health, drug, and alcohol problems. Figure 5.6 details some of these issues for parolees released from prisons in 1999. These numbers show a few of the many problems connected to supervising and assisting the U.S. parolee population. Drug and alcohol use numbers are huge, with more than 80% using one or the other at the time they committed crimes; almost 25% depended on alcohol and 59% were using drugs within a month of their crimes. In addition, over 14%

Figure 5.6

The Prevalence of Mental Illness, Drugs, and Alcohol among Released Parolees, 1999

Characteristic	Percent of Expected Releases
Alcohol or Drugs Involved at Time of Offense	83.9
Alcohol Abuse	
Alcohol use at time of offense	41.5
Alcohol dependent	24.9
Drug Use	
Drug use in month before offense	58.8
At time of offense	45.3
Intravenous use in the past	24.8
Committed offense for money for drugs	20.8
Mentally Ill	14.3
Homeless	11.6

Source: Hughes, Timothy, Doris James Wilson, Allen J. Beck (2001) Trends in State Parole, 1990–2000. Washington, D.C.: U.S. Department of Justice, Office of Justice Programs, Bureau of Justice Statistics.

reported suffering from some mental illness. (Because based on self-reporting rather than a medical diagnosis, this figure may be an underestimate.) Almost 12% of parolees said they were homeless at the time of their arrests; because these are national averages, this figure is probably far higher in cities than in suburban or rural America.

Moreover, in the opinion of Joan Petersilia, perhaps the country's leading authority on parole and community corrections, parolees have an almost infinite need for other services: "They [parolees] remain largely uneducated, unskilled, and usually without solid family support systems, and now they bear the added burden of a prison record and the distrust and fear that inevitably results."[26] While Petersilia reports that in the 1960s parolees had full-time employment rates of approximately 50%, "today, full-time employment for parolees is rare."[27] Compounding this already bleak situation is that states have started to cut many of the general employment and job-training programs for which parolees were already at the back of the line, due to most states' budget shortfalls at present.

Given all the social, economic, and health deficits of those coming out of prison, it becomes less than surprising that so many parolees are sent back to prison for rule violations. When one combines these problems with conditions that are routinely set for parole—no drug use, having a permanent address, having or actively pursuing employment, keeping all reporting and treatment appointments—a recipe for failure results.

Moreover, the drug and alcohol abuse, mental illness, and homelessness that affect so many people on parole guarantee that this is a population with enormous needs for treatment and varied social services. In addition, parolees also clearly need employment and educational opportunities. But, while this is a moment when more people are coming out of prison onto parole supervision with more needs and problems than ever before, such treatment, employment, educational, and other social services are largely absent from the American parole system, for two reasons. One entails resources, and the second relates to parole's recently changed mission from a rehabilitation-oriented focus on counseling, social services and assistance to a more law enforcement–oriented focus on monitoring, supervision, and violation.

The resource issue is fairly straightforward. Petersilia writes that the average cost of a parolee under active supervision is $1,500 a year, including supervision and resources. But an effective treatment program costs between $12,000 and $15,000 per year.[28] She also says that over 80% of parolees are supervised on caseloads of 69:1 (or 69 parolees to every 1 parole officer) and are seen only twice a month. According to criminologist Elliot Currie, writing in a similar vein, "Many probation and parole agencies, especially in big cities, are stretched well past the point of effectiveness, their ability to provide meaningful supervision of offenders drastically eroded by years of fiscal starvation and caseloads that can run into the hundreds."[29]

This combination of more parolees with increasing needs and dwindling parole resources has created a situation where the parole system is almost structurally incapable of providing the help that its population requires. On the other hand, these constraints do allow for strict monitoring and control of parolees, a point that brings us to the second reason behind the current deemphasis on treatment in parole. The political backlash against rehabilitation that occurred in the 1980s and 1990s, coupled with decline of resources provided for parole and probation agencies, has led many large corrections and community supervision agencies to adopt what Malcolm Feeley and Jonathan Simon have called "the new penology."[30] In essence, correctional agencies now perceive their mandates as involving risk management and avoidance; their institutional focus has shifted from concerns about rehabilitating or reforming individual offenders to minimizing the risks these offenders seem to pose. Correspondingly, agencies' strategies have moved away from counseling and program intervention toward actuarial calculation and controls via classification systems, offender-based data systems, and drug-testing technologies. As parole agencies have come to manage their caseloads by using technology and exceptionally efficient parole violation procedures that can quickly send parolees back to prison, Simon notes: "The result is a system that has shifted from supervision to the mechanics of adjudication and punishment."[31]

For sociologist David Garland, the risk-management focus of corrections agencies is symptomatic of larger societal trends that involve collective social outrage at and demonizing of criminals and the lower class more than risk and economic efficiency on the part of organizations per se. In Garland's words:

> Punitive policies such as the War on Drugs, "prison works," and the death penalty, may claim to be cost-effective forms of risk management but the calculations involved are far from actuarial. Rather, they

are motivated by an unstated but well-understood sentiment that view the offenders targeted by such acts (recidivists, career criminals, "sexually violent predators," drug dealers, pedophiles) as wicked individuals who have lost all legal rights and all moral claims upon us. The motivating mind set here is not actuarial prediction or careful risk-management. It is a hard, self-righteous intolerance produced by stereotypical images of danger and negative evaluations of moral worth.[32]

But regardless of the explanation offered for parole agencies' shifts in focus over the last two decades, organizationally speaking, these agencies did adopt the methods and rationale of risk prediction and management through most of the 1980s and 1990s. Moreover, whether these agencies are successful at their purported task (and usually they are not), the techniques they have adopted are efficient and almost perfectly attuned to a time of fiscal crisis insofar as they result in quick identification and apprehension of violators.

For, unlike expensive program interventions such as job training and placement, counseling and mental health treatment, drug treatment, and housing, the technologies and processes of "violation detection" are exceptionally cheap. In-office or at-home drug testing for thousands of people is also easy and, for the most part, determinative: you have either used drugs or you have not. In administrative parole violation hearings, this evaluation requires only a "preponderance of evidence"; that is, a positive drug test is usually all that is necessary to send a parolee back to prison. Deeper questions about why the parolee is using drugs and what can be done to ameliorate his or her problem, have become more exceptional than normal to ask. Instead, positive results on a drug test—"dirty urine"—have turned into a standard violation of parole, one that in many states can automatically land the parolee back in prison. Indeed, drug-testing protocols and the subsequent violation process are the perfect antidote for parole agencies that are resource-starved, risk-averse, data-driven, and now forced to operate in a political and social environment that became, over the past twenty years, openly hostile to the very notion of rehabilitation.

In this political and economic environment, the bureaucratic task that most parole agencies have given themselves—identifying and apprehending rule violators—is the metaphorical equivalent of shooting fish in a barrel. Recall the extent to which homelessness, drug and alcohol use and addiction, mental illness, unemployment, and lack of education characterize the nation's present parolee population. Now match this population with some of the standard conditions of parole. According to a national survey of parole boards undertaken in 1988, the most common standard conditions of parole—other than the obvious "obey all laws"—were gainful employment, "pay all fines and restitution," and "do not associate with other convicted felons."[33] Simply matching the problems associated with the parolee population with these conditions leads to the conclusion reached by Norman Holt in an essay titled "The Current State of Parole in America": "Thus, we design systems so that almost all parolees are likely to fail at some point."[34] The empirical evidence on parole in America has proved him correct.

So far, then, this chapter has contended that parole's changed mission from rehabilitation to risk management—taking advantage of new technologies and making the best of a severe lack of funding—has resulted in many parole agencies using violations as their primary tool of supervision and monitoring. Other factors have fueled this trend as well. From the standpoint of the imaginary parole officer I mentioned when opening this chapter, continually sending parolees back to prison doesn't cost him anything, he knows that while parole agencies are constrained by low and finite budgets, prisons are not. From their perspective, too, almost every state has allowed parole agencies to use the technical violation process unencumbered by limitations. With the exception of a handful of states that have started to address the issue of technical violators flowing back into prisons—most notably Texas, Washington, Kansas, and North Carolina—most states have let this process take place as if it were a law of nature. Indeed, the same state that takes a hard line on any increases in parole expenditures for more staff or programs may be willing to spend tens of millions of dollars incarcerating technical parole violators who comprise a third that state's prison admissions. Why?

One reply is impressionistic. Having traveled around the country over the last couple of years talking to a variety of state legislators about this issue, I have noticed that many legislators do not recognize that technical parole violations are costing their states so much money. This is not entirely surprising, given that how so many parole violators are returned to prison has been one of the most under-the-radar processes in government. Who, outside a small circle of criminal justice practitioners, academics, and government bureaucrats, knows about this at once mundane and simultaneously complex process? The answer is almost no one, since very little legislative oversight and review occurs. Therefore, parole officers are not likely to perceive any limit on their ability to flood state prison systems with technical violator readmissions. The same legislators who hold down budgets for parole spend many more times their states' parole budgets on technical rule violators who have been sent back to prison. Moreover, since parole agencies are not spending money inside agencies themselves (i.e., they are not increasing their own budgets), their representatives do not need to appear before legislative appropriations or budget committees to request more funds. Then, on the prison side of the equation, parole admissions are simply calculated as part of the baseline used to determine prison population levels and, in turn, funding. Consequently, the uniqueness, complexity, and general ignorance involved in this process allow the issue to escape most legislative oversight.

Finally, parole officers themselves are generally allowed enormous discretion in their caseload management. The parole officer job itself is quite entrepreneurial. Officers have their own caseloads and are frequently in the field by themselves; they are the primary, and usually the only, contact that the parolee (and perhaps his or her family) has with the parole agency. The decisions made by individual parole officers are what generally determine the fate of parolees, unless they are arrested for a new crime; in the latter eventuality, the criminal justice system takes over. This level of discretion brings significant power. Parole agents carry firearms and have the legal authority to arrest and search parolees, their residences, and their property without the requirements imposed by the Fourth Amendment, since parolees are still technically state prisoners. As Jonathan Simon describes, "The ability to arrest, confine, and in some cases imprison the parolee makes the parole agent a walking court system for those people directly affected by the civil and criminal conduct of the parolee."[35] This power is all the more daunting if parole officers have an institutional bent toward law enforcement, violation, and revocation. Mona Lynch, who did an ethnographic study of a California parole field office, found that while the agents themselves did not necessarily mirror the conceptual risk-management strategies attributed to the organization's management, they were still very much focused on enforcement. Of the parole officers she writes: "Rather, to control the risk presented by the clientele, they seemed to model themselves after traditional police officers."[36]

It should be underscored that nothing here should be taken as an indictment of individual parole officers. Parole officers are doing what parole systems ask them to do; they work with few resources and experience constant pressure, including anxieties about whether someone on their caseload will be the next murderer of a Polly Klaas. Indeed, a combination of high caseloads, few internal resources, and frequent political condemnation makes their job one of the most difficult and stressful in the criminal justice system. I headed a probation department in New York City where the average probation officer's caseload approached 200 cases per officer; most officers attempted valiantly, even heroically, to stay on top of their caseloads. But it simply couldn't be done. This was not the fault of the probation officers but a systemic problem. Analogously, the current state of parole is not the fault of frequently maligned parole officers who have been asked to do impossible jobs under impossible circumstances.

Similarly, nothing in this analysis is meant to overlook that even in highly underfunded parole agencies, such as California's, specific programs and units may well be doing exceptional work with parolees through innovative programs because their motivation and willingness to try something different is great. But even with all the good work done by parole officers, and even though interesting programs exist in some places that could become models for other states as well, systemwide the fact remains that one of the most common "outcome" measures for parole officers is technical violations resulting in reincarceration.

One more point still needs exploring with regard to the technical violation process: Where do considerations of public safety fit in? This is no easy question to answer, but it is hard to make a compelling case that public safety is greatly enhanced by this practice. Yet the overriding rationale given by parole agencies for high rates of revoking parole and returning technical violators to prison is that unless they do so, more serious criminal conduct will result. The problem with this rationale is that no extant research demonstrates any connection between rule-breaking behavior of the kind involved in technical violations and future crime. Arguably, then, the whole enterprise is thrown into question by this lack of any cause-and-effect data connecting technical violations and crime.

Given the high rate of drug use among people going to prison, some might ask whether a wholesale policy of violating parolees who use drugs makes sense. After all, didn't their use of drugs land them in prison in the first place? Isn't there some sort of connection between drugs and crime? These are reasonable concerns that require several responses. The first is perhaps the most facile: while the majority of those who entered prison used an illegal drug, most people who use illegal drugs never go to prison. But second, and more to the point, is that given the geometric increases in the numbers of people sent to prison for drug offenses over the past decade and a half—most of whom do not receive drug treatment while in prison—it should come as no surprise that drug use among parolees is common. The key question, then, is how parole agencies should respond. While reacting with sanctions to such parole violations is understandable, using prison as one of the sanctions is not. For one thing, especially with regard to drug-related crimes, prison sentences simply don't work. Recidivism rates of 50% within three years for formally incarcerated drug offenders is an indication that a prison stay for this group as a whole is not particularly effective. Why would another prison stay, for a much shorter duration, work a second time?

A final response is that, according to criminologists Al Blumstein and Allen J. Beck, drug offenders who constitute the bulk of the parole violators sent back to prison are particularly vulnerable to technical violations because of failing urinalysis tests. This means that the public safety benefits of high levels of technical parole violations are dubious at best. As Blumstein and Beck put this point:

> There is no clear indication that either approach [high or low technical violation rates] results in any meaningful difference in the criminal activity of the released prisoners, at least to the extent that the recommitments for new offenses provide an indication on that issue. If that lack of a difference is found to be the case even when the other crime-preventive aspects of technical conditions of parole are taken into account, then that must raise the question of the value of technical violations. Technical violations involve significant cost and effort for the parole system, frequent admissions to prison, even if for a short time, and frequent disruption to the lives of parolees and their attempts to reintegrate into society.[37]

Blumstein and Beck also address the huge variation in rates of technical violators admitted to prison in California, New York, Illinois, and Florida. California, with an incarceration policy of "catch and release" and a parole policy of "violate and recommit," generates a high volume of the nation's prison releases and recommitments. New York, Illinois, and Florida have policies that result in longer terms of imprisonment followed by longer times free under parole supervision. Blumstein and Beck conclude that while the volume and timing of prison recommitments may differ, there is no clear link to variations in public safety.[38]

A whole range of legitimate responses and sanctions for not complying with the rules of parole exist that fall short of prison. Prison, in most cases, should not be the first option for violations of parole. Drug treatment, increased supervision, or other intermediate program interventions are preferable. Many of these programs have rates of success superior to that of prison time. But also, given both the financial costs of prison and its long-term consequences for those sent back and their families, it is hard to imagine that using these alternatives is not better —especially when noted criminologists like Blumstein and Beck do not see public safety benefits from returning offenders to prison for positive drug tests. On the contrary, the wholesale return of so many parolees to prison for technical violations, especially for drug use, has the effect of drawing funds away from interventions that could bring substantial safety benefits.

None of this is to say that some parolees should not be sent back to prison for violating the conditions of parole. If a sex offender begins hanging around schools, if someone who has committed robberies with a gang is seen back with the old group, if someone who has committed domestic violence disregards an order of protection, then returns to prison are certainly appropriate. But the overriding problem with many states' use of the technical parole violations process is their wholesale reliance on prison as a primary sanction—a reliance that evidence does not show is contributing significantly to increased public safety.

The other rationale for revoking parole and sending people back to prison on technical violations is that some crime is prevented as a result of incarcerating parolees for some period of time. While this seems indisputable, the effect has to be quite small given the relatively short lengths of time that technical parole violators, on average, spend in state prisons. For instance, in California and New York, the average length of stay for technical parole violators is approximately five and six months, respectively. While it may well be that a six-month prison stay for a population that has been in and out of jail and prison has some incapacitation effect, such short lengths of stay would seem to minimize it. In addition, other costs are associated with sending these violators back to prison, including loss of employment (however meager), housing, and harm to families and children. Any study of the public safety benefits of reincarcerating this population for a matter of months should attempt to calculate the effects, both on public safety and otherwise, of removing so many people from their communities once again for such short periods of time.

To summarize, parole agencies in the United States are structurally underfunded and almost incapable of providing meaningful program and rehabilitative services. Yet they have just about every political, organizational, and fiscal incentive to identify, apprehend, and incarcerate technical parole violators. Moreover, this entire process has received virtually no attention in the form of oversight or review by state legislatures. Taken together, these factors have significantly fueled the size and continued expansion of the American prison system.

RESTRUCTURING PAROLE

The current system of parole supervision badly needs restructuring. Prison costs alone and the sheer volume of parole failures render this conclusion easy to reach. Consequently, this section aims at showing what options exist and could be used productively by states concerned with restructuring their parole systems. I begin, though, with various suggestions that have been offered in theory.

First, however, it should also be noted that over the past few years, academics, policy analysts, and some practitioners have evinced renewed interest in problems of postprison release. In the late 1990s, after then-Director Jeremy Travis authored a short report titled "But They All Come Back," the National Institute of Justice continued to play an instrumental role in calling attention to such issues.[39] The report succinctly highlighted the huge numbers of people returning from prisons to their communities and the importance of focusing on this population, given their high rates of return. Indeed, following this report and the discussions it provoked, the term "prisoner re-entry" was coined. Prisoner re-entry encompasses efforts aimed at preparing prisoners for their release back into communities as well as assistance intended to ease prisoners' transition back into neighborhoods, families, jobs, and drug-free lives. This focus has gained the attention of academic and policy analysts, and even some policy makers, around the country.[40]

In the past decade, too, several proposals have been put forward to remake the current U.S. parole system. Some advocate getting rid of discretionary parole release and supervision altogether; some propose strengthening and refocusing existing parole and community corrections infrastructures; still others envision entirely different forms of postprison community supervision. Several such proposals are worth reviewing, since they can provide a framework for state policy reforms. However, while these proposals are helpful, it should be emphasized that states have very different legal, criminal justice, and political cultures. While most states need to rethink how their parole systems work, more than one way of changing parole will eventually be adopted. Ultimately, some states may reject all these suggestions, choosing to keep their current systems intact; others might end up with a hybrid of these options, or come up with their own completely new concepts. Still, these proposals, all from seasoned experts in criminal justice and parole, are very useful in stimulating debate and discussion; they may offer practical and valuable elements that can be adopted by states, leading thereafter to a fairer and more rational system of postprison supervision.

Eliminate Parole Supervision

Perhaps the most radical suggestion about how to reform parole has been offered by Martin Horn, currently the New York City Correction and Probation Commissioner and the former Pennsylvania Corrections Commissioner and Executive Director of the New York State Division of Parole. In an article published in *Corrections Management Quarterly*, Horn proposed completely eliminating parole supervision and replacing it with a "personal responsibility" model.[41] Horn's notion is that discretionary parole should be eliminated entirely, since prison should be reserved for dangerous offenders; the purpose of prison, in Horn's view, should be punishment. Thus good behavior should not be used to mitigate a sentence primarily aimed at punishing. In any event, it is impossible to predict exactly who will be rehabilitated. As he wrote:

> Achievement of a college degree, willing performance of assigned duties, or speculative progress toward "self realization" and internaliza-

tion of social controls do not appreciably change that [prisoners being incarcerated as long as necessary]. If imprisonment for ten years is required to satisfy society's need for retribution, to preserve social order and prevent social anomie, good behavior in prison—which should be the norm—does not change that.[42]

He proposes that while in prison, inmates should be taught to read and write. ("Shame on us if we don't teach inmates to read and write in the 21st century. Prisons are good at those things, better than they are at psychotherapy.")[43] Toward the end of their release, prisoners would be put in halfway houses to ease their "graduated re-entry" back to communities. This is the point at which Horn's proposal becomes radical. Upon release, ex-prisoners would sign an agreement to obey the law and would receive vouchers that could be used, at the discretion of the ex-prisoner, for drug treatment, job training, or counseling. The vouchers would be funded through the complete elimination of all parole supervision. He offers New York as an example where the savings from the elimination of parole supervision would enable paying for all such voucher services, still saving the state $50 million after the vouchers were funded. However, the coercive part of this plan involves its adding two years to any sentence handed down for a new crime committed within two years of release.

Consequently, other than through the provision of vouchers and new punishment added for new crimes, in Horn's plan the state absents itself entirely from the ex-prisoner's postprison life. This is because "the flaw in the current system of parole is that it places responsibility for the success or failure of parolee on the state rather than the offender."[44] For Horn, then, the benefits of this plan are threefold: sentences are set and "transparent"; the onus for law-abiding behavior is on the parolee; and fiscal savings are potentially considerable. This last benefit is an especially important one. Quoting Horn one last time:

Public budgeting is a zero sum exercise. Dollars spent on imprisonment are not available for tax reduction. We cannot speak about increased investment in corrections today without allowing that those dollars will have to come from policing, teen pregnancy prevention programs, pre-natal and peri-natal programs and increasingly public education."[45]

In this plan, budget savings would emanate both from the elimination of parole supervision and the elimination of technical violations of conditions of parole. With no parole, there can be no parole violators. However, while potential cost savings from this plan are indeed considerable, funds have to be added back in for the two years added to the sentences of those released who, within two years, are convicted of new crimes.

Clearly, a host of thorny political and practical issues adhere to this proposal. The first is that many law makers and criminal justice analysts will not be comfortable with a system that completely eliminates postprison supervision. Given the tremendous problems of those coming out of prison—for instance, drug use, skill and educational deficits, and mental illness—many will hesitate about having these ex-prisoners fend for themselves with only some vouchers in hand. Second, many states will not be politically comfortable with eliminating after-prison supervision, since doing so will likely result in a nervous public and battles with labor unions who represent parole officers. Consequently, thus far only two states—Maine and Virginia—have eliminated postprison supervision. The decision to eliminate this function entirely may be difficult for many states, though the fiscal benefits likely to result might ease their discomfort.

Reinventing and Reinvesting in Parole

After interviewing many U.S. correctional efforts about parole, criminologist Joan Petersilia proposed a completely different approach to reform.[46] According to Petersilia, this new model

> should incorporate at least four components: the identification of dangerous and violent parolees, for whom surveillance through human and technological means is a top priority; the delivery of quality treatment (particularly substance abuse) and job training programs to the subgroup of offenders for whom research shows it could be most beneficial; the establishment of intermediate sanctions and other means of diverting technical parole violators to community-based alternatives and away from expensive prison cells; and committing to a community-centered approach to parole supervision. This approach requires a commitment to manage offender risk in those neighborhoods where parolees live and means forming active partnerships with local police,

community members, offenders' families, neighborhood associations, and other indigenous groups. Some refer to this as "neighborhood" parole.[47]

This proposal calls for strengthening the programmatic parts of the parole system that have been so decimated over the last two decades, including drug treatment and job training. But the plan also contains elements of the risk-management approach to handling high-risk parolees through the use of sophisticated monitoring and supervision technologies such as voice verification systems and phone breathalyzers. To curtail the flow of technical violators into prisons, the creation of intermediate sanctions would allow parole agencies to "step up" parolees who begin to violate the conditions of parole into programs other than prison, such as day treatment centers or short-term boot camps. The overall rationale for this plan is that dangerous people are on parole, and that it is the state's mandate to use intensive monitoring and control to ensure that they do not commit any more crime. On the other hand, Petersilia understands the scope of remedial services needed by huge numbers of people if they are to make a successful transition to productive and law-abiding citizens. Like Horn's proposal, Petersilia's recognizes the costliness of sending so many people back to prison through technical violations. To address this issue, she proposes to divert people into nonprison alternatives; this would be less expensive than present practice of sending technical violators back to prison but more expensive than Horn's effective elimination of technical violations altogether.

In a more recent book on parole, Petersilia specifically calls for the following: more education, work, and rehabilitation opportunities in prison; instituting discretionary parole release based on recidivism (risk) prediction instruments; better use of parole classification instruments and more targeted services to high-need and high-risk offenders; and more partnerships with service providers, formally incarcerated persons, law enforcement, family members, victim advocates, and neighborhoods. She also strongly recommends that the most intensive services and surveillance should begin immediately upon release. Since the great majority of recidivism occurs during the first six months to a year, these services should be frontloaded to that time period. Moreover, Petersilia recommends giving parolees the ability to significantly shorten their lengths of time under supervision by meeting key objectives early on in their supervision, such as remaining drug-free, remaining employed, engaging in community service, and/or attending rehabilitation programs.[48]

Petersilia's proposals would be much more likely to attract the support of people in the "field" of corrections; it might interest some state legislators as well. Because community supervision would both continue and expand, this plan avoids many of the political and labor-related issues inherent in Horn's proposal. Indeed, Petersilia's proposal might be popular with many community corrections and treatment organizations for expanding these organizations' size and scope; nor does the proposal raise the specter of possibly drug-addicted and mentally ill ex-prisoners walking around unsupervised.

But problems would arise in Petersilia's plan as well. For one thing, the plan obviously maintains parole even though, according to Horn, doing so is only "throwing good money after bad" and "enlarging an already inefficient and unfair bureaucracy."[49] In addition, improving the present parole system as Petersilia recommends would require quite a bit of up-front investment to strengthen that system's programmatic aspects and create intermediate sanctions to handle technical parole violators. In the current fiscal climate, such new investment might be hard to procure. Also, sending some technical parole violators to newly created intermediate sanctions has the potential to increase costs rather than save money. Finally, though the politics of this proposal are less incendiary than Horn's, the task of convincing legislators to expand the parole system would still be exceptionally difficult. Obtaining up-front investment is difficult in any case, but especially in a time of fiscal constraint, legislators perceive little political capital to be gained from beefing up parole systems. Hence the onus on this proposal's proponents is considerable in terms of convincing legislators that the plan is worthwhile, cost-effective, and capable of increasing public safety.

Finally, this proposal is essentially reformist in character, leaving the essential structure of the parole enterprise intact. The same cannot be said for a third proposal, which has been put forward by Jeremy Travis, now the President of the John Jay College of Criminal Justice.

Ending Parole as We Know It

In a May 2002 talk delivered at the Vera Institute of Justice, Jeremy Travis declared, "It is time to end parole as we know it."[50] In explaining this statement, Travis proposed that the executive branch of government no longer determine sentence lengths in the form of parole boards making discretionary release decisions. He cited research on declining rates of parole release prior to elections and changes in release rates from one administration to another as evidence of the highly politicized and inherently unfair nature of this method of release. For Travis, the fact that all but a few prisoners come home is far more important than the method by which they are released from prison. "It does not matter whether they are sentenced under indeterminate or determinate sentencing schemes, released by parole boards or by operation of law, they all return to live in free society."[51] Instead, he recommended that all sentences for technical parole revocations be made by either sentencing commissions or sentencing judges, but not by the administrative parole process. Sentencing commissions would have the role of developing standards for the reentry process (Travis's primary concern), and sentencing judges would not only impose a determinate sentence but "be expected to create and review re-entry plans for each person sent to prison, just as they now approve supervision plans for those on probation."[52] This would lead to the creation of reentry courts from which judges would oversee the period after prison. A court-based position of reentry liaison would also be created; this person would visit the prisoner once a month in prison to help develop a release plan, and the prisoner would then appear once a month in the reentry court postrelease.

In a departure from current practice, Travis recommends, as does Petersilia, that expenses devoted to reentry be frontloaded into the first three months of supervision, this being the time period when the highest rate of failure occurs.[53] According to Travis, if a state spent the same amount of money on the first three months after release as it does on prison in the three months prior to release, $7,000 would become available for significant assistance in transitional housing, counseling, job training, drug treatment, and other services. This compares with $265 a month that parole currently spends on the first three months postrelease. This funding would also help create a Community Justice Corporation (possibly a public or private/public benefit agency) that would replace parole supervision as a distinctly community-based entity created to oversee the reintegration of released offenders. The remainder of funding would come from "reduced incarceration" and would be further supplemented with resources from housing, drug treatment, workforce development, and social service programs.[54] Finally, on the issue of technical violations, Travis merits quoting at some length:

> In my view, there are only two reasons to deprive someone of liberty after he has been released from prison. First, if he has committed a new crime, in which case that crime should be prosecuted like any other crime, not under the guise of a parole violation. Second, if he has failed to abide by a critical component of a transition plan, such as attending a drug treatment program, staying away from an intimate partner if there is a history of abuse, working at an approved job or staying drug free. I would cap these sanctions at a low level, perhaps five days in jail, and cap the exposure to these sanctions to the first three months after release from prison, renewable in three month extensions up to a year, upon a showing that continued judicial supervision is needed to reduce public safety risk. By considerably shortening the period of transition between three and twelve months, we could take all the money now spent on parole, front load it, and create, in effect, a system of intensive transitional support, with focused supervision.[55]

Travis's idea is that shortening the period on supervised release to as little as three months and capping technical violations with a five-day jail stay would free up enough resources to fund this entire scheme and then some.

Like Horn's, Travis's proposal is a fairly dramatic reworking of the current parole system. Note that both proposals would eliminate parole supervision, whether (in Travis's case) as we know it or (in Horn's) entirely. But the proposals are quite different in conception and approach. Travis clearly sees a major, albeit shortened and more limited, role for the state in supervising and assisting released prisoners; Horn essentially eliminates the state from all activities once prisoners are released. In addition, unlike Horn's but like Petersilia's, Travis's proposal would more likely to be received warmly by legislators and practitioners.

Nonetheless, this proposal would not simply be embraced; more probably it, too, would encounter obstacles. First, while the idea of reentry courts is appealing and analogous in many ways to the nation's system of specialized drug courts, states' court systems would have to be significantly expanded to handle a new workload of over half a million people released from state prison, who would now swell regular court workloads. Moreover, just when ways are being sought to save money, new judges, support staff, and courtrooms would require a significant influx of funds to the nation's courts. Second, while this proposal does not emulate Horn's call for the elimination of supervision and assistance for ex-prisoners, Travis does call for the elimination of parole agencies; again, therefore, political and labor issues would likely ensue. The proposal also calls for significantly increased funding for supervision in the first few months after release. Though the argument is that funds would be freed up through shorter supervision periods and many fewer technical violations, legislatures would have to be convinced that these monies would indeed quickly materialize in the exceptionally short term in order for them to proceed with these investments.

Finally, the creation of a public/private benefit corporation to direct all community supervision, liaise with courts, and make decisions about how and where to invest savings from decreased incarceration would be a difficult political task. Legislatures are not fond of creating "off-line" agencies that are not part of the regular governmental structure or subject to the same kinds of oversight, control, and budget process as regular government agencies. Though models do exist in states that have local development corporations receiving state and other funding, creating new organizational entities tends to be resisted. This would be especially true of community-based organizations with the power to make spending decisions outside the legislative process.

A Hybrid Proposal

The last proposal I mention here blends elements of the suggestions previously discussed. In an important article on parole trends, Jim Austin suggests that a high proportion of parolees are low-risk in terms of both public safety and their chances of being rearrested.[56] Austin further proposes that these parolees be identified through a risk analysis and their terms on parole shortened or eliminated. According to Austin, this would make sense since, at present, many high-risk parolees wind up receiving the same minimal supervision as those who are low-risk. Obviously, the former cases should be receiving more intensive levels of supervision and monitoring. Yet, even here, the decision to eliminate or greatly reduce parole supervision for released prisoners faces difficulties similar to the ones that would predictably ensue from the proposals reviewed above.

All these proposals are thoughtful. But perhaps most in need of emphasis is that individual states—with their own distinctive political landscape, particular level of economic distress, and legal and criminal justice culture—will vary greatly in the elements they lift from such proposals for the purpose of restructuring their parole or postprison supervision systems.

Regardless of how an individual state's parole system is reconfigured, though, several "principles" should be an essential part of any parole or postprison supervision system. These principles, my own suggestions for change, are as follows:

1. Move Parole Resources Up Front

Extant research on both new arrests and technical violations shows that the first several months to one year postprison are the most crucial period for a person to make a successful transition from prisoner to citizen; indeed, this is precisely when most violations occur. People who leave prison do not want to come back. But the key to this actually happening is providing the right kinds of targeted programming to address the areas of greatest need for recently released prisoners. A prisoner's greatest need may be in the area of drug treatment, mental health counseling, temporary housing, or job training. While all these programs are cheaper than prison, each costs money; some programs, such as transition housing or job training with a supported work component, can cost several thousand dollars a year. Yet parole agencies cannot simply count on more and more funding to create these programs. Consequently, they need to "collapse" resources currently available and to concentrate them at the beginning of the parole process, in order to keep violations from occurring in the first place.

It makes no sense for government to have spent $2,000 to $3,000 per month on someone in prison for years and then, beginning postrelease, to devote only $100 to $200 per month to the same person. Given that parolees tend to violate quickly, as well as their known desire to succeed upon first leaving prison, most of parole's resources should be concentrated in the first several months after release. For instance, instead of spending $15,000 on a parolee under general supervision over a five-year period, parole should spend, say, $8,000 in the first year, devoting this money not to more enforcement or monitoring but to programs designed to successfully transition those released from prison back to their communities. Some of this funding should be used at the latter

stages of incarceration, when specific postrelease plans should be formulated. These last several months of incarceration are when plans
should be made for numerous postprison activities such as treatment,
employment or job training, and, if necessary, temporary housing.

If this is to work, parole agencies will have to ensure that funds are
used not simply to detect more violations but to provide more services.
For the goals and outcomes of greater first-year funding must be to reduce new crimes and technical violations, not to send more people back
to prison for violating the terms of their parole. Thus this principle involves more than simply changing parole's ongoing funding stream. In
addition, a strong message must be sent from the executives that run
parole to parole officers about just what they wish to see happen.

Once a parolee makes it through the first year, chances of success increase enormously. Accordingly, levels of supervision—and spending
—can be stepped down and even eliminated. While such collapsing
of resources may not be appropriate for everyone leaving prison—for
example, sexual predators and pedophiles may require constant and
ongoing supervision—this strategy does make sense for most people
leaving prison.

2. Use Risk Instruments to Determine Initial and Ongoing Level of Supervision

Not everyone leaving prison presents the same public safety risk or
requires high levels of supervision. Sex offenders and those who have
committed violent crimes (especially recently) generally require higher
levels of supervision than other nonviolent prisoners. In contrast, aged
prisoners, of whom there are many, present a far lower risk to public
safety than young prisoners. Likewise, released prisoners who return to
a permanent place to live, have supportive families, and do not have
drug or mental illness problems tend to require far less intervention and
supervision than those who leave with no housing, job prospects, or ad-
dictions to drugs. In light of these variations, the use of sophisticated
risk and need instruments can help parole agencies to make sound
judgments about where and for how long to use their limited resources,
as opposed to treating everyone on supervision equally despite people's unequal needs. For instance, Jim Austin, a criminologist who
works with a number of state prison systems around the country, has
created risk instruments for parole agencies that are designed to iden-

tify relatively low-risk parolees who require only minimal, if any, supervision. Conversely, this instrument can identify high-risk parolees who require more supervision and monitoring.

3. After an Initial Period of About One Year, the Resources Dedicated to Supervision and Programming Should Decrease

In general, those who receive intensive intervention and supervision should be moved after approximately one year to an "administrative" caseload entailing minimal levels of supervision. In many cases, as per Petersilia, supervision can end entirely after only a year or so of successful adherence to parole conditions. Except for some classes of parolees (again, for instance, sexual predators) and individual cases that represent an ongoing public safety risk, almost everyone should be "stepped down" to lower supervision levels—or released from parole entirely once a shortened period of compliance is met. The advantage of this proposed intensive first year followed by minimal (if any) supervision thereafter is that violations should decrease in the first year, when they happen most frequently; after the first year, though, there will be less of an effort (or no effort at all) to simply catch those who technically violate parole, since funding levels will not allow it. Those who do commit new crimes later were most likely have done so in any event. Moreover, the lack of attention to purely technical violations, especially after the first year, will continue to realize huge prison savings—some of which can again be reinvested into this initial transition process. In fact, part of the ongoing savings can be redirected back to parolees in the form of vouchers (as per Martin Horn) that allow people to take advantage of services on their own once their supervision levels have decreased or ended.

4. Create Uniform Responses to Technical Violations That Make Use of Graduated Sanctions, the Last of Which Are Short Stays in Jail or Prison

Incarceration should be a decision of last resort, used only after a number of other, graduated responses have been exhausted. These could range from strict warnings from parole supervisors or judges (where it is made clear to the parolee that any subsequent violation will result in immediate placement back in prison), to the use of day centers, to, finally, short-term use of incarceration. Day centers are facilities where those under community supervision can go, up to seven days per week, to attend treatment programs, and where they can also perform community service. Another variant on these day centers are secure technical violation centers where violators might be housed for short periods of time while attending all mandated treatment programs. The lengths of stay here might be only one or two months, as opposed to many more months parolees might usually serve in prison (without any treatment).

Policy makers must ensure that their staffs know about and use such alternatives to prison, turning to very short prison stays only when all other sanctions have failed. Of course, in some cases, long stays in prison may be appropriate for some technical violators, such as those who flee their jurisdictions or who have or attempt to obtain weapons. However, most technical violators do not fall into these categories, so an initial decision to send someone back to prison for six months to one year represents a significant waste of resources.

5. State Policy Makers Must Take an Active Oversight Role in Parole and Postprison Supervision to Ensure That Current Parole Incentives Are Changed

Parole agencies should not be allowed to operate virtually independently; the ramifications for public safety, and for the number of resources that may be poured into prison unless oversight exists, are too great. All the incentives that now exist for parole agencies—namely, catching people violating parole and then sending them back to prison for a period ranging from several few months to a year or more—must be changed by legislative bodies and governors' offices, since redistribution of resources from prisons to community programs and parole will, by law, be required. But such changes also entail altering organizational culture, ensuring sound strategic planning, and maintaining legislative oversight to ensure that parole agencies use their resources, and state prison resources, wisely. For, again, it is precisely a lack of oversight and involvement by legislatures that has contributed to the massively inefficient parole system that currently persists in many states. The situation cannot improve short of active, ongoing, and substantive participation and oversight on the part of state law makers. While state legislatures have been quite involved in issues around parole abolition, few have bothered themselves with the details of what actually happens on parole.

6. Eliminate Structural Barriers to Successful Reentry

States that disenfranchise former prisoners by not allowing them to vote should change these policies. Once someone has been released from prison, and perhaps completed a period of community supervision, their voting rights should be restored. Nothing can more dramatically symbolize the welcoming back to the community of someone who has erred and paid his debt to society than restoring perhaps the most important and symbolic right of being a citizen: the right to vote. States that disenfranchise ex-prisoners are continuing to marginalize and help prevent the successful reintegration of several hundred thousand, disproportionately minority, people annually.

States should also make sure that prisoners can obtain the variety of licenses and identification necessary for employment. While it obviously makes sense to bar people convicted of certain crimes from particular occupations—for example, sex offenders from day care centers or those who have committed elder abuse from nursing homes—states should allow former prisoners as much latitude as possible in finding employment. It is difficult enough for this population to secure meaningful and decent-paying jobs without states restricting the availability of these jobs.

The federal government should rework its ban on categories of prisoners who are not eligible for public housing, food stamps, college loans, or welfare benefits. Given all the hardships and deficits that ex-prisoners face upon release, the absence of these basic benefits only increases their chances of failure. The Legal Action Center recently released a report on the barriers to successful reentry for prisoners in every state. States would do well to closely examine these different laws, regulations, and policies with an eye not only toward fairness but also toward increasing public safety.[57]

IN SUM

As defined by recidivism and reincarceration for technical violations, parole supervision's failure is staggering. Moreover, this failure exerts a major influence on many state prison systems' ongoing expansions. More parolees are returned to prison for violating rules of parole than for committing new crimes. The public safety benefits of this process are questionable, but its costs are not. California alone spends about $1 billion annually to incarcerate technical parole violators; obviously, these funds are then unavailable for badly needed improvements to address educational, health care, or other high-priority government services. Since parole agencies have come to see their mission as one of enforcement and monitoring, and because they are simultaneously starved for resources, they have come to make efficient use of relatively cheap and available technologies to monitor compliance and revoke paroles. As parole caseloads continue to grow and resources stay constrained, this tendency to manage risk through violation will only increase, since every political and organizational incentive conspires to push parole officers toward returning parolees to prison.

This situation has inspired extremely interesting suggestions about how the current system of postprison release and supervision could be reformed. All four reform proposals discussed in this chapter are thoughtful and were suggested by nationally recognized leaders in the corrections and parole fields. Though the proposals differ, some of their concepts and proposed practices are similar. Yet each proposal would be objectionable in one way or another to legislatures, governors, and labor unless accompanied by the sort of larger political and fiscal strategies I suggest in the next chapter. I have listed some of the more obvious objections or barriers that would emerge in reaction to these or any other proposals that called for meaningful and long-term structural reform. But again, it must be kept in mind that there are 50 different governments and political cultures in the United States wherein reforms need to be proposed. This means, at minimum, that no one way, no grand theory, is likely to emerge about how all states ought best to treat prisoners as they transition back into communities.

While it may be unrealistic to think that any one plan can change the back end of the criminal justice system, certain guiding principles like those listed above can be used as broad guidelines. For key to overcoming the sorts of objections described in this chapter is to frame these principles in ways that can concretely assist law makers as they deal with problems of declining revenues and rising public demands for other services such as education and health care. The next chapter seeks to provide this framework.

6

Success Stories and Works in Progress

ON THE SURFACE, California, Connecticut, and Louisiana could not be more dissimilar. Each state's political landscape is different. Their sizes range from small to middle to huge, both in population and acreage; from the West to the South to the Northeast, not only regional but cultural diversities become apparent. Despite this variety, all three states have in common a struggle to reduce the size and cost of their corrections systems.

Policies aimed at helping states downsize prisons must have elements that apply across the board, to all states, while simultaneously taking state-by-state differences into account. But what, specifically, would such policy suggestions look like in practice, not only in theory?

This chapter focuses on these states because, as later explained, I have done extensive research within them precisely because of their clear-cut differences. However, taken together, they offer exemplars of changes needed at the national level, since almost all 50 states in America presently suffer from severe budget constraints and spiraling corrections costs. To illustrate both the general and the specific nature of what I am proposing, then, a list of general principles follows. These principles are purposely formulated in broad terms so that they can be tailored to state-specific plans for prison reform. Afterward, I apply these general concepts to case studies of California, Connecticut, and Louisiana, in order to illustrate concretely how policy changes can be implemented. The purpose of these state-specific plans is not to impose a strategy that a given state would necessarily follow; indeed, for any state-based plan to be successful, it must be developed by state officials who themselves are best aware of the local context in which they operate. Rather, my goal is to provide a framework wide enough in scope and complexity that individual states can adopt it as they develop their own large-scale, and necessarily individualized, reforms.

PRINCIPLES OF REFORM

1. Reform Must Be "Homegrown"

Any plan for state-based prison reform must be developed by state officials themselves—perhaps in partnership with universities or research institutes—in order to encompass and address differing political, legal, and criminal justice cultures. While outsiders or consultants can provide technical assistance, state officials have to be the driving force for prison reforms; only this can ensure "buy in" by a variety of government agencies and staff, and that political issues and pitfalls will be adequately worked through. In other words, it is axiomatic that strategic plans for change must be "homegrown."

By extension, this means that the process of developing statewide strategic plans is likely to be difficult substantively as well as politically. For one thing, disparate actors need to be brought together: legislatures, governors (including the corrections, parole, and budget directors), and, in some states, the judiciary and attorney generals as well. In itself, this is no easy task, since one or more of these actors may have myriad reasons for resisting change. However, the compelling and overriding state interest in reforming the prison system and funding other priorities favored by these same institutional actors provides a strong motivation to see the process through. In some states, reform-oriented groups might be headed by a powerful legislator or the governor's chief of staff or a member of the judiciary. But the specific breakdown of the group charged with mapping out reform would be less important than its overall commitment to the reform effort itself. For instance, in 2001, Nebraska created a statewide working group to examine community corrections that comprised representatives from all three branches of government; the outcome was draft legislation for a new community corrections system, which passed in 2003. In 2003, New Mexico converted its statewide statistical analysis center into a formal sentencing commission, again with all three branches of government represented, to review the state's incarceration policies. Arizona and Wisconsin likewise recently created new sentencing commissions with the same mandate.[1]

Again, the main reason states need to chart their own course of reform is that each state has a unique set of political and organizational circumstances and history. For instance, some states have had a long-lasting antipathy to the creation of state sentencing commissions. For such states, the barriers to having a new nonpartisan body that removes the legislature from direct control of sentencing policy may be too strong to overcome, even in dire fiscal times; these states will have to either fashion acceptable alternatives or decide that present circumstances warrant breaking heretofore insurmountable political obstacles.

Ultimately, many state efforts at prison reform will feature many of the same elements. Certain commonalities exist: every state prison system has grown dramatically over the last 20 years; every state system now incarcerates more and a higher percentage of drug offenders than two decades ago; every state struggles with high recidivism rates (though some are higher than others); and virtually every state holds prisoners for significantly longer periods than even one decade prior. Consequently, all reform efforts will face some, or all, of these realities; at the same time, "getting there," which includes deciding the specific priorities and "look" of reform, will vary greatly from state to state.

2. Strategies Must Confront and Surmount Local Obstacles to Reform

Not all states pose the same institutional or political obstacles to reform. Chapter 2 discussed many impediments, but it is a rare state that confronts them all. For instance, a complex variety of factors in New York State bequeaths conditions at once conducive and not conducive to reform. New York has very powerful corrections unions but absolutely no private prisons. The state does have a prison system that provides significant economic development to its rural areas. On the other hand, efforts aimed at changing New York's severe Rockefeller Drug Laws have recently gained momentum, and the size of the state's prison system has contracted over the past several years.

By contrast, New Mexico has a small and not particularly powerful corrections union; this state also has the highest percentage of prisoners in the nation (43%) who are in private facilities.[2] As a result, not surprisingly, the private prison industry has a significant and influential presence in New Mexico. Nonetheless, a recently departed Republican governor made drug reform one of his top political priorities (though his proposed reforms have not yet been adopted by the legislature), and the state has created a Corrections Population Control Commission to make recommendations on drug reform to the legislature.

A third example: Illinois has powerful public labor unions but no private prisons. It also had a governor, George Ryan, who was the first in the nation to reexamine the use of the death penalty by declaring a moratorium on capital punishment in January 2000. Ryan also publicly discussed the possibility of early release from prison of first-time non-violent offenders.

Each state has a particular mixture of obstacles to reform and promising areas where change has already begun (or has potential to commence). Consequently, all state reform efforts must initially identify obstacles as well as opportunities, thereafter developing plans to overcome the former and build upon the latter.

3. Some Obstacles to Reform Can Become Part of the Solution

While private prison companies and high recidivism rates for released prisoners are two very different kinds of impediments to reducing incarceration, both can be turned into reasons for implementing reforms. For instance, while private prison operators wield significant political clout, they also provide states with the opportunity to make immediate reductions in prison contracts without the loss of state jobs. Reducing or eliminating contracts for private prisons also results in immediate budget savings. In states that want to protect public employee jobs and also have private prisons, these contracts provide an opportunity to meet two important political and fiscal goals: saving public jobs and realizing immediate budget savings by canceling private contracts. Indeed, in 2002, Governor Ronnie Musgrove of Mississippi closed a Correction Corporation of America prison and realized an almost immediate $4 million savings.[3]

Likewise, while high return rates for released prisoners are a major cause of prison expansion, this "bad news" can offer a substantive and political opportunity (thereafter leading, paradoxically, to prison contraction). Take California, for instance, where about a whopping 85,500 of 115,000 parolees are sent back to prison each year for either technical violations (approximately 71,200) or new crimes (approximately 14,300).[4] Given the magnitude of these numbers, even marginal reductions in this state's disturbingly high recidivism rates would have a large impact on the size of the prison system. Thus, ironically, states that have high recidivism rates for those on parole or in other forms of post-prison supervision may actually be better poised to significantly reduce incarceration—through policies aimed specifically at ameliorating high recidivism rates—than states with relatively low recidivism and return to prison rates.

Even more specifically, parole reform—especially if focused on those who are returned to prison on technical violations—has the potential for dramatic impact in a state like California, where parole violators make up 70% of prison admissions. By contrast, in Florida, where parole violators constitute only 6% of all prison admissions, parole reform would have a minimal effect.[5] Still, precisely because the national percentage of prison admissions of parole violators is 36%,[6] the majority of states would potentially reap huge benefits from changing the organizational structure of institutions that fail to keep large numbers of people from returning to prison.

4. Wherever Possible, Labor Reductions Should Occur through Attrition

In most cases, prison systems can reduce staff through natural attrition and by not replacing staff, rather than through layoffs. This means that, as reforms take hold, gradual prison contraction will result simply by not hiring additional classes of corrections officers. For instance, if a prison system experiences even a low rate of turnover each year due to retirements or officers taking new jobs elsewhere—for argument's sake, let's assume this rate is 6%—this measure alone would translate into substantial annual savings. Thus, in a system with 5,000 officers making an average salary of $45,000 and an additional $12,000 in benefits and pension plans, 250 officers costing an average of $57,000 would leave naturally at an annual savings of $14.3 million. Further cost savings would result from lower administrative and support costs.

From a strictly managerial point of view, some administrators might counter that targeted layoffs are more desirable than attrition. Through targeted layoffs, staff reductions can be made in specific areas; by contrast, attrition happens across the system and in areas where staff reductions were not needed (say, a uniformed chief of security has retired, leaving a job that must be replaced). While it is true that attrition can thus lead to problems of replacing key positions (and sometimes retraining people to fill these positions), layoffs should be an absolute last resort, for reasons both ethical and political. Moreover, corrections unions, many of which know they have shrinking memberships, will be much more cooperative and might well participate in efforts to retrain and reassign officers if they understand that their ranks are not going to be forcibly reduced by layoffs.

5. Private Prison Contracts Should Be Reduced

Private prison contracts should be reduced or eliminated for three reasons. The first is that in states that have begun to reduce their prison populations, cutting or eliminating existing contracts provides an immediate, and possibly the best, opportunity for achieving budget savings. Second, extant research indicates there is no reason to believe that, as a general rule, private prisons are cheaper than public prisons.[7] In fact, even though debate whirls on this subject, the overwhelming evidence shows no differences in cost between operating private and operating public prisons. Finally, prioritizing private prisons for initial budget reductions will help win the cooperation of public corrections unions and associations to actively participate in long-term reforms to downsize prison systems.

6. Budget Savings Must Be Reflected in the Budget

It is essential that any planned savings from state reform efforts be reflected in the adopted budget. The savings must be clearly shown, and if a state does a multiyear budget, these should continue and grow in later years. This serves the obvious function of actually moving funds out of corrections. But it also highlights where savings are being used, in cases where states have simultaneously decided to increase spending on higher education, for instance, or to protect particular programs from elimination as a result of the corrections savings. Budgets can show these decisions quite clearly.

Depending on the level and timing of savings, the prison budget might actually decline or the amount of expected increase in the prison budget be far smaller than anticipated. It might be the case that simple increases in collective-bargaining contracts, inflation, lease and rent costs, increasing fuel costs, and so on will cause the prison budget to increase even with a small decrease in population. This is still a budget savings for states that plan or budget for out-year (later-year) expenditures. For states that have only current, one-year budgets, having a smaller-than-expected increase in corrections funds remains a savings, even if this is more difficult to show than in cases of actual decrease. This is not an insurmountable obstacle: state and legislative budget offices can easily figure out how to clarify that funds have been saved due to population reductions. Still another possibility is that, in some cases, reduction in prison populations will not immediately save operating funds, due to rising budget costs in other areas. However, a declining or lower-than-expected prison population may well prevent the building of another prison. This kind of cost avoidance is also real budget savings: again, state officials need to emphasize this in their budgets.

Finally, continuing and increasing reductions in the later years of a budget maintains a sense of pressure for implementing successful reforms and achieving meaningful savings. Assuming that a solid plan and strategy are in place, funds must be removed from corrections in anticipation of reforms. This tends to make corrections officials nervous, since funds will be removed from their budgets prior to specific reforms taking hold. However, a benefit of removing funds in advance is that all the actors in the system have a joint interest in seeing that specific reforms happen according to a preexisting timetable. Nothing mobilizes state agency officials to act like seeing a significant portion of their funds disappear: no one wants to go back to the governor or legislature for more money because she was not able to successfully implement an already agreed-upon reform strategy.

7. Sometimes You Have to Spend Money to Save Money

Depending on the particular method of achieving reduced correctional expenditures, a state may have to invest some funds in a particular program or part of the criminal justice system, or in community-based service providers, to achieve savings. An obvious example is if a state decides to provide intensive prerelease planning for prisoners about to leave state custody and significant community support services immediately upon these prisoners' release. After attempts to reallocate existing funds are exhausted, this might require investing new funds to create or expand these services. Yet, during budget crises, allocating new funds or reinvesting savings in new programs is difficult to justify—even more so when the new funds are earmarked to "help" current or ex-prisoners, not necessarily the most politically popular use of scarce resources.

A good response, though, is as follows: the ultimate result of these investments is likely to be reductions in the prison budget, due to re-duced recidivism of ex-prisoners now able to receive essential support services that can keep them from reoffending—in other words, more public safety at less cost. Again, these prison savings should be reflected in the budget alongside new funds, so that everyone—in the legislature as well as the general public—can see the connection between these two actions. For new funding and savings are intertwined: the savings cannot happen without the investment, and given the tremendous cost of prison, savings will almost always be many times the size of new investments.

Ideally, the investment and at least some portion of the savings should occur in the same year, so that resulting prison savings wholly or partially offset new funding; this will make initial investment much easier. However, some programs require an initial investment and will not show significant budget savings for one or two years and will re-quire, especially in states with tremendous budget shortfalls, a large measure of political will to implement. For instance, a major political "lift" will be needed to invest in job training and drug treatment for prisoners or parolees at the same time that a state may be laying off hun-dreds or thousands of teachers. This can happen only if law makers clearly explain to the public that this short-term investment of funds in an area that might not be their highest priority will bring huge savings in a year or two that can then be used to address their priorities.

It is worth noting in this context that policy makers must be com-fortable that money is being spent on programs that work. Criminolo-gists and criminal justice policy makers actually know quite a bit about what works and what doesn't. We know from a number of program analyses and meta-analyses that a number of *in prison* treatment pro-grams work to reduce recidivism. Among these are academic skills training, vocational skills training, cognitive skills programs, and drug treatment and sex-offender intervention programs.[8]

In addition, we know quite a bit about after-prison programs. Much of the literature concludes that treatments that are targeted and well de-signed and implemented can likewise reduce recidivism and result in budget savings. The key here is to develop or replicate those programs that have shown clear-cut evidence of success. For instance, the Center for Employment Opportunities in New York, which provides jobs, job training, and placement for parolees returning to New York City, has been successful; other employment programs in Texas and Chicago have shown good results as well.[9] We know that targeted interventions with parolees and their families can bring down drug use and crime, as has happened with New York's La Bodega de la Familia program.[10] Here, many researchers around the country as well as nonpartisan and not-for-profit groups such as the Vera Institute of Justice and the Urban Institute can provide invaluable assistance to policy makers in learning which programs in different areas have demonstrated records of success.

When considering investments in new programs, then, policy makers need to be assured that programs that begin in prison and those which continue outside prison can increase public safety and save money. Happily, evidence exists to reassure them. Sometimes the differences may not be that large; yet even marginal differences translate into significant savings and less crime. Creating or expanding these programs in a structured and rigorous way also takes effort, time, and sustained managerial attention. It is more than worth it.

To repeat, this will not be easy. Battles for scarce funds are intense during tight budgets, and the competition includes critical social needs such as early childhood education, infant mortality clinics, and day care. Still, investments that may be initially unpopular can aid in better funding other services in the future. At the same time, these investments are designed both to save money and to increase public safety by reducing new crimes and parole violations; the public stands to benefit by feeling more secure as well as by seeing their priorities better responded to than they have been in recent state budgets. Thus there is a "good news" story here, even though this point is not easy to underscore, and newspaper headlines that blare "Politicians Fund Programs for Criminals as Kindergarten Class Size Skyrockets" are easy to imagine. Still, if politicians are straightforward and clear in explaining how public safety and fiscal benefits accrue from seemingly disconnected expenditures, changes in budget allocations should be possible to achieve.

THREE "REAL WORLD" EXAMPLES OF HOW PRISON REFORM MIGHT WORK

At present, almost every state in the nation is struggling with increasing prison budgets amid constrained revenues. In this section, I examine three states in detail: California, Connecticut, and Louisiana. I selected these states for several reasons. One relates to these states' diversity. They are geographically diverse (representing the West, the Northeast, and the South, respectively); have different population sizes (representing a large, small, and medium-size state, respectively); and have interestingly divergent political landscapes and commitments to grappling with increased corrections costs. The second reason for selecting these particular states is that each is at a different stage of needing to, or already starting to make, reforms. California has just begun this process, though I try to make a strong argument for the potential benefits of changing this state's present policies; Connecticut has passed significant legislation that reduces corrections costs and reinvests some savings back into community programs; and some reforms have begun in Louisiana, but in a "mixed" manner—that is, changes have occurred in some areas but not others. Finally, I chose to look in more detail at Connecticut and Louisiana because, in both places, I personally have been involved in trying to influence reform as both an academic and a policy analyst.

The purpose of these case studies of how prison reform might work in these states is to illustrate concretely the feasibility of such reform even in varied local circumstances. Again, given the importance of states' finding their own way, my aim is to provide ideas, not a rigid road map. Yet by the end of this section it should be clear that any state, regardless of its particular political, legal, and criminal justice culture, can begin to significantly reduce its prison populations. For each case below, I commence by briefly summarizing how and why recent prison growth occurred in the state. I then discuss the political environment in which reform must happen before, finally, presenting a proposed reform agenda for each state.

California

Prison Growth and Its Causes

The nation's largest state among the lower 48 also has the largest prison population. The population of the California Department of Corrections (CDOC), 34,640 in 1982, ballooned to 162,317 in 2002, representing a 369% increase in two decades. In 1982 those convicted for drug sales and possession made up 6.6% of the prison population; 20 years later, this figure had risen to 22%. By contrast, the number of males incarcerated for violent crimes made up 59.6% of the prison population in 1982; by 2002, this figure had fallen to 49.7%.

Perhaps the most dramatic change in the California prison system through the 1980s and 1990s is reflected in the number of parolees sent back to prison for failing parole. In 1982, 6,009 parolees were sent back to prison, 2,113 for technical violations of parole, and the rest for committing new crimes while on parole. By 2002, those numbers had increased to 85,574 parolees sent back to prison; 71,246 of these returns were for technical parole violations.[11] This amounts to an increase of more than 34 times the 1982 number of parolees sent back to prison without new criminal convictions and has become one of the most important factors behind the state's 20-year increase in prison population.

The impact on California's prison system of parole failures, both for technical and new crimes, is also highlighted by examining their percentages of the total prison population. In 1982, parolees sent back to prison for all reasons represented 16.9% of the total population; by 2002 that figure had increased to 40.6%. Another way of looking at how parolees have poured into the prison system is to compare their admission numbers to those sent to prison for the first time. In 1982, 15,262 new first time prisoners were admitted, compared to 6,009 parole violators returned to prison. Two decades later new admissions increased about 2.5 times to 38,662, while all parole violators increased by over 14 times to 85,574.[12] More than any other single factor, parole failures have driven the growth of California's prison system.

Other factors in the incarceration increase include a number of sentencing changes over this period, most notably the 1994 three strikes law that required life in prison for any third felony conviction. Finally, the majority of those incarcerated in California prisons, like those in most states, have been convicted of nonviolent crimes. About 52% of the California prison population have been convicted of a nonviolent crime: 21% are property offenders, 24% are drug offenders, and the remaining 7% have been convicted of other nonviolent crimes.[13] The 2004–2005 budget for the CDOC is $5.3 billion.[14]

Political Issues

With this astounding growth in the state's prison population has come hugely increased power of the correctional officers union, the California Correctional Peace Officers Association (CCPOA). With 30,689 sworn peace officers working in California's prisons and parole system,[15] the CCPOA has an enormous membership. As described in Chapter 2, the CCPOA has become one of the most powerful political groups in the state, if not the most powerful, making large campaign contributions and receiving exceedingly generous collective-bargaining settlements in the midst of an extreme fiscal crisis. Clearly, the CCPOA would be a major obstacle to any prison reform that it perceived was harmful to its members (for example, having fewer of them).

Like most of California's recent governors, the recently recalled Governor Gray Davis (defeated by Arnold Schwarzenegger in California's October 2003 recall election) was conservative on crime. Davis poured resources into the state's prison system, refusing to reduce prison funding even during one of the worst fiscal crises in the state's history; he rarely granted parole, even in cases where it was recommended by his parole board.[16] California's legislature has also been conservative on crime issues, passing a host of "get tough" legislation during the 1980s and 1990s and, like the governor, showing a strong willingness to make inordinate expenditures on prison expansion.

Yet, of late, public opinion in California has registered increasing tolerance for using alternatives to prison for those convicted of drug crimes and a strong preference, in the current budget crisis, for cutting prison funding. In 2000, Californians voted overwhelmingly for Proposition 36, mandating drug treatment in lieu of incarceration for tens of thousands of drug sellers or possessors who would have otherwise gone to prison. The measure passed overwhelmingly, 61% to 39%.[17] More recently, in a statewide public opinion poll about the budget taken in June 2003, the only service a majority of Californians thought should be reduced was prisons and corrections. In terms of which services the public wanted to protect from cuts, prisons and corrections ranked far behind public schools, health and human services, higher education, and transportation.[18] These findings mirrored those in a Field Poll in California taken a year earlier that asked what services should be the first to be cut.

The State of the Budget

In fiscal years 2003 and 2004, California had a combined budget deficit of over $38 billion, as well as a protracted battle between the governor and the legislature about how to close this massive budget hole.

California remains, according to one *Los Angeles Times* characterization, "the nation's fiscal basket case."[19] Part of what explains California's dismal economic condition is that expenditures on Medicaid exceeded budgeted amounts by over $1 billion in fiscal years 2002 and 2003.[20] In addition, revenue collections have been in a free-fall since the national economy entered a recession in 2001 and California's dotcom industry virtually collapsed. In fiscal year 2003 alone, tax collections of personal income taxes came in $5 billion below projections; collections for sales tax were almost $600 million less than projected; and the corporate income tax was approximately $900 million less than expected.[21]

During fiscal year 2003, attempting to cope with such massive deficits, the governor and legislature instituted a number of new fees, laid off state employees, enacted across-the-board reductions to state agencies (corrections was largely exempted), slashed aid to cities and counties, and encouraged early retirement for state employees.[22] However, even after all these revenue-increase and expenditure-reduction actions, California ended fiscal year 2003 with a deficit of nearly $4.5 billion.[23]

Going into fiscal year 2004, former Governor Davis recommended an increase in the sales and tobacco taxes, the creation of new tax brackets for the personal income tax, additional fee increases, and a 6.4% reduction in Medicaid spending (in the preceding two years, Medicaid spending had grown by over 14%).[24] In addition, the governor proposed continuing the prior year's hiring freeze and permanently eliminating up to 20,000 vacant jobs.[25] One thing the governor did not propose, though, was significant cuts to the Department of Corrections. In fact, his proposed budget included $160 million in new one-time costs for a CDOC headquarters and an additional one-time investment of $220 million to renovate San Quentin's deteriorating death row. Overall, the agency's proposed budget actually increased by $40 million annually.[26]

Upon taking office on November 17, 2003, one of the first acts Governor Arnold Schwarzenegger carried out was eliminating a highly unpopular fee increase for car registrations that former Governor Davis had proposed. This increase would have raised approximately $4 billion in new revenue but was so unpopular with Californians that it doubtless contributed to Davis's recall. Upon the rollback of this fee increase, the California deficit grew by an additional $4 billion, totaling more than $15 billion in fiscal 2004 alone. The main way in which

Governor Schwarzenegger successfully raised the revenue to solve the state's 2004 budget crisis was to borrow about $15 billion through the sale of state bonds. Even with this new revenue and other proposed service reductions, the California Legislative Analyst's Office projects a budget deficit in 2006–2007 of $8 billion.[27]

A Proposed Plan of Prison Reform

In an interview with the *Los Angeles Times*, Stephen Greene, an Assistant Secretary of the California Youth and Adult Correctional Agency, commented, "Contrary to what people think, we have a budget that is very difficult to cut. The only way . . . is to let a bunch of people out early, and the governor does not want to do that."[28] However, politics aside, the corrections budget is not difficult to cut; moreover, various ways of reducing this budget without letting people out early do exist (though a number of low-level, low-risk offenders could be "let out early" with almost no risk to public safety).

Law makers must play a critical role in setting the stage for correctional reform in California. As indicated in Chapter 2, former Governor Davis was a huge beneficiary of CCPOA campaign contributions and showed no willingness to do anything other than continually increase the prison population and prison system's budget. All indications are, however, that Governor Schwarzenegger is, unlike his predecessor, willing to take this issue on directly. Thus, in this particular state's context, the governor and the legislature have already begun a drive for prison reform.

In California's case, the governor and legislators have started to paint a picture of a state not only in dire fiscal crisis, where education and health care budgets have been decimated (that picture has already been painted), but also where intelligent correctional reform is an attractive alternative both to increasing taxes (a point capable of garnering Republican support) and to far more draconian cuts in heath care and education (a point capable of garnering Democratic support). Further, they have to make the public case that although California has had an impressive crime-rate decline in the last decade, a number of other states have had even larger increases with far smaller increases in prison population. They can point to states such as Mississippi, Louisiana, Alabama, and Texas, all exceedingly conservative "tough on crime" states that in different ways have tackled sentencing practices or parole reform. In doing so, legislators can underscore that California lags behind many states across the country that have been grappling with controlling and shrinking their prison expenditures.

Last but not least, legislators and the governor still require a specific program of reform that can substantively and politically achieve the goal of reducing huge prison populations. In California, such a program might include the following elements.

Changing Parole Incentives and Operations

The numbers of parolees sent back to prison must be drastically cut. How might this happen? First, a "cap" should be placed on how long a parolee can spend in prison for a technical violation. At present, the average length of stay is slightly over five months for all categories of technical violators returned to prison.[29] Yet what a few months' prison stay can achieve in terms of public safety is questionable at best. Definite, though, is that these stays take tens of thousands of young (and mostly minority) men out of their neighborhoods, removing them from their families, the job market, and any possibility of social services; simultaneously, their chances of making viable reentries into their communities are disrupted. Thousands are sent back because parole officers are angry at people who are not adhering to their parole conditions; other parole officers just want to get their attention (and get them off their caseloads) by sending them back to prison. The fact is, you can get someone's attention by doing a number of things aside from sending him or her back to prison for a few months, and if incarceration is for some reason the only way left to refocus a parolee, this can be done just as well in many cases by reincarcerating the individual for a weekend or a few weeks, rather than a few months. The first thing to be done, then, is to greatly reduce the length of stay for parolees returned for technical violations. Enacting legislation that limits a technical parole violator's length of stay in prison can do this.

For example, let's suppose that the state legislature decided to draft legislation that limited the time certain "technical violators" could spend in prison but wanted to be specific about exactly what kind of violators the law would apply to. According to the CDOC, many of the technical violators who have been sent back to prison were actually involved in some sort of criminal activity, but the parole violation process was used to dispose of the case. This in and of itself is somewhat bizarre. The CDOC has determined that there were 78 homicides, 524 robberies, and 384 rapes committed by parolees that were handled as technical parole violations, wherein the individual had an administrative parole hearing and served a little longer than nine months in prison.[30] It is hard to imagine that district attorneys would allow these kinds of alleged violent crimes to be disposed as technical parole violations with a nine-month prison stay.

Beyond this, the use of the technical parole violation process as a vehicle to handle alleged serious crimes raises a host of troubling issues. As Jeremy Travis asked in his testimony to California's Little Hoover Commission: "Has California simply created a parallel system of criminal adjudication, with lower burdens of proof and lesser adversarial process? Why should these criminal events be adjudicated in a process where the maximum prison term is one year?"[31] Of the entire process seemingly being used to handle new allegations of serious criminal behavior, Travis concludes: "The use of this mechanism [the administrative parole violation process] to imprison people for criminal behavior raises profound questions about the role of this form of adjudication and punishment in our criminal justice system."[32]

Putting aside for the moment this particular important issue, the CDOC data also show that there were 24,085 technical violators returned to prison in 2001 for drug use, possession, and other nonserious "miscellaneous violations," and these violators served an average of 4.4 months in prison.[33] These lengths of stay are actually quite long and, according to Travis, are harsher than the most severe sentences would be if drug courts handled these cases as new crimes, and even longer than those imposed by traditional courts.[34] Additionally, according to the CDOC, another 11,556 parolees were sent back for what it calls "administrative violations" that have nothing to do with allegations of any additional crimes.[35] If the legislature passed legislation requiring that these categories of technical violators spend no more than 60 days in prison, as the State of Washington did, then this relatively simple and marginal reduction would save slightly more than 7,000 prison beds at an annual budget savings of almost $190 million.[36] By limiting this initial legislation to low-level administrative violations or violations based in nonviolent drug use or possession misdemeanors (which, by definition, refer to relatively small amounts of drugs), the legislature can take the public position that it is not reducing the length of stay of any technical violator who might have engaged in a serious or violent crime. This will help deflect "soft on crime" charges, especially in a state where the public seems overwhelmingly supportive of alternatives to prison for those convicted of drug crimes.

This action would immediately begin to free up savings, a portion of which could be used by the legislature and the governor for other high-priority programs such as education and health care, and a portion of which could be used for a variety of other prison and community-based programs that would further decrease recidivism and increase prison savings. For instance, if $50 million were reinvested in a variety of community-based programs such as drug treatment, employment training and job placement, and mental health services, a statewide system of important support services for ex-prisoners could be created. This system would serve as a way to respond to initial technical parole violations in lieu of prison and would also begin to provide important services to a population in desperate need of some help. This, in turn, would begin not only to reduce the number of technical violators returned to prison but also to cut down on the number of new crimes committed by parolees.

These additional resources would have to be accompanied by serious changes in the way the parole division operates. Uniform standards or guidelines would have to be created and implemented regarding when to begin technical violation proceedings and what the responses to violations should be before prison is used. The $50 million investment in community-based programs would allow these alternatives to be created and available to parole officers. (North Carolina, for example, has developed a system of graduated responses to technical violations, but California could also have an extensive support system to help create new alternatives to prison.) Along with these increased resources, there would have to be new strong management in the parole division that emphasized support and assistance in lieu of simple technical violations but also a uniform rational and graduated response to those who continuously break the rules of parole. The importance of this management change cannot be overemphasized. In 2004, Governor Schwarzenegger appointed a new secretary for the California Youth and Adult Correctional Agency and a new corrections director. The combination of a new governor and new correctional leadership might bode well for this kind of reform.

One result of a significantly enhanced community-based treatment system and managerial changes in how the parole division responds to technical violations is that fewer technical parole violators should be sent back to prison and fewer parolees should commit new crimes. If, for instance, this additional support and these management changes resulted in 50% fewer parolees being returned to prison for purely technical violations and just 10% fewer committing new crimes (that either get disposed as technical violations or new convictions), then new and significant savings would begin to materialize. In this scenario, the total "bed savings" from these reductions in the number of parolees returning to prison would be about 6,300 prison beds, at a total budget savings of almost $170 million annually.[37]

Again, a significant portion of these savings should be reinvested in prison, parole, and community programs to further address successful reentry. Let's assume that in this case $70 million is reinvested into these program areas, leaving $100 million for other state purposes. This $70 million would allow prisons to begin in-prison services as well as comprehensive prerelease planning efforts in the months prior to release; and parole and community-based programs would be funded to provide intensive services (not more monitoring or supervision) upon release, such as assistance with temporary housing, immediate life-skills training, supported work, and job training. Because the majority of parole violations happen within the first several months after release, resources should be focused on this time period, not evenly spread out over the entire period of parole.

The state might also decide to create parole reentry courts, modeled on many of the nation's successful drug courts, to provide clear judge-based supervision, support, and graduated sanctions, as Jeremy Travis recommends.[38] The state might decide to institute risk-based discretionary release, designed to identify those prisoners most likely to succeed under community supervision based upon a scientific assessment of risk, as Texas did in 2001. This approach is recommended by both Joan Petersilia[39] and James Austin.[40] Perhaps California might decide to become the first state to adopt a commission modeled on state sentencing commissions, to draft guidelines and even legislation that specifically recommends under what circumstances and when technical parole violators should be sent back to jail or prison, and for exactly how long. As Travis asks about this particular proposal, "Why shouldn't we apply the lessons from our experiments with sentencing guidelines and structured sentencing to develop and codify, after public debate, simple revocation guidelines that specify the range of sanctions that are proportionate to the underlying offense?"[41]

There are other, more radical approaches to California's "parole problem" that, while having some merit, likely won't work, at least in the short run, in this particular state. For instance, Horn's proposal to eliminate postprison release supervision and replace it with a voucher system for services used voluntarily by those released from prison is intriguing and has been discussed more fully in Chapter 5.[42] If this were to happen in California, the budget savings would be enormous and include the several hundred million dollars that funds the parole system, as well as several hundred million dollars from the elimination of the flow of technical violators back into prison (since there would be no parole supervision, technical violations would cease to exist). The savings would be partially offset by the cost of providing the services to be redeemed by the vouchers, and it could be argued that new crimes would be reduced as well, since there would be a variety of new services available to parolees. In this system, the responsibility for rehabilitation is put squarely on the ex-prisoner. Aside from whatever substantive arguments there are about the merits of this proposal, it would require layoffs of over 3,000 parole employees—not a particularly likely scenario in California, where most of them are members of the state's most politically powerful union. There may be other states where this proposal is far more realistic.

Clearly, though, there are a host of policy and legislative actions that can and should be taken, in addition to the two relatively simple ones suggested here. The advantage of beginning reform with simply cutting down the length of stay of nonviolent technical violators and then using a portion of the savings to fund targeted programming designed to cut recidivism and produce more savings and increased public safety is that these things can happen fairly quickly and don't involve, at the outset, the more difficult political project of altering or eliminating particular criminal sentences. The politics of this kind of reform may have the greatest likelihood of succeeding in a state like California, which has so many structural impediments to reform. In this case, the CCPOA, while seeing some loss through attrition of its corrections officers, will simultaneously see a strengthened community corrections program. Additionally, Governor Schwarzenegger seems willing confront the CCPOA politically. The public will see a continuation of the kind of policy it overwhelmingly approved in the form of Proposition 36—one that continues to provide treatment and programming for a nonviolent population. The politics of starting with marginal

reductions in prison time for nonviolent parolees in exchange for significant budget savings during a fiscal crisis, as well as the opportunity
to increase public safety by cutting recidivism (and getting even more
savings), could attract enough support to get this change underway. In
this scenario alone, the total savings to the state from lowering lengths
of stay for a group of technical violators and from slightly decreasing
rates of parolees who return to prison is about $360 million annually. In
this case, I have suggested a total reinvestment of $120 million back into
community-based programming to fund alternatives to prison for technical violators and for targeted efforts at reducing overall parolee recidivism. This reinvestment into community programs will be difficult
in a fiscal crisis, but the argument must be made that it is essential to
achieving far greater savings, both fiscally and in terms of public safety.
This leaves $240 million annually for California to fund other pressing
needs, such as in health and education, or to protect these areas from
further erosion due to declining state revenues. Even in California, this
is real money.

The amount of savings and reinvestment can continue to grow, as
can increased public safety resulting from lowered recidivism rates, as
this reform program is built upon by some of the other ideas suggested
above. The cumulative effect of implementing some of these reforms
would be that the California prison population, which the CDOC is projecting will remain relatively stable at around 157,000[43] until 2009 (this
projection was prior to an unanticipated rise of 5,000 in the prison population in the spring of 2004), can start to begin a long-term decline
without having any negative impact (and indeed, likely with a positive
impact) on public safety.

To this end, Governor Schwarzenegger proposed in his 2005 budget
to reduce the California Department of Corrections budget by a total of
$477 million. Most of this reduction, or $300 million, is based primarily
on one-time concessions from the CCPOA's new contract that requires
negotiation between the governor and the union. About $85 million is
projected savings from reductions in parolee recidivism as a result of
better prerelease planning and alternatives to prison for technical parole violators.[44]

These cuts to the California prison system by a Republican governor are a tremendously important and symbolic act. Given the state's
huge fiscal problems, that it is difficult to paint Schwarzenegger as a

"soft on crime" liberal, and that he ran without support from the California prison union, he is in a unique position to lead the first serious reform effort of the largest state prison system in the nation. Thus far, he is willing to push that reform.

Two other factors have contributed to enhancing the political environment in California in favor of prison reform. The first is a highly publicized series of stories about abuses in the prison system fostered by an officer "code of silence" and by huge budget overruns in the Department of Corrections.[45] The second is the appearance of a ballot initiative that would amend the current three strikes law by requiring increased sentences only for violent (rather than for any) third offense. This ballot initiative also requires specific violent or serious offenses for the second "strike." This would be a major revision to the toughest three strikes law in the country. As of June 2004, the California public opinion polls showed overwhelming support for this change by a margin of 76% for and 14% against the change. Interestingly, support for this measure was approximately the same among both Republicans and Democrats.[46]

Even in California, then, with perhaps more structural impediments to reform than any other state, the governor and legislators under tremendous pressure to cut budgets have taken it upon themselves impose reform on a correctional system that had been hugely resistant. The combination of a catastrophic budget, a series of public hearings on parole reform conducted by the state's Little Hoover Commission during the legislative session, intense media coverage and legislative hearings on prison abuses that came to light in the beginning of 2004, a fair amount of community and editorial advocacy for reforming corrections, and the arrival of a new governor willing to make changes to the state's prison system contributed to this shift.

Now that this change has occurred, it may well be possible for California to continue and build on what could be the first step toward long-term correctional reform.

Connecticut

Prison Growth and Its Causes

On the opposite coast, and with a significantly smaller and less complex prison system than California's, Connecticut is nonetheless struggling with huge increases in its prison population. Unlike California and most other states, Connecticut has no county jail system. This means the prison system also houses pretrial detainees and those who serve short-term misdemeanor sentences. Connecticut's overall prison and jail population as of the middle of 2003 was 19,263,[47] relatively small compared to those of many of the country's larger states. However, from 1995 to 2002, the Connecticut prison population (sentenced prisoners) has increased by 35.2%, a faster rate of growth than the 23.6% for all states and five times the 6.9% rate of growth for all states in the Northeast during the same period.[48] More recently, the state's prison population grew by 7.9% in a single year, from 2001 to 2002, while the rest of the country's state prison systems grew by only 2.4% and the rest of the Northeast increased by 1.9%.[49] Only two states grew at a faster rate than Connecticut during this time period.[50]

One of the primary explanations for the increase in Connecticut's prison population is that the average length of sentences for violent offenders increased dramatically from 1993 to 1997. In 1993, persons convicted of violent crimes were serving, on average, 38 months in prison, compared to 43 months nationally. Four years later, those convicted of violent crimes were serving 53 months, an increase of almost 40% and a significantly larger rate of increase than the 14% national growth in prison time for the same kind of prisoners. In fact, by 1997, Connecticut's violent offenders, who were serving five months less time than the national average in 1993, were serving four months longer than the national average.[51] One of the driving forces behind these increased lengths of stays is that in 1995 Connecticut's legislature ended all "good time" credit for prisoners.[52] This quickly drove up the prison population, as thousands of prisoners began to stay beyond the point they would have been released prior to the legislation.

Another reason the prison population has increased is that in 2002 5,600 prison admissions, or almost 18% of all prison admissions, were technical violators of probation, parole, or a community supervision program run by the State Correction Department. Probation violators alone made up almost 4,000 of these admissions. At any one time, a minimum of 2,250 prisoners, or about 17% of the total prison population, are incarcerated for technical violations of their community supervision.[53]

Unlike California, where technical parole violators are helping drive the size and growth of the prison system, Connecticut's probation violators are one of the main causes of its prison growth. Connecticut has only 2,255 people on parole, while there are almost 51,000 on probation.[54] With so many people under probation supervision and caseloads approaching 200 per officer, it is not surprising to find large numbers of technical probation violators being sent back to state prison. As in the California parole system, there are scant resources available in Connecticut to prevent or deter violations or to find alternatives to prison for those who begin to break the conditions of probation.

Although probation and parole are very different functions, they have remarkably similar conditions. Both require regular reporting, no drug use, and strict attendance at all mandated programs. Some conditions are unique to probation, such as paying restitution to crime victims, but generally the same behaviors are expected for probationers and parolees.

Like many states, Connecticut incarcerates a high percentage of people who have been convicted of nonviolent crimes. Only 30% of the Connecticut prison population has been convicted of a violent crime. Drug offenders make up 23% of the population, property offenders constitute 12%, probation violators are 14%, and the remaining 21% have been convicted of other nonviolent crimes.[55]

Finally, though Connecticut has a relatively low overall incarceration rate compared to the rest of the United States and the incarceration rate for whites is below the national average, the rate for Blacks is far above the national rate, making the discrepancy between the white and Black incarceration rates among the highest in the nation. The state's incarceration rate for Hispanics is double the national average.[56]

Political Issues

The governor of Connecticut from 1995 to 2004 was a moderate Republican, John Rowland, who was generally considered conservative on fiscal and criminal justice issues and more liberal on social issues. He resigned as governor on June 21, 2004, in the face of a growing scandal and legislative impeachment hearings concerning a host of financial improprieties. The remainder of his term will be served by the lieutenant governor, M. Jodi Rell, who is also a Republican. She has said she will shake up Rowland's cabinet, which, along with her as yet unknown priorities and relationship with the legislature, will certainly greatly complicate Connecticut's politics and policy making in the short run.

The Connecticut state legislature—both the House and the Senate —is currently controlled by Democrats, though their majority is not solid enough to override vetoes. Both the governor and the legislature have in the last decade passed tough-on-crime legislation, such as "truth in sentencing" that lengthened sentences and elimination of prison "good time."

Connecticut has sent about 500 of its prisoners out of state to Virginia due to its prison capacity constraints. This has created a backlash among some community activists and families of prisoners, angry about the movement of prisoners out of state, and the corrections officers' union, worried about job losses. Because of overcrowding in Virginia prisons in 2004, that state informed Connecticut that it must take those 500 prisoners back, putting even more pressure on Connecticut's already crowded prison system.

Unlike California, there have long been visible and active legislative "champions" of prison reform in both the House and Senate. Representative Mike Lawlor, Co-Chair of the Judiciary Committee, a Democrat from East Haven, has been a longtime supporter of trying to control prison growth through alternatives to incarceration. In addition, Representative William Dyson, a Democrat from New Haven and the powerful Co-Chair of the Appropriations Committee, has made one of his top priorities controlling and shrinking the prison population and reinvesting some prison savings in community-based programs. Representative Robert Farr, a Republican from West Hartford has joined Lawlor and Dyson as someone who believes that prison spending can be reduced while protecting public safety. Having powerful legislators from both parties who have a public commitment to prison reform is a tremendous advantage in the attainment of structural prison reform. In addition, former Governor Rowland had signaled that he would be supportive of some legislative and policy changes that would begin to slow the growth of Connecticut's prisons.[57]

Clearly, the state politics are currently far more conducive to serious prison reform in Connecticut than in a number of other states. There are powerful state legislators who publicly support reform, a (former) Republican governor who was receptive to some legislative and policy changes, and community activists and a corrections union that might also welcome some changes if it meant that a lowered prison population could result in prisoners no longer being shipped out of state. Like California, the state's budget problems are creating an environment where some tough and unpopular decisions must also be made.

The State of the Budget

In fiscal year 2003, Connecticut had a $500 million deficit to contend with, which was projected to grow to $1 billion in fiscal 2004. With a total state budget of about $13.4 billion, the potential 2004 deficit represented 7.5% all state spending—a significant shortfall, especially given the half-billion-dollar deficit that preceded it the year before.[58]

Despite the fact that Connecticut is one of the wealthiest states in the country, with one of the highest concentrations of millionaires anywhere, and that the state boasts two huge casinos that provide a constant source of state revenue, the state has clearly not escaped the economic ravages of the national recession. As in many other states, the combined impact of a national recession, the fallout from the September 11 attacks, and a tax-cutting fervor in the early to mid-1990s combined to wreak havoc on Connecticut's revenue collections. From 1992 to 2000, while the national economy was growing, Connecticut reduced taxes by over $2.5 billion, a huge amount given the overall size of the state's budget.[59] Finally, Medicaid expenses grew by 14% in the two fiscal years of 2002 and 2003, resulting in expenditures of $94 million over budget in 2002 alone.[60]

As a result of all these factors, the state has had to struggle with two straight years of massive budget deficits. In 2003, Connecticut raised taxes and a host of fees, laid off thousands of state workers, encouraged early retirements, reduced local aid to counties and cities, and enacted across-the-board service reductions to state agencies.[61] The state also depleted its rainy-day fund, made deep cuts to social services and mental health programs, and even issued short-term debt to raise additional revenue.[62]

Even with a combination of raising revenue and all these expenditure reductions, the state ended fiscal year 2003 with a deficit of almost $100 million, larger than every other state in the country except Wisconsin. In fiscal 2004, the state managed to balance its budget by raising taxes and fees. However, because of the political pain wrought by these new taxes, the legislature and the governor were initially at a standoff and actually began the fiscal year without a budget. To balance its fiscal 2005 budget, the state is planning additional tax increases on tobacco products and alcohol.[63]

A Proposed Plan of Prison Reform

The advantages of having even a few legislators committed to prison reform, especially if they happen to be chairs of key committees, can be seen in the case of Connecticut.

In 2003, the Council of State Governments (CSG) received grants from the Open Society Institute (OSI) and the JEHT Foundation to identify and work with a couple of states that might be ready to undertake a serious effort at corrections reform. CSG would offer the states free technical assistance in the form of analyzing the specific reasons and driving forces behind the state's prison growth and providing the state with a menu of legislative and policy options that could drive down the prison population. This analysis would also provide the state with detailed cost-benefit analyses of the realistic prison savings resulting from these various initiatives and what costs, if any, would result from specific policy interventions to divert nonviolent offenders from prison. The state would be provided with geo-coded maps that would show specifically what neighborhoods were "feeding" the prisons, as well as where in those neighborhoods ex-prisoners, probationers, and parolees lived. The maps would also show how much the state spent in prison, probation, and parole costs on people who lived in those neighborhoods. In fact, these maps, presented at a large public joint hearing of the Appropriations and Judiciary Committee in May 2003, were instrumental in getting legislators to see just how many prisoners, parolees, and probationers were concentrated in just a few of the towns in Connecticut and neighborhoods in Hartford and New Haven. They also showed how much money was being spent to incarcerate those residents. This particularly powerful visual aid at the least reinforced the resolve of many of the legislators in pushing for prison reform.

In return for being selected as one of the CSG's "national demonstration sites," the state would have to agree to reinvest a portion any prison savings in community-based programs that could serve the specific population that was now being sent to prison or probation, as well as in the neighborhoods from which they came.

The head of CSG's Criminal Justice Programs, Michael Thompson, selected Connecticut as one of the states where reform had a good chance of success due to the interest of several key legislators coupled with the state's massive budget problems. Representatives Dyson and Lawlor welcomed CSG's assistance, and Dyson, who as Co-Chair of the legislature's Appropriations Committee had tremendous political power in shaping the state's budget, was very interested in re-investing some of the potential prison savings in community-based programming.

The analysis of the causes of the state's prison growth, policy and legislative recommendations, and cost-benefit analyses were provided by James Austin and this author.[64] The mapping was provided by Eric Cadora of OSI, a foundation created by financier George Soros that funds a number of corrections and sentencing-related initiatives around the country.

The analysis determined the state's prison growth was due, as the prior section indicated, to huge numbers of technical probation violations and increased lengths of stay mainly as a result of the elimination of good time. The analysis also found that technical probation and parole violators spent, on average, over one year in prison as a result of their violations. This is a long time to spend in prison for a technical violation (usually drug-related) of the conditions of probation. Additionally, Austin found that prisoners who were eligible for parole stayed, on average, nine months beyond their parole eligibility date before they were released. Austin found that there were thousands of nonviolent prisoners serving short sentences who were eligible for release but not being released through the Department of Corrections (DOC) Transition Supervision or Community Release Programs. (These programs are community-based programs to transition low-level offenders back into the community through early supervised release.) Those who were being released to these transitional DOC programs were also being returned back to prison for technical violations at the same high rates as probation. Based on these findings, Austin and Jacobson submitted a report to Representative Dyson[65] that made the following recommendations:

Require all prisoners with sentences greater than two years to serve no more than 85 percent of their sentence unless they are special management problems. This would address the lack of any good time provisions for prisoners in Connecticut and bring the state in line with much of the rest of the country. This change alone would save 843 prison beds.

Reduce, on average, the amount of time paroled prisoners are incarcerated beyond their parole eligibility date from nine to five months (or a net savings of 4 months). This marginal change in release dates for parolees would save 459 prison beds.

Reduce the number of technical probation violation admissions by 25 percent. This particular change requires a host of policy changes by the state's probation department in terms of providing alternatives to prison for technical violators and creating a uniform system of graduated sanctions on the "back end" of probation to address probation violators. This also requires some additional funding for probation. This change would save the state 488 prison beds.

Reduce, on average, the length of stay for the remaining technical probation violators by three months. This change requires that the Legislature and the Governor work with the state's prosecutors and judges to persuade them that these average lengths of stays for probation violators are far longer than necessary and a three month reduction would still leave an average stay of nine months—still a very long time—with no impact on public safety. This change would save 341 prison beds.

Release 25 percent of the prisoners with sentences under two years who are not being released via Transitional Supervision or Community Release who are now serving 6–7 months. This change would release more eligible non-violent prisoners to these DOC community based transition programs. This change would save 279 beds.

Reduce the 1,700 persons being returned to the DOC from Transitional Supervision, Community Release, and from parole as technical violators and to reduce their current lengths of stay. Divert 25% of each type of violator from prison. This would reduce the number of those on parole and DOC community based programs from being sent back to prison as technical violators and would also marginally reduce their length of stay. Like the probation recommendation, this would require an initial investment to create "back-end" sanctions other than prison for these technical violators. This change would save 268 beds.[66]

All told, these recommendations would save 2,678 prison beds, or promote a roughly 14% reduction in the size of the entire prison system. Using very conservative cost calculations, the state could save almost $50 million annually with all these changes.[67] The report also recommends that several million dollars of this savings be reinvested in community programs both to create the alternatives to prison required for technical violators and to help strengthen the communities from which most of these offenders are sent to prison.

By the end of July 2003, the governor and the legislature finally reached a budget agreement. Contained in the budget was $7.5 million set aside for the next two years to reinvest in number of community-based programs that would be designed to stem recidivism.[68] Interestingly, the legislature did not implement any of the reductions to the DOC budget that were recommended by Austin and Jacobson. Half of the strategy was accomplished (funding for community-based programs) and half was not (the reductions to DOC designed to reduce population and generate savings).

However, in the next 2004 legislative session, the other half of the prison reform effort was passed by both houses of the legislature and signed into law by the governor two weeks before he resigned. The bill (HB 5211) sets forward an aggressive reentry strategy for the Department of Corrections, including creating a 500-bed Community Justice Center in Hartford that will serve as transitional housing for released prisoners. It adopts many of the recommendations put forward by Austin and Jacobson, including requiring earlier parole hearings for prisoners who have served either 75% or 85% of their sentences depending on the conviction charge. It also requires the DOC to submit to the legislature a plan to reduce by at least 20% all probation and parole violators returning to prison.

Thus, in the midst of a severe budget crisis, Connecticut was able over two legislative sessions to enact the most significant justice reinvestment legislation in the country. That is, through the creation of new legislation, Connecticut law makers and the governor reduced correction expenses by making greater use of parole and speeding up the parole process, reducing technical probation and parole violations, and creating a large transitional or halfway-house center in Hartford that is designed to smooth reentry and reduce recidivism. The legislation then reinvests $7.5 million into community corrections and community development projects that are designed to further reduce recidivism. One additional benefit of this strategy is that, as the prison population declines, Connecticut will no longer have to send a portion of its prisoners out of state, an issue that was very important to many of the prisoners' families, to community activists, and to the correction union.

This legislative effort at reducing prison populations and reinvesting funds into community-based corrections and community development projects, even with its relatively small scale, can serve as a model for the rest of the country. For this effort ultimately to be successful, however, a number of tough bureaucratic, management, and political hurdles remain.

A number of policy changes must occur that will require organizational and management attention and commitment. The probation department must immediately begin to adopt technical violation guidelines and create a graduated set of sanctions for those who begin to break the rules. This will require intensive staff training as well as a clear commitment from the top of the organization to make these changes. It will also require a great deal of development work in creating new or expanding different programs to keep probationers from violating their conditions, and to respond to them if they do. The probation department and the state court system (of which probation is a part in Connecticut) must be held accountable for implementing these changes aggressively and ensuring that the result of the infusion of new funds, along with these organizational changes, is not simply "net-widening." That is, the state must make certain that the new funds and efforts result in fewer probation technical violations and that fewer of those who violate wind up in prison. The governor's office as well as the state legislature must keep constant pressure on the agency to hold it accountable for implementing the reforms and adhering to specific outcome measures.

In addition, the governor must make clear to his parole board that once either 75% or 85% of sentences are served, depending on the conviction charge, the assumption is that parole should be granted absent any evidence of threat to public safety. This same pressure needs to be applied by the governor and legislature to DOC to release eligible short-term and nonviolent prisoners to its community supervision programs, and also to create systems to respond to their violations in ways other than returning them to prison. The DOC must restructure its operations and organizational incentives in much the same way as probation, and a part of that effort should be to begin serious prerelease planning months before someone leaves state prison. Both efforts can be enhanced through the use of risk-based instruments in identifying the lowest risk candidates for community supervision. Connecticut should quickly begin to make use of these kinds of tools. In terms of reducing lengths of stay for probation violators, the governor must use all her powers of persuasion to convince state prosecutors and judges to agree to marginally reduce their stays in prison.

Careful thought and consideration must also be given to those community-based programs that will be the beneficiaries of increased funding. There will obviously be competition for these dollars among underfunded community organizations, but the funding must be used parsimoniously to create or expand programs that are geared to assisting either this criminal justice population or the neighborhoods in which they live. This can take the form of organizations that provide temporary housing or job training and placement as well as efforts to provide economic development, lending, and job creation to entire communities.[69] The overall goal of any new infusion of resources into community-based programs must be that the short- and long-term results are fewer people returning to prison for technical violations or new crimes, and ultimately, less crime and fewer people going to prison at all. Getting the funding to do this is an important and essential step, but the more difficult task in many ways is determining the specific needs of this population and their communities and making an assessment of existing capacity to address those needs and to build and create programs that serve those needs.

As a general rule, both probation and parole, in addition to everything else they have to do in this effort, must begin to shift the focus of their supervision resources up front. Since we know that most violations occur early on in supervision, it makes no sense to spread supervision resources equally over an extended period of time. Early on, these agencies should target their existing resources (and a good number of additional resources) to address the serious issues that these ex-prisoners and probationers face, such as lack of housing, joblessness and drug addiction. An intensive support effort initially—one that emphasizes service and support, as opposed to pure monitoring and violation—will doubtless reduce the number of violations (technical violations as well as new crimes) over the long term. It is in the interest of public safety to make this intensive effort early on: to provide structure, stability, and treatment and then to step down the level of supervision and monitoring, rather than to continue a constant level of supervision with minimal program resources for years.

It should be clear by now that a tremendous amount of commitment and effort is required for this kind of program to be successful. It is not simply a matter of passing legislation and moving on to the next big issue. It is not as "easy" as simply changing sentence lengths or eliminating minimum mandatory sentencing. Once those sentencing changes are made, no organizational effort at all is required to reduce prison population. Of course, actually getting legislatures to make those sentencing changes is far from easy. Even if states begin seriously to roll back many of the harsh sentences passed over the last decade and a half (which they should), these changes to community supervision practices, along with strengthening communities that feed prison systems, must be done. Given the numbers of people returning to prison from community supervision, this kind of effort must be made even if states do tackle the issue of sentencing reform.

Ultimately, these kinds of program changes, which can result in both reduced prison populations and increased public safety in the form of lowered recidivism rates, can provide a huge political impetus for achieving systematic sentencing reform.

Louisiana

Prison Growth and Its Causes

Larger than Connecticut but significantly smaller than California, Louisiana has a large prison population and an incarceration rate that surpasses any other state in the country. With a state prison incarceration rate of 794 per 100,000 residents, Louisiana's per capita incarceration is almost twice the U.S. average of 427 per 100,000 for all state prison systems.[70] Its prison population of 35,736 (as of 2002) makes Louisiana's prison system the ninth largest in the country. Though its prison population remained relatively stable between 2001 and 2002, since 1995, Louisiana has seen a growth of almost 42%, one of the fastest rates of growth in the United States and almost twice the national average of 23.6%.[71]

One of the distinguishing characteristics of the Louisiana prison system is that fully 45% of all its prisoners are housed in local jails, by far the highest percentage of locally held prison inmates in the country.[72] This system has existed for decades and has a number of implications for both correctional practice and the political power of locally elected sheriffs who house these prisoners and receive significant funding in the form of state reimbursement. Prisoners held in local facilities for years spend their period of incarceration housed primarily with short-term detainees who are the main population of local jails and receive little, if any, correctional programming in facilities designed for rapid turnover. There is little question that keeping long-term felony-sentenced state prisoners in bare-bones local facilities is exceptionally poor correctional practice. (The sole advantage it might have is that the prisoner might be held closer to his community if the jail is in his county of residence.) The political power that comes along with sheriffs having this responsibility is discussed further in the next section.

One of the reasons for the large numbers and recent growth in Louisiana's prison population is that the state system has an exceedingly high number of parole violators, who constituted 61% of all prison admissions in 2001. Only California has a higher percentage of parole violators being admitted to state prison. Moreover, in just over a decade, from 1990 to 2001, Louisiana saw its percentage of parole and probation violators admitted to prison grow from just 15% to 61%, the second highest rate of growth in the country.[73]

The success rate (defined only as completing the term of parole without any violations for new crimes or technical violations) for parolees alone in Louisiana has diminished substantially in the last decade. In 1990, almost 62% of parolees were successfully discharged from parole, a figure that declined to 47% by 1999.[74] The national state average for successful discharge on parole, not including California (its numbers are so enormous it disguises what the rest of the country is doing), is 53%.[75] As more parolees find their way back to prison in Louisiana, the number of prison admissions has also increased substantially. In 1994, there were 12,094 total admissions to Louisiana prisons. By 2002, admissions had increased to 15,454, an increase of 28%.[76]

Unlike both California and Connecticut, the Louisiana Department of Corrections (LDOC) contains both the parole and probation functions, in addition to its central mission of running prisons. Thus, one agency controls the largest alternative to prison (probation), the prisons themselves, and all postprison supervision (parole). Also unlike most states, Louisiana probation officers handle both parole and probation cases; that is, they have a mixed caseload. It is not surprising, then, that in addition to large numbers of parole violators returning to prison, the same is true for probation cases. If all parole and probation violators who return to prison are combined, then at least 63% of all Louisiana's prison admissions in 2001 were either parole or probation violators.[77]

Louisiana classifies those revoked from community supervision (both parole and probation) and sent back to prison into three categories: violators convicted of a new crime, technical violators, and "waiver" cases comprising those facing a new criminal charge but who choose to waive their parole violation hearings and return to prison without a new conviction. In 2001, of the 10,103 violation admissions to prison, 1,338 were there for a new crime, 4,773 were technical violators, and 3,992 were waiver cases. Thus, almost half of all violation admissions in Louisiana are "pure" technical violators, and the number of technical-violation prison admissions increased by over 50% over seven years, from 3,164 in 1994 to 4,773 in 2001.[78] The number of waiver cases also increased dramatically, from 1,308 in 1994 to 3,992 in 2001—an increase of over 200%. Only violations for new convictions stayed relatively stable during this period, going from 1,483 in 1994 to 1,338 in 2001.[79]

Unlike California, where the average length of stay for technical violators is several months, prison stays in Louisiana are exceptionally long. Those technical violators returning to Louisiana prisons spend, on average, 19 months in prison, and those returning on waiver cases spend a bit less (somewhat surprising, since they are facing new criminal charges as opposed to technical violations)—16 months in prison.[80] This means that in 2001, technical violators took up 5,838 beds, or 16% of all prison beds, and waiver cases required 4,626 prison beds, or 13%. Thus, these two categories of violators use almost 30% of Louisiana's prison system.[81]

Clearly, then, the rising numbers of prison admissions who are technical and waiver violators, coupled with their exceptionally long lengths of stay are what has been driving the recent increases in Louisiana's prison system.

It is also striking how few prisoners who have been convicted of nonviolent crimes are released on parole. For example, only 12.3% of those convicted of drug possession, 8.6% of those convicted of theft, and 9.9% of those convicted of simple burglary were released by the state's parole board.[82] These are very low release rates for nonviolent crimes, and this policy further contributes to the size and growth of the state's prison system.

Political Issues

Louisiana has a long and storied political history. Ever since Huey Long, perhaps the state's best-known governor, was assassinated in 1935 in the rotunda of the state capitol in Baton Rouge, the state has had a number of "colorful" political figures, many of whom have found their way into prison. Most recently, former Governor Edwin Edwards, a Democrat who served three terms (1972–1980, 1984–1988, and 1992–

1996), was sentenced in 2001 to 10 years in federal prison for 17 counts of fraud and racketeering.

The state that gave rise to David Duke, the nationally known Klansman and presidential candidate, is also one of the poorest in the country, with almost 18% of its population living below the poverty line. (Only New Mexico has a higher proportion of its population living in poverty.)[83] African-Americans constitute almost one-third of the state's population.[84]

From the last half of the 1990s up until 2004, Louisiana has had a Republican governor and a solidly Democratic legislature. The legislature is controlled by a strong majority of Democrats (by about a two-to-one ratio) in both the State Assembly and the Senate.[85]

On November 16, 2004, Kathleen Blanco, a Democrat from Lafayette and the lieutenant governor under Mike Foster (who was prohibited from running again due to term limits) became the new governor of Louisiana. In a close race, she defeated her conservative Republican opponent, Bobby Jindal, by 52% to 48%.

Though having the highest incarceration rate in the United States, and thus considered one of the toughest of the tough-on-crime states, Louisiana nevertheless was one of the first states in the country to pass legislation to eliminate a number of mandatory minimum sentences created during the 1990s. In 2001, Louisiana adopted new legislation (Senate Bill 239 and House Bill 665) that eliminated mandatory minimum sentences for 19 nonviolent crimes, amended the penalties for multiple felony convictions, lowered the minimum and maximum sentences for a number of drug violations, allowed the courts to suspend the sentences for certain drug violations, and lowered the sentences for third-time or more "driving while intoxicated" (DWI) convictions.[86] Though it has been estimated that the actual effect on the prison population from these measures will not be especially significant,[87] the political symbolism of these sentencing changes cannot be underestimated. For a state considered by many to be the most conservative in the country in terms of punishment to be the first to repeal or revise even some of the harsh legislation passed in the prior decade and a half sent a powerful message, inside the state and out, that serious sentencing reform was possible and that Louisiana might well be ready to undertake even more measures to reduce its prison population.

The impetus for these reforms came from two different directions. On the one hand were African-American members of the legislature who had long been interested in changing many of the state's harsh sentencing laws; some, such as Senators Donald Cravins and Paulette Irons, are senior and influential members. On the other hand, the state's huge budget crisis forced other legislators who otherwise would never have been sympathetic to these kinds of changes to support them as a way to save money.

United in opposition to these changes were the state's locally elected sheriffs. These law enforcement officials are, not surprisingly, quite conservative on issues of law and order and punishment and wield a tremendous amount of political power in the state. They have their own political action committee, and their support is considered key in gubernatorial campaigns. In August 2003, the candidates running for governor all attended the Louisiana Sheriffs' Association and, in the words of the state's largest newspaper, "took no chances at the sheriffs' annual convention promising oodles of money that the state doesn't have."[88]

One of the great sources of the sheriffs' power is that they are responsible for housing just under half of all the state prisoners in Louisiana. Even with a relatively low reimbursement rate of $23 per day,[89] the Louisiana Department of Correction paid the state's sheriffs $154 million in 2003.[90] This money not only allows sheriffs to build and staff jails, but with the profit from the reimbursement, they can hire additional deputies to perform highly visible and politically popular law enforcement functions in their counties.

In 10 years, from 1993 to 2003, this payment to state sheriffs increased dramatically, from $40 million to $154 million—an almost fourfold increase.[91] Obviously, the state's sheriffs have seen their funding multiply geometrically from this policy, and the revenue stream has become, in both political and substantive terms, essential. Not surprising, any attempt to reduce this revenue by lowering the state's prison population would be met with coordinated and aggressive resistance.

The political landscape, then, is mixed in terms of achieving prison reform. There are active legislative proponents of change who have already been successful in passing sentencing reform in 2001. However, the state is very conservative on criminal justice issues, and the sheriffs are guaranteed to oppose any effort to significantly lower the prison population if it will affect their revenue stream. Like California, Louisiana also had a change of governors in 2004: Kathleen Blanco took office in January. As of this writing, it is too soon to tell how Governor Blanco will approach the issue of correction reform.

The State of the Budget

Louisiana has not experienced the same kind of budget turmoil as either California or Connecticut, despite being a much poorer state. Louisiana has not had to raise taxes or fees and has thus far avoided the kinds of massive layoffs, furloughs, and early retirements that California and Connecticut had to undertake. Louisiana's Medicaid expenditures were not over budget in 2003, and its revenue targets were generally on target. As opposed to both California and Connecticut, it ended the 2003 fiscal year with a small surplus.[92]

The state still faces a tight budget over the next two years. It used some "one-time" revenue to balance the 2003 budget; and these funds did not materialize again in 2004.[93] Though 2004 was a tight year for the Louisiana budget, the state did not have to resort to large service reductions or layoffs to balance the budget. In order to balance the budget for fiscal year 2005, the governor is proposing to raise an additional $160 million in sales tax by permanently eliminating sales tax exemptions for certain businesses.[94] Though the state continues to face a very constrained budget, the pressure to cut services to balance the budget is not as intense as in either California or Connecticut. Nevertheless, as the state with the second-highest percentage of its population living in poverty in the nation, Louisiana continues to have enormous needs in the areas of education, health care, and housing.

A Plan for Prison Reform

Louisiana was the other state that was selected as a demonstration site for the Council of State Governments (CSG) to receive a variety of technical and analytical assistance. As in Connecticut, CSG offered to provide assistance if the goal of the effort was to achieve prison savings by lowering prison population and then reinvesting a portion of savings into communities. James Austin and this author provided technical assistance by analyzing the reasons for prison population growth and making recommendations for policies to reduce that trend. Also, like Connecticut but in contrast to California, Louisiana had legislators willing to publicly push the issue of prison reform. Senator Don Cravins, the Chairman of the Louisiana Senate's Judiciary and a member of the Joint Legislative Committee on the Budget, took the lead on prison reform in the legislature; he and his colleague, Senator Paulette Irons, became the primary legislative "champions" of this issue. Senate President John J. Hainkel was also involved in the early stages of discussing strategy for lowering prison population and using some of the savings for community-based reinvestment. However, his direct involvement ended early into the effort—perhaps foreshadowing, as I explain below, the final result. Senator Cravins's positions on the Judiciary and Budget Committees, as well as his prior role in pushing Louisiana's sentencing reform, made him a natural choice for taking the legislative lead on this difficult issue.

Given the factors that have been driving Louisiana's prison population, a number of recommendations were made that could substantially reduce it. First and most obvious, Louisiana could immediately lower its prison population by again placing a cap on the amount of time a technical parole or probation violator could spend in prison. Instead of the average 18 months in prison, if technical violators spent no more than 12 months in prison (still more than twice the length of stay for California technical violators), 1,400 prison beds would be saved in the first year and increase to 2,000 three years later.

Second, like Connecticut, the state should lower the numbers of technical violators who return to prison by creating other, community-based sanctions. If the state diverted 25% of its almost 4,800 purely technical violators from prison, simply going back to the number of technical violators who were returned to prison in Louisiana in 1996, 1,200 prison beds could be saved annually. While achieving this number of saved beds might take three years (since some investment of resources and effort would be needed to create alternatives to prison), the state could still, conservatively, save 400 beds in just the first year.

Third, if Louisiana increased the parole release rates for nonviolent and low-risk prisoners, savings in prison beds would once more be substantial. For example, if approximately 10% more of the almost 8,000 prisoners convicted of nonviolent crimes were released only several months earlier by the state's parole board, about 200 beds would be saved in the first year and about 525 by the third year of this practice.

Why should parole boards consider releasing nonviolent, low-risk prisoners a few months earlier than they now do? The primary reason is that standardized risk instruments now exist and are in use that are designed to identify those prisoners who pose the lowest public safety risk. Parole boards should take advantage of this technology to better target the lowest-risk prisoners who are eligible for parole. These risk instruments are not perfect and cannot always predict recidivism correctly, but they are an important supplemental tool in release decision making.[95]

Were all three of these relatively straightforward initiatives to be tried, total beds saved in the first year would be approximately 2,000; three years later, this figure would rise to approximately 3,725. Using a conservative cost estimate of $27 dollars per day per prisoner (this combines daily reimbursement costs for sheriffs and marginal DOC costs for operating a prison bed), the state could save $19.7 million in the first year; this figure rises to $36.7 million in the third year. Even with Louisiana reinvesting as much as a quarter of its savings in creating alternative sanctions for technical violators and community-based programs, the amount of savings for this state would be substantial. Since the state's prison population is projected to stay relatively stable (absent any of these new initiatives),[96] this population overall could decline by as much as 10%.

But here is where Louisiana is different from both California (where reforms have just begun) and Connecticut (which has completed some significant reform). In Louisiana, even though the legislature and governor initially agreed to a series of reforms and reinvestment to lower the prison population, these measures did not pass during the state's 2003 legislative session. Several reasons can be identified for this failure. For one, during this legislative session, the state did pass groundbreaking legislation that completely reformed its juvenile justice system. That legislation (HB 2018) required that, within 18 months, the state discontinue the use of the infamous Tallulah Prison (where, allegedly, juvenile inmates suffered physical abuse and brutality) as a juvenile facility. The legislature also created a new cabinet-level agency, the Department of Juvenile Justice, that would alone take responsibility for handling all the state's issues regarding juvenile justice.[97] In and of themselves, these were gigantic changes; perhaps, then, it would have simply been too much for the legislature to deal with juvenile justice and adult prison reform in the same session. On a more hopeful note, Senator Cravins agreed to push prison reform once again in the next legislative session.[98]

Unfortunately, none of the proposed prison reform legislation was passed during the 2004 session as well. The proposed reform itself was designed very similarly to Connecticut's. Bills were proposed that made more use of parole, cut the number of parole and probation violators, and significantly reduced their lengths of stay. In addition, a significant percentage of the savings would have been set aside for investment in community-based programs.

One of the reasons for the inaction was that the bills' champions, Senators Donald Cravins and Paulette Irons, both lost their important leadership positions as a result of changes in the leadership of the Senate. Senator Cravins had been the Chair of the powerful Judiciary Committee and Senator Irons had been the Vice Chair of the influential Finance Committee. As a result, neither senator was any longer in a position to forcefully guide these bills through the legislature. Additionally, a couple of weeks before the end of the legislative session, an off-duty police officer was killed by someone who had been in prison. The killing naturally provoked outrage and an understandable outpouring of sympathy for the slain officer: the funeral procession stretched 14 miles. In this environment, reminiscent of the year before, when a series of Baton Rouge killings also created hesitations, it became difficult to push for legislation that might be interpreted as "soft on crime."

Nonetheless, reasons remain to be optimistic about prospects of reform in Louisiana. The state's correction commissioner, Richard Stalder, is committed to decreasing the number of returned parole and probation violators. The corrections department is about to open a technical violation center designed to divert hundreds of technical violators from prison. Finally, Governor Blanco seems personally committed to reducing Louisiana's incarceration rate. At the end of May 2004 she stated, "I have charged the Department with reducing the state's incarceration and recidivism rates by increasing educational and work programs for inmates that will better prepare them to become productive, law-abiding citizens upon their release."[99]

Thus, Louisiana is still poised to undertake serious reform. The state that began much of the nation's recent prison reform in 2001 by repealing many of its mandatory-minimum sentences has the substantive strategy and political dynamics to bring down its prison population—even after the two failed legislative attempts just described.

CONCLUSION

The three states discussed in this chapter are all very different and very much alike. Each state has seen its prison system increase dramatically over the last decade, and in the case of Connecticut, in just the last couple of years. Each state has a problem with technical parole or probation violators coming back in huge numbers and this being a main cause of prison growth. The states are all in different levels of fiscal distress, with California experiencing worst fiscal problems in the country, though Connecticut has suffered its own fiscal crisis and Louisiana has entered a period of fiscal constraint.

At the same time, these states are quite different in size, geography, and politics. While Connecticut and Louisiana have made strong legislative attempts to reform their corrections system (one successful and one not), such an effort may be in its infancy in California. Neither Connecticut nor Louisiana has anything equivalent to the power enjoyed by the California correction officers' union. Louisiana is one of the poorest states in the country with the country's highest incarceration rate, while Connecticut is one of the richest states with a low incarceration rate. Obviously, too, the political landscape is very different in each of these states (as in all the states).

The point most in need of emphasis here is that, despite these differences, significant reform is possible in all these states (though California may be the most challenging state). None of these states was making any serious effort at prison reform as recently as 2000, but political and fiscal circumstances have made reform in each a real possibility. Louisiana and Connecticut have tackled the issue head on, and even in California reform might be starting to take hold.

While a sample of three states is hardly enough to generalize to the all states in the country, most states contain at least a few of the features highlighted in the contexts of California, Connecticut, and Louisiana. The most common features are growing prison systems with attendant fiscal and social costs; severely constrained budgets; tremendous needs in education and health care systems; and a growing willingness to look more closely at corrections budgets. The majority of states have large numbers of probation and parole violators returning to their systems who could be handled without prison or who could, with targeted efforts, be supervised far more effectively in the community. This would lead full circle, resulting in lower violation rates to begin with.

Thus, almost every state can be analyzed in the way used in the three examples here. Specific reasons for population growth can be made clear; policies to address those issues can be developed (especially those that revolve around probation and parole); key legislators

can be identified (even in California); and the politics of beginning to reduce prison costs and benefiting other high-need areas can be made to
work in almost any state. And while every state contains structurally
based impediments to reform as well, strategies can be developed to
deal directly with many or all such problems.

Many states already have legislators willing to champion such reform efforts. This is especially true lately, since parole and probation reform can be made to work politically, and because potential correction
savings can be rechanneled to meet publicly agreed-upon needs. Given
the fiscal crunch that states face for the foreseeable future, as well as the
high priority that the public places on quality education and health
care, a "window" for prison reform efforts has opened all around the
country. These efforts can lead to more large-scale efforts at sentencing
reform, too. What happened in Connecticut and almost happened in
Louisiana can occur in states across the country, regardless of what political party controls the executive or legislative branch.

But this window won't stay open forever. States should take advantage of a historical moment when significant prison reform is not
only possible but, done carefully, can and should become politically
popular as well.

7

Downsizing Prisons

ON AUGUST 11, 2003, Supreme Court Justice Anthony M. Kennedy told the attorneys gathered for the American Bar Association's 2003 annual conference, "Our [prison] resources are misspent, our punishments too severe, our sentences too loaded." He then added, "I can accept neither the necessity nor the wisdom of federal mandatory minimum sentences. In all too many cases, mandatory minimum sentences are unjust."[1] Almost one year later, in a speech to the American Bar Association on sentencing discretion, he said, "Tough on crime should not be a substitute for thoughtful reflection or lead us into moral blindness."[2] The timing of these powerful and unambiguous critiques of the excessiveness of punishment and the scale of imprisonment, especially coming from a conservative Supreme Court Justice appointed by President Ronald Reagan, is not accidental.

In 2004, nearly 2.2 million people are incarcerated in United States prisons and jails.[3] At current incarceration rates, almost one-third of Black men born today are likely to spend some time in prison, more than seven times the 4.4% of white men likely to serve prison time.[4] States are struggling to provide basic services as they cut education, social service, and health programs and increase taxes and fees to cope with their most precarious financial situation in decades. Still, spending on corrections continues to grow, despite studies that show little relationship between increasing incarceration and crime reduction. Simultaneously, however, public opinion polls have shown a long-term trend toward prioritizing health care and education over crime; the public also appears to have grown more tolerant of using alternatives to prison for nonviolent, especially drug, offenders.[5]

In one respect, it seems surprising that a conservative Supreme Court Justice would be so openly critical of current U.S. punishment and incarceration policy. In another, it is not astonishing at all that greater numbers of senior-level officials across branches of government have started to perceive structural flaws inherent in our incarceration policies, as well as the direct impact those policies have on other essential areas of government.

In fact, on June 23, 2004, two Republican and two Democratic members of the House of Representatives introduced the Comprehensive Federal Reentry Legislation, otherwise known as the Second Chance Act of 2004 (HR 4676). The legislation not only proposes removing a variety of federal barriers to successful reentry (such as the denial of federal housing, financial aid, and welfare benefits) but also proposes more funds for job training, drug and mental health treatment, and transitional housing. The legislation proposes that continued funding be based on states' ability to reduce their recidivism rates. This is an extraordinary development not only because of the clear bipartisan sponsorship of the legislation but also because it has the potential to have the reverse effect of the 1994 Crime Bill that encouraged states to build prisons and increase criminal sentences. This can possibly have the opposite effect: it rewards states for reducing the number of people who return to prison. This proposed legislation would have been unimaginable even just a few years ago, and it is another sign that the political dynamics of correctional reform have changed. Whether or not the legislation passes, it is yet another hopeful sign that this country is ready for serious and structural changes in our corrections policies.

This is the time to start developing state-based strategies for penal reform. The next few years offer what is probably the best opportunity of the last 25 years for altering the way in which the United States has used incarceration. I have argued that, in many states, this can initially take the form of making large-scale changes in how parole and probation agencies operate; this can serve both to decrease the use of incarceration and create desperately needed community-based services for people returning home from prison. As prison length of stays for technical parole violators are reduced and alternatives to prison offered, additional targeted investments can be made that can further reduce recidivism in the dual forms of new crimes and technical violations. This strategy will also free up real savings to use for education and health care, providing states with much-needed budget relief.

Some states might want to begin their reform programs with substantial diversion programs centering on treatment provision in lieu of incarceration of low-level drug offenders; this was recently undertaken in Kansas and, as mandated by referenda, in California and Arizona as well. Like parole reform, these strategies are likely to require the active involvement of state legislatures and—even if requiring community-based treatment capacities to be built from scratch—will quickly result in huge budget savings. As shown in previous chapters, these savings can then be used to further strengthen treatment capacity and for other investments that can help prevent people from returning to prison.

Either or both types of reform efforts can lay the political groundwork for systematic change to a host of sentencing policies including reducing the glut of mandatory minimum sentences and three-strike laws that have contributed much to the nation's growth in incarceration and (especially in the case of nonviolent and increasingly elderly prisoners) so little to public safety. As these initial parole/probation reform or diversion strategies take hold and demonstrate success at reducing prison costs and either maintaining or lessening recidivism, the political environment will be far more receptive to sentencing changes that can also bring long-term reductions in prison populations.

I have tried to show in this book, concretely, that reform efforts can work. Conservative states such as Louisiana and Mississippi have already enacted sentencing reform, and Louisiana, after passing a huge juvenile justice reform bill, continues to grapple with parole and probation reform. Texas successfully enacted policy changes that hugely reduced the numbers of technical parole violators returning to prison and mandated probation and treatment for certain first-time drug offenders. Washington State passed legislation setting a 60-day limit on jail stays for technical violators and ended postrelease supervision for some nonviolent offenders. Michigan rolled back most of its mandatory minimum drug sentences. Kansas passed legislation mandating diversion for first- and second-time nonviolent drug offenders. Idaho imposed a 2% surcharge on liquor sales to fund drug courts.

Clearly, then, numerous and varied states have taken first steps aimed at controlling their prison populations. This does not mean that these states have gone far enough; and many other states have yet to begin their own serious efforts at reform. But my contention is that each state should have a political and substantive "road map" of how and in what sequence reforms can be implemented. Though each state has a particular set of political, financial, and public safety concerns that shape its individual approach to downsizing prisons, just about all confront escalating concerns about long-term prison growth, serious budget shortfalls, and yawning needs in education and health care.

Ironically, the issue of how to control skyrocketing prison expenditures has become less a partisan issue between Democrats and Republicans and more a problem that both parties are trying to grapple with substantively and politically. "We have a Republican Governor and a Democratic legislature, and we are definitely on the same page when it comes to figuring out a way to bring these costs under control without affecting public safety," observed state legislator Michael Lawlor, the Democratic Co-Chair of Connecticut's Joint Judiciary Committee.[6] Likewise, Ray Allen, the conservative Republican Chair of the Texas Legislature's House Corrections Committee, remarked about attempting to control prison costs, "I'm a hardcore conservative back home and I sound like the liberals that I came in to displace."[7] In fact, thus far Republican governors have taken the lead on the issue of providing alternatives to prison for nonviolent drug offenders.[8]

Most if not all states, then, currently have an interest in controlling and shrinking prison spending. But many states need assistance in forming specific reform plans that address their own political, criminal justice, and social needs. The challenge for states is to develop a strategy that not only works politically and substantively but also saves money in the short run, a portion of which can be reinvested in efforts to further reduce recidivism and provide alternatives to prison for particular classes of offenders. Budget savings also need to be made available for other essential services as part of an overall package that can appeal to the widest possible constituency.

The politics of this kind of reform are tricky and can always change in an instant with the commission of a high-profile crime. For instance, Louisiana was roiled by highly publicized serial killings just when it was considering prison reform; this doubtless contributed to failure to enact legislative changes in the 2003 session. Hence, two considerations need to be kept in mind at the same time that reforms are being undertaken. First, states have to be reminded of the experience of other states, and of cities such as New York, that have significantly decreased crime while increasing prison use at far less than the national average; in the case of New York City, crime decreased as prison use, too, was actually decreasing. Second, and flowing from this first consideration, is that practitioners and legislators from states that have successfully implemented reform must provide testimony, formal and otherwise, as to how they were able to do so. Legislators always find it useful to hear from their peers around the country about how and why they overcame political hurdles and successfully passed reform measures. For a state that is considering reform, academic and substantive policy expertise is essential, but it does not substitute for legitimacy of the kind that can be conveyed by legislators such as Ray Allen from Texas, Donald Cravins from Louisiana, Cal Hobson from Oklahoma, and Michael Lawlor from Connecticut, each of whom has been intimately involved with some aspects of prison reform in his respective state.

While every state regards itself as having a unique political culture, legislators are extremely interested in how other state legislators have handled both the politics and substance of prison reform in their states. State legislators who can explain to their colleagues how they can overcome political resistance to change or, perhaps more important, how they were able to frame issues in a way that did not hurt their reelection prospects are an incredibly valuable resource in making change possible in many states.[9]

However, I reiterate once more, in concluding, that none of this will be easy. The political obstacles to shrinking prison systems and actively moving funding to other uses are dramatic. These obstacles can be overcome, but in all states this will take a thoughtful, ongoing, and committed effort by those in and out of government. Perseverance in the face of suddenly changing politics, the commission of a high-profile crime, and the unexpected appearance of other priorities that divert attention from the issue, is crucial. Moreover, larger successes can follow smaller ones, and temporary "failures" can be regarded as just that: temporary. For instance, Louisiana eliminated many of its mandatory minimum sentences in 2001; two years later, while failing to reform its adult corrections system, the state did succeed in completely revamping its troubled juvenile justice system. And even though Louisiana came up short on prison reform in 2003 and 2004, Commissioner of Corrections Richard Stalder is implementing a number of internal reforms designed to divert technical parole violators from prison. Senator Cravins, the prime legislative architect of Louisiana's plan to reduce the size of the prison system, has also vowed to make continuing efforts at reform through the legislature.[10]

Of course, none of these strategies can be developed without the use of good and current data. In this respect, states are in remarkably different shape. Some states have the ability to know exactly who is in their prison systems at any time, for how long, and for what conviction charges; these states even know an individual's entire criminal history.

Other states barely know who is in their prison systems. Hence, it is crucial that all strategies, both substantive and political, be based on solid and reliable data. Knowing what kinds of offenders populate prisons should assist in shaping plans to reduce prison populations. Are the numbers of nonviolent drug offenders increasing? Are there a significant number of simple drug possession cases in prison? To what extent do technical probation and parole violators take up prison beds? Are lengths of stay for nonviolent offenders significantly increasing and, if so, for terms longer than the national average? What statewide capacity exists for drug treatment or employment programs? These and other questions must be answered before any reform plans can be intelligently forged and implemented. For the answers to many of these questions will affect not only the contents of reforms but political strategies as well. Legislators may think that most people in their prison system are in for violent crimes, but the realization that a significant number are low-level, nonviolent drug offenders and technical violators will contribute to an educational process that can make supporting prison reform much more attractive for legislators as well as the general public.

Several national nonpartisan organizations such as the Vera Institute of Justice's Corrections and Sentencing Program, the Urban Institute, the Council of State Governments, and Jim Austin's JFA Associates are invaluable assets to states in their analytical and planning efforts. All these organizations enjoy excellent national reputations and have worked with numerous states, sentencing commissions, and corrections agencies. A number of local universities and research institutions can also add greatly in states' varied reform efforts.

But even after all data have been collected, strategies have been developed, legislative and/or executive champions have been found, and reforms have passed in the form of new legislation or executive or administrative policies, a host of challenges remain. It is one thing to pass legislation that mandates drug treatment in lieu of incarceration, or to divert technical parole violators from prison, or to have governors intelligently concentrate their resources on programmatic needs of parolees in their first months out of prison. It is quite another thing to actually do it. Reform does not end with legislation or an executive order. Rather, longer-term changes of a more structural character take ongoing attention, evaluation, and maintenance from prison, parole, probation, and sentencing officials, as well as treatment providers and community-based organizations. Analogously, ongoing oversight and support will be required from state legislators, especially since, in many cases, organizational "missions" and resources will be subject to near-complete overhauls. For, in many instances, parole or probation agencies will have to move from what has become a purely risk-management and enforcement focus to making service provision and recidivism reduction their priorities. Other states may have to create community-based treatment and support resources that currently do not exist.

Consequently, given that reforms of the scope I have advocated in this book are not easy to make, it is essential that these be done well. If not, ramifications may extend beyond the disappointment of simply having made an unsuccessful effort. In addition, the public, and the media reporting on political developments, may come to the unfortunate and inaccurate conclusion that nothing can be done to alter correctional policy. This conclusion then moves policy around in circles, benefiting only politicians who may wish to continue or return to "easier" policies of endless investment in more prisons.

But even where reform efforts have already been successful, can they be maintained and expanded—even in a social and political environment that remains very punitive in the contemporary U.S. context, so much so that Berkeley sociologist Loïc Wacquant characterizes present strategies as a "queer form of anti-poverty policy and camouflaged racial control"?[11] I think, and hope, that the answer to my own question is yes. Despite the myriad social, political, and economic obstacles to prison reform summarized in Chapter 2, sufficient structural incentives remain to allow reform efforts to take hold with their own kind of permanency.

But a second, concluding question is whether this book's analysis implies that reforms would reverse if states were to once again become flush with revenue and could once more afford to build prisons while still delivering tax cuts and fully funding Medicaid and education. This is especially germane if the changes I have advocated here are undertaken for pragmatic more than political reasons, making "virtues of necessity." What will happen if, around the same time, crime again were to begin to increase year after year—won't it be inevitable that states will again respond with new ways of increasing incarceration? Here, my response is that no level of reform can guarantee things will not revert to the way they used to be; indeed, upturns in the economy, as in some types of crime, are more common than rare. In this case, though,

I believe the dynamic of shrinking prison systems while maintaining and even increasing public safety can, along with a number of burgeoning community-based prison reform movements, itself shift the political environment in the United States in a direction more inclined toward continuing and expanding prison reform than ending it. The trick is to be able to point to successful and intelligent state examples of the kinds of reforms I have been advocating; for the public and media to see prison populations shrink and crime decline or remain stable in the aftermath of altered policies; and to insist that budgetary savings be rechanneled into badly underfunded areas such as education and health care.

Consequently, my goal has been to make a contribution by providing a guide capable of taking us "from here to there." Returning to a point I raised by way of introduction, while sociologists and criminologists have long provided extremely valuable and well-documented criticisms of present incarceration policies, nowhere near adequate changes have resulted. For instance, in *Sentencing Matters,* criminologist Michael Tonry calls passionately for "a just sentencing system" that would include, among other reforms, the following:

> First, legislatures would repeal all mandatory minimum penalties, including "three-strikes" laws;

> Second, legislatures would invest the funds needed to establish credible, well-managed noncustodial penalties that can serve as sanctions intermediate between prison and probation;

> Third, authority for creation of rules of sentencing would be delegated to an administrative agency, often but not necessarily called a sentencing commission. . . .[12]

However well-argued the need for these goals (and Tonry makes his case well indeed), critiques of this kind may be rendered "utopian" in our present political environment to the extent that policy makers, the public, and the media are not convinced such changes are desirable and pragmatic. Thus, in the case of corrections, it has not been enough simply to advocate ending mandatory sentences; in and of itself, calling for these sentences' demise has not resulted in their abolition. Rather, what I have attempted to offer here—combining academic research with my background as a corrections and probation administrator and, presently, a policy consultant—is an addendum to such calls through practical suggestions designed to achieve specific results. Focused strategies that incorporate multidimensional political and fiscal realities can only improve the likelihood that "What is to be done?" issues in corrections (and, by analogy, other social problems) will eventually result in concrete transformations. Further, I would contend that pragmatic strategies are even likely to assist, and perhaps contribute to forming and expanding, the strength of anti-incarceration social movements by rendering those movements' goals more attainable.

So many challenges: strategies still need developing, and collective perseverance is required to implement and sustain new legislation and diverse program initiatives. But the goals, if difficult to attain, are extraordinarily worthwhile. For how can it not be worthwhile to heighten social justice, to have healthy and stable communities, to spend fewer of our scarce public dollars on prisons and more on learning and health? How can it not be worthwhile to halt a 30-year policy of constantly increasing the rates at which we incarcerate our citizens, especially those who are overwhelmingly poor and of minority groups?

Present policies have produced more harm than good, and it is time to stop.

It's time to stop.

Notes

NOTES TO THE INTRODUCTION

1. Garland, David (ed.) (2001) *Mass Imprisonment: Social Causes and Consequences.* New York: Sage.

2. See specifically, from among the most recent to the least recent of these critiques, Garland, David (2001) *The Culture of Control: Crime and Social Order in Contemporary Society.* Chicago: University of Chicago Press; Wacquant, Loic (2001) "Deadly Symbiosis: When Ghetto and Prison Meet and Merge." *Punishment and Society* 3:1; Tonry, Michael, and Joan Petersilia (eds.) (1999) *Prisons.* Chicago: University of Chicago Press; Mauer, Marc (1999) *Race to Incarcerate.* New York: New Press; Petersilia, Joan (2003) *When Prisoners Come Home: Parole and Prisoner Reentry.* New York: Oxford University Press; Parenti, Christian (1999) *Lockdown America: Police and Prisons in the Age of Crisis.* New York: Verso; Currie, Elliot (1998) *Crime and Punishment in America.* New York: Henry Holt & Co.; Irwin, John, and James Austin (1997) *It's About Time: America's Imprisonment Binge.* Belmont, CA: Wadsworth; Zimring, Franklin E., and Gordon Hawkins (1995) *Incapacitation: Penal Confinement and the Restraint of Crime.* New York: Oxford University Press; Tonry, Michael (1995) *Malign Neglect: Race, Crime and Punishment in America.* New York: Oxford; Clear, Todd R. (1994) *Harm in American Penology.* Albany: State University of New York Press; Garland, David (1990) *Punishment and Modern Society: A Study in Social Theory.* Oxford: Clarendon Press; and Morris, Norval (1974) *The Future of Imprisonment.* Chicago: University of Chicago Press.

3. In fact, state prison population growth has slowed over the last few years and from 2000 to 2001 remained remarkably constant, though from 2001 to 2002 state systems began to grow once more (albeit at a lower rate than in the 1980s and 1990s). By the first half of 2003, state prison populations had increased by the largest rate since 1999. As a result, spending on state prison systems continues to grow even in states that have relatively stable populations, and most states' prison populations continue to grow. The federal prison system, too, continues to grow at an even faster rate than state systems.

4. See, for example, Cullen, F. T., and P. Gendreau (2000) "Assessing Correctional Rehabilitation: Policy, Practice, and Prospects." In J. Horney (ed.), *Criminal Justice 2000.* Vol. 4: *Policies, Processes, and Decisions of the Criminal Justice*

System (pp. 109–175). Washington, D.C.: National Institute of Justice, U.S. Department of Justice; and MacKenzie, D. L. (1997) "Criminal Justice and Crime Prevention." In L. W. Sherman, D. Gottfredson, D. MacKenzie, J. Eck, P. Reuter, and S. Bushway (eds.), *Preventing Crime: What Works, What Doesn't, What's Promising* (pp. 9.1–9.76). Washington, D.C.: National Institute of Justice.

5. International Center for Prison Studies, "Prison Briefs for France, Italy, Germany, the Netherlands, Spain, Australia and South Africa." Available at www.prisonstudies.org.

6. Elkins, Mike, and Jide Olagundoye (2001) "The Prison Population in 2000: A Statistical Review." Home Office, London, England. Available at www.homeoffice.gov.uk/rds/pdfs/r154.pdf.

7. Tournier, Pierre W. (2002) "The Prisons of Europe, Prison Population Inflation and Prison Overcrowding." Centre de Recherches Sociologiques sur le Droit et les Institutions Penales, France.

NOTES TO CHAPTER I

1. "Before Being Sentenced to Die, Killer Disrupts a Courtroom." *New York Times* (September 27, 1996), p. A16.

2. Garland, David. (2001) *The Culture of Control: Crime and Social Order in Contemporary Society.* Chicago: University of Chicago Press; Beckett, Katherine (1997) *Making Crime Pay: Law and Order in Contemporary American Politics.* New York: Oxford University Press; Tonry, Michael (1995) *Malign Neglect: Race, Crime and Punishment in America.* New York: Oxford University Press; Sutherland, Edwin (1950) "The Diffusion of Sexual Psychopath Laws." *American Journal of Sociology* 56, pp. 142–148; Cohen, Stanley (2002) *Folk Devils and Moral Panics.* New York: Routledge.

3. Beckett, *Making Crime Pay*, p. 6.

4. There were 753,141 persons on parole and 3,995,165 on probation as of December 31, 2002. Bureau of Justice Statistics. Key Facts at a Glance Correctional Population, 2004. Available at www.ojp.usdoj.gov/bjs/glance/tables/corr2tab.htm.

5. Hughes, Timothy, Doris James Wilson, and Allen Beck (2001) *Trends in State Parole, 1990–2000.* Washington, D.C.: Bureau of Justice Statistics, U.S. Department of Justice, Office of Justice Programs.

6. Austin, James, John Clark, Patricia Hardyman, and D. Allen Henry (October 1999) "The Impact of 'Three Strikes and You're Out.'" *Punishment and Society* 1(2), p. 131.

7. Young, Jock (2003) "Merton with Energy, Katz with Structure: The Sociology of Vindictiveness and the Criminology of Transgression." *Theoretical Criminology* 7(3), pp. 403–404.

8. Christie, Nils (1981) *Limits to Pain.* New York: Oxford University Press.

9. See Tonry, *Malign Neglect*; and also Garland, *Culture of Control.*

10. Garland, *Culture of Control*, p. 4.

11. National Advisory Commission on Criminal Justice Standards and Goals (1973) *A National Strategy to Reduce Crime: Final Report.* Washington, D.C.: Government Printing Office, p. 358 and 597; as cited in Garland, *Culture of Control*, p. 1, n. 1.

12. Taken from the American Correctional Association's Web site's Legislative Position statements. Available at www.corrections.com/aca/government.

13. Garland, *Culture of Control*, p. 1.

14. Martinson, Robert (1974) "What Works? Questions and Answers about Prison Reform." *Public Interest* 35, pp. 22–54, p. 22.

15. Martinson, Robert (1979) "New Findings, New Views: A Note of Caution Regarding Sentencing Reform." *Hofstra Law Review* 7, pp. 242–258.

16. Fine, Michele et al. (2002) "Changing Minds: The Impact of College in a Maximum Security Prison." The Graduate Center of the City of New York and Women in Prison at the Bedford Hills Correctional Facility.

17. A frequent issue raised by social scientists is whether the research on prison education and recidivism overstates the importance of education. People question if prisoners who take advantage of these programs are already self-motivated and, therefore, not necessarily comparable with other prisoners who do not take advantage of these programs. This may be a legitimate question. However, the existence of educational programs allows self-motivated prisoners opportunities without which their futures might be bleak, and their recidivism rates might eventually rise.

18. See Steurer, Stephen J., Linda Smith, and Alice Tracy (2001) *OCE/CEA Three State Recidivism Study.* Correctional Educational Association; Beck, Allen, and Bernard Shipley (1989) *Recidivism of Prisoners Released in 1983.* Washington, D.C.: Bureau of Justice Statistics, U.S. Department of Justice, Office of Justice Programs; Harer, Miles D. (1994) *Recidivism among Federal Prison Releases in 1987: A Preliminary Report.* Federal Bureau of Prisons, Washington, D.C.; Jenkins, David H., Jennifer Pendry, and Stephen J. Steurer (1993) *A Post-Release Follow-up of Correctional Education Program Completers Released in 1990–1991.* Maryland Department of Education; Open Society Institute (1997) *Education as Crime Prevention: Providing Education to Prisoners.* Research Brief, Occasional Paper Series No. 2. New York: OSI Center on Crime Communities and Culture.

19. Lawrence, Sarah, Daniel P. Mears, Glen Dubin, and Jeremy Travis (2002) *Practice and Promise of Prison Programming.* Washington, D.C.: Urban Institute, p. 8.

20. Fine, et al., "Changing Minds," pp. 16–17

21. Riveland, Chase (1999) "Prison Management Trends, 1975–2025." In Michael Tonry and Joan Petersilia (1999) *Prisons.* Chicago: University of Chicago Press, pp. 174–175.

22. See Clear, Todd R. (1994) *Harm in American Penology: Offenders, Victims and Their Communities.* Albany: State University of New York Press; Clear, Todd, Dina Rose, and Judith Ryder (2000) *Drugs, Incarceration and Neighborhood Life: The Impact of Reintegrating Offenders into the Community.* Washington, D.C.: U.S. Department of Justice, Office of Justice Programs, National Institute of Justice; Clear, Todd, and Dina Rose (1999) *When Neighbors Go to Jail: Impact on Attitudes about Formal and Informal Social Control: Summary of a Presentation.* Washington, D.C.: U.S. Department of Justice, Office of Justice Programs, National Institute of Justice; The Vera Institute of Justice (January 1996) *Unintended Consequences of Incarceration: Papers from a Conference Organized by Vera.* Available at www.vera.org/publications.

23. See Tonry, *Malign Neglect*; Mauer, Marc (1999) *Race to Incarcerate.* New York: New Press; Wacquant, Loic (2001) "Deadly Symbiosis: When Ghetto and Prison Meet and Merge." *Punishment and Society* 3(1).

24. See Tonry, Michael (1996) *Sentencing Matters,* New York: Oxford University Press; Shichor, D., and D. K. Sechrest (eds.) (1996) *Three Strikes and You're Out: Vengeance as Public Policy.* Thousand Oaks, CA: Sage; Zimring, Franklin E., and Gordon Hawkins (1995) *Incapacitation: Penal Confinement and the Restraint of Crime.* New York: Oxford University Press; and even DiIulio, John (12 March 1999) "Two Million Prisoners Are Enough," *Wall Street Journal,* A14.

25. See Petersilia, Joan (ed.) (1998) *Community Corrections: Parole, Probation and Intermediate Sanctions.* New York: Oxford University Press; Tonry, Michael, and Norval Morris (1990) *Between Prison and Probation: Intermediate Punishments in a Rational Sentencing System.* New York: Oxford University Press; and Gendreau, Paul, and Robert Ross (1987) "Revivification of Rehabilitation: Evidence from the 1980's." *Justice Quarterly* 4(3), pp. 349–407.

26. Langan, Patrick, and David Levin (2002) *Recidivism of Prisoners Released in 1994.* Washington, D.C.: Bureau of Justice Statistics, U.S. Department of Justice, Office of Justice Programs.

27. Harrison, Paije M., and Jennifer C. Karberg (2004) *Prison and Jail Inmates at Midyear 2003.* Washington, D.C.: Bureau of Justice Statistics, U.S. Department of Justice, Office of Justice Programs.

28. $60.3 billion spent in fiscal year 1999. Bauer, Lynn (May 2004) *Justice Expenditures and Employment in the United States, 2001.* Washington, D.C.: Bureau of Justice Statistics, U.S. Department of Justice, Office of Justice Programs.

29. See Echols, Alice (1989) *Daring to Be Bad: Radical Feminism in America, 1967–1975.* Minneapolis: University of Minnesota Press; McAdam, Doug (1988) *Freedom Summer.* New York: Oxford University Press; and Morris, Aldon (1984) *The Origins of the Civil Rights Movement: Black Communities Organized for Change.* New York: Free Press.

30. Bureau of Justice Statistics Prison (June 30, 2003) *Statistics: Summary of Findings.* Available at www.ojp.usdoj.gov/bjs/prisons.htm.

31. Mauer, Marc (1999) *The Crisis of the Young African American Male and the Criminal Justice System.* Prepared for the U.S. Commission of Civil Rights, Washington, D.C., April 15–16. Available at www.sentencingproject.org.

32. Bonczar, Thomas (August 2003) *Prevalence of Imprisonment in the U.S. Population, 1974–2001.* Washington, D.C.: Bureau of Justice Statistics, Office of Justice Programs, U.S. Department of Justice.

33. California's Proposition 36, to divert drug offenders from prison to treatment, passed overwhelmingly, 61% to 39%, largely because of a public education campaign by the referendum's sponsors about the prevalence of nonviolent drug users in the California prison system.

34. 1,209,640 in state prisons as of December 31, 2002. Harrison and Karberg, *Prison and Jail Inmates at Midyear 2003.*

35. 140,741 in federal prisons as of June 30, 2001. Harrison and Karberg, *Prison and Jail Inmates at Midyear 2003.*

36. LeonHardt, David (November 4, 2001) "Recession: Almost Official." *New York Times,* Final, Section 4, p. 2; Padgett, Tania, and James Toedtman (November 1, 2001) "Evidence Points to Recession: Economy Shrinks at Fastest Rate in Decade." *Newsday,* p. A45.

37. Stevenson, Richard W. (November 27, 2001) "Economists Make It Official: U.S. Is in a Recession." *New York Times,* Business/Financial Desk.

38. DeParle, Jason (October 8, 2001) "A Mass of Newly Laid Off Workers Will Put Social Safety Net to the Test." *New York Times,* National Desk.

39. National Conference of State Legislatures. *State Fiscal Update, June 2002.* Available at www.ncsl.org/programs/fiscal/sfo2002.htm.

40. Ibid.

41. National Governors Association and the National Association of State Budget Officers (June 2003) *The Fiscal Survey of States.* Washington, D.C.

42. National Association of State Budget Officers (Summer 2001) *2000 State Expenditure Report.* Washington, D.C., p. 5.

43. Wilhelm, Daniel F., and Nicholas R. Turner (2002) *Is the Budget Crisis Changing the Way We Look at Sentencing and Incarceration?* New York: Vera Institute of Justice.

44. National Association of State Budget Officers, *2000 State Expenditure Report.*

45. See *The Criminal Justice Sourcebook* (2002) Table 2.1: "Attitudes toward the Most Important Problem Facing the Country, 1983–2003." Sourcebook available at www.albany.edu/sourcebook.

46. *Criminal Justice Sourcebook.* Table 2.2: "Attitudes toward the Important Issues for the Government to Address, 1993–2003." Sourcebook available at www.albany.edu/sourcebook.

47. National Association of State Budget Officers, *2000 State Expenditure Report,* p. 5.

48. *The New Politics of Criminal Justice: A Research and Messaging Report for The Open Society Institute* (February 2002) Peter D. Hart Research Associates, Inc.

49. Ibid., pp. 14–15.

50. Ibid., p. 16.

51. Bureau of Justice Statistics. *Four Measures of Serious Violent Crime.* Available at www.ojp.usdoj.gov/bjs/glance/tables/4meastab.htm.

52. I use 1993 as the baseline year for comparison here, recognizing that crime in New York City actually started its decline in 1991. Violent crime actually declined by 9% from 1991 through 1993. There are two reasons 1993 is used as the baseline. First, it is the beginning of a very different form of policing strategies, initiated by Commissioner Bill Bratton in Mayor Giuliani's first term. Second, the rates of crime decreased sharply beginning in 1993. However, even if 1990 were used as the baseline year for this analysis, the story would be much the same.

53. New York Police Department (NYPD) (2004) *CompStat.* Available at www.nyc.gov/html/nypd/html/pct/cspdf.html.

54. DCJS, *Criminal Justice Indicators.* Available at www.criminaljustice.state .ny.us; and Federal Bureau of Investigation (FBI) (1993–2002) *Uniform Crime Reports.* Available at www.fbi.gov/ucr/ucr/htm.

55. DCJS, *Criminal Justice Indicators* (1993–2000).

56. FBI (1993–2002) *Crime in the United States, Uniform Crime Reports.* Washington, D.C.: U.S. Department of Justice.

57. Bureau of Justice Statistics. *National Prisoner Statistics, Data Series (NPS-1).* Available at www.ojp.usdoj.gov/bjs/abstract/cpusst.htm. Beck, Allen J., and Paige M. Harrison (2003), *Prisoners in 2002.* Washington D.C.: Bureau of Justice Statistics, U.S. Department of Justice, Office of Justice Programs (also Bureau of Justice Statistics Data online, *Violent Crime Totals,* available at www .ojp.usdoj.gov/bjs).

58. Harrison and Karberg, *Prison and Jail Inmates at Midyear 2003.*

59. Langan and Levin, *Recidivism of Prisoners Released in 1994. Special Report.*

60. State of California Department of Corrections Offender Information Services Branch, Estimates and Statistical Analysis Section, Data Analysis Unit. *California Prisoners and Parolees 2002.* Available at www.cdc.state.ca.us.

61. California Department of Corrections Data Analysis Unit. *Historical Trends, 1982–2002,* and *California Department of Corrections Facts.* Available at www.cdc.state.ca.us.

62. Data on number of parolees returned, average length of stay for returned parolees, and average cost per day for incarceration available from the California Department of Corrections, at www.cdc.state.ca.us.

63. The Bureau of Justice Statistics does have state-level data on parole violators, but it cannot in any great detail break out the reasons for technical vio-

lations, such as how many dirty urines or missed appointments before a violation is filed. BJS does have two large data sets from 1991 and 1997 that are based on prisoner interviews, and there are questions about the nature of any technical violations that might have been the reason for their current admission. The limitations of these data involve all the limitations that go along with self-reporting but, even more important, the data cannot be broken down by state, given the overall sample size.

64. Young, "Merton with Energy."

NOTES TO CHAPTER 2

1. American Civil Liberties Union (December 9, 2003) *A Question of Innocence.* Available at www.aclu.org/DeathPenalty/DeathPenalty.cfm?ID=9316&c=65.

2. The Gallup Organization, Inc. (2003) *The Gallup Poll.* Available at www.gallup.com/poll/topics/death_pen.asp.

3. Bureau of Justice Statistics (2004) *Four Measures of Serious Violent Crime.* Available at www.ojp.usdoj.gov/bjs/glance/tables/4meastab.htm.

4. At mid-year 2003, the rates of incarceration in prison or jail were: 4,834 per 100,000 Black males; 1,778 per 100,000 Hispanic males; and 681 per 100,000 white males. Source: Bureau of Justice Statistics (June 30, 2003) *Prison Statistics: Summary of Findings.* Available at www.ojp.usdoj.gov/bjs/prisons.htm.

5. Bonczar, Thomas P. (2003) *The Prevalence of Imprisonment in the U.S. Population, 1974–2001.* Washington, D.C.: U.S. Department of Justice, Office of Justice Programs, Bureau of Justice Statistics.

6. See, for example, Reiman, Jeffrey (2000) *The Rich Get Richer and the Poor Get Prison: Ideology, Class and Criminal Justice.* Boston: Allyn & Bacon.

7. See Mauer, Marc (1999) *Race to Incarcerate.* New York: New Press; Miller, Jerome (1996) *Search and Destroy: African-American Males in the Criminal Justice System.* New York: Cambridge University Press; Tonry, Michael (1995) *Malign Neglect: Race, Crime and Punishment in America.* New York: Oxford University Press; and Parenti, Christian (1999) *Lockdown America: Police and Prisons in the Age of Crisis.* New York: Verso.

8. Substance Abuse and Mental Health Services Administration (2003) *Results from the 2002 National Survey on Drug Use and Health: National Findings.* Rockville, MD: Office of Applied Studies, NHSDA Series H-22, DHHS Publication No. SMA 03-3836.

9. See Egan, Timothy (February 28, 1999) "War on Crack Retreats, Still Taking Prisoners." *New York Times,* p. A1; and Rudolph, Alexander, and Jacquelyn Gyamerah (September 28, 1997) "Differential Punishment of African Americans and Whites Who Possess Drugs: A Just Policy or a Continuation of the Past?" *Journal of Black Studies,* pp. 97–111.

10. See Wacquant, Loic (2001) "Deadly Symbiosis: When Ghetto and Prison Meet and Mesh." In David Garland (ed.) *Mass Imprisonment: Social Causes and Consequences.* London: Sage; and Beckett, Katherine, and Bruce Western (1999) "How Unregulated Is the US Labor Market? The Penal System as a Labor Market Institution." *American Journal of Sociology* 104, pp. 1030–1060.

11. Huling, Tracy (May 10, 2000) "Prisoners of the Census." *Mother Jones*; Dugan, Molly (July/August 2000) "Census Dollars Bring Bounty to Prison Towns." *Chicago Reporter.*

12. Tonry, Michael (1994) "Racial Politics, Racial Disparities and the War on Crime." *Crime and Delinquency* 40(4), pp. 491–492.

13. Wacquant, "Deadly Symbiosis: When Ghetto and Prison Meet and Mesh." *Punishment and Society* 3(1), p. 97.

14. Ditton, Paula, and Doris James Wilson (1999) *Truth in Sentencing in State Prisons.* Washington, D.C.: U.S. Department of Justice, Office of Justice Programs, Bureau of Justice Statistics.

15. King, Ryan S., and Marc Mauer (August 2001) *Aging behind Bars: "Three Strikes" Seven Years Later.* Washington, D.C.: The Sentencing Project. Available at www.sentencingproject.org.

16. See Tonry, Michael (1996) *Sentencing Matters.* New York: Oxford University Press; Zimring, Franklin E., and Gordon Hawkins (1995) *Incapacitation: Penal Confinement and the Restraint of Crime.* New York: Oxford University Press; and Tonry, Michael, and Norval Morris (1990) *Between Prison and Probation: Intermediate Punishments in a Rational Sentencing System.* New York: Oxford University Press.

17. Ditton and Wilson, *Truth in Sentencing in State Prisons.*

18. Bureau of Justice Statistics, *Number of Persons in Custody of State Correctional Authorities by Most Serious Offense, 1980–2001.* Available at www.ojp.usdoj .gov/bjs/glance/tables/corrtyptab.htm.

19. Mauer, *Race to Incarcerate,* p. 111.

20. Tonry, *Sentencing Matters,* p. 8.

21. See Rose, Dina R., Todd Clear, and Judith A. Ryder (2001) "Addressing the Unintended Consequences of Incarceration through Community-Oriented Services at the Neighborhood Level." *Corrections Management Quarterly* 5(3), pp. 62–71; Rose, Dina R., and Todd Clear (1998) "Incarceration, Social Capital and Crime: Implications for Social Disorganization Theory." *Criminology* 36(3), pp. 441–480; Mauer, *Race to Incarcerate*; The Vera Institute of Justice (January 1996) *Unintended Consequences of Incarceration: Papers from a Conference Organized by Vera.* Available at www.vera.org/publications.

22. Rose and Clear, "Incarceration, Social Capital and Crime," pp. 441–480.

23. Snell, Tracy L. (n.d.) *Women in Prison: Survey of State Prison Inmates, 1991.* Washington, D.C.: U.S. Department of Justice, Office of Justice Programs, Bureau of Justice Statistics.

24. See Gabel, Katherine, and Denise Johnston (1997) *Children of Incarcerated Parents*. Lanham, MD: Lexington Books.

25. Mumola, Christopher (2000) *Incarcerated Parents and Their Children*. Washington, D.C.: U.S. Department of Justice, Office of Justice Programs, Bureau of Justice Statistics.

26. Ibid.

27. Western, Bruce, and Katherine Beckett (January 1999) "How Unregulated Is the U.S. Labor Market? The Penal System as a Labor Market Institution." *American Journal of Sociology* 104(4), p. 1052. This work is not without its critics. David Greenberg thinks, for instance, that Beckett and Western significantly underestimate the employment levels of people entering prison, thus overestimating the impact of prison on unemployment rates. He also notes that the growth of prisoners in the 1990s is too small to explain aggregate drops in unemployment. See specifically, Greenberg, David (January 2001) "Novus Ordo Saeclorum? A Commentary on Downes, and on Beckett and Western." *Punishment and Society* 3(61), p. 81–93.

28. Mauer, Marc, and Meda Chesney-Lynd (eds.) (2003) *Invisible Punishment: The Collateral Consequences of Mass Imprisonment*. New York: New Press.

29. Bureau of Justice Statistics (1980–2002) *Key Facts at a Glance: Correctional Populations. Number of Persons under Correctional Supervision*. Available at www.ojp.usdoj.gov/bjs/glance/corr2.htm.

30. *Probation and Parole in the United States, 2000. Press release*. Washington, D.C.: U.S. Department of Justice, Office of Justice Programs, Bureau of Justice Statistics. Available at www.ojp.usdoj.gov/bjs/pub/pdf/ppus00.pdf.

31. Petersilia, Joan (1998) "The Current State of Probation, Parole and Intermediate Sanctions." In Joan Petersilia (ed.) *Community Corrections: Probation Parole and Intermediate Sanctions*. New York: Oxford University Press.

32. Stephan, James J. *State Prison Expenditures, 1996*. Washington, D.C.: U.S. Department of Justice, Office of Justice Programs, Bureau of Justice Statistics.

33. Rothman, David J. (1980) *Conscience and Convenience: The Asylum and Its Alternatives in Progressive America*. Boston: Little, Brown, p. 83.

34. Walker, Samuel (1998) *Sense and Nonsense about Crime and Drugs*. 4th ed. Belmont, CA: Wadsworth Publishing Co., p. 221.

35. Petersilia, "The Current State of Probation, Parole and Intermediate Sanctions."

36. *Mayor's Management Report* (February 2002). New York: Office of the Mayor, Office of Operations.

37. Los Angeles Probation Department Web site: probation.co.la.ca.us/adult/aspecial.html.

38. Petersilia, "The Current State of Probation, Parole and Intermediate Sanctions."

39. See Leaf, Robin, Robin Arthur Lurigio, and Nancy Martin (1998)

"Chicago's Project Safeway: Strengthening Probation's Links with the Community"; Morgan, Terry, and Stephen D. Marrs (1998) "Richmond, Washington's SMART Partnership for Police and Community Corrections"; and Corbett, Ronald P., Jr., Bernard L. Fitzgerald, and James Jorday (1998) "Boston's Operation Nightlight: An Emerging Model for Police-Probation Partnerships." All in Petersilia (ed.), *Community Corrections.*

40. Gendreau, Paul, Francis T. Cullen, and James Bonta (1998) "Intensive Rehabilitation Supervision: The Next Generation in Community Corrections?" In Petersilia (ed.), *Community Corrections.*

41. Gaes, Gerald G., Timothy J. Flanagen, Laurence L. Motiuk, and Lynn Stewart (1999) "Adult Correctional Treatment." In Michael Tonry and Joan Petersilia (eds.) (1999) *Prisons.* Chicago: University of Chicago Press, p. 414.

42. Clear, Todd, and George Cole (2000) *American Corrections.* Belmont, CA: Wadsworth Publishing Co., p. 487.

43. At national recidivism rates of 51%, many of these communities see a churning of people going in and out of prison over the course of two to three years.

44. Langan, Patrick A., and David J. Levin (2002) *Recidivism of Prisoners Released in 1994.* Washington, D.C.: Bureau of Justice Statistics, U.S. Department of Justice, Office of Justice Programs.

45. Tonry, Michael, and Joan Petersilia (1999) "American Prisons." In Tonry and Petersilia (eds.), *Prisons,* p. 8.

46. Spelman, William, "What Recent Studies Do (and Don't) Tell Us about Imprisonment and Crime." In Michael Tonry (ed.) (2000) *Crime and Justice: A Review of Research.* Vol. 27. Chicago: University of Chicago Press, p. 481.

47. Gainsborough, Jenni, and Marc Mauer (2000) *Diminishing Returns: Crime and Incarceration in the 1990's.* Washington, D.C.: The Sentencing Project.

48. Spelman, "What Recent Studies Do (and Don't) Tell Us," p. 485.

49. Ibid., p. 487.

50. See, for instance, Zedlewski, Edwin W. (July 1987) *Making Confinement Decisions.* Washington, D.C.: National Institute of Justice; and Miller, Ted R., Mark A. Cohen, and Brian Wiersema (1996) *Victim Costs and Consequences: A New Look.* Washington, D.C.: U.S. Department of Justice, National Institute of Justice.

51. See Mauer, *Race to Incarcerate*; and Zimring, Franklin, and Gordon Hawkins (1991) *The Scale of Imprisonment.* Chicago: University of Chicago Press.

52. Zedlewski, *Making Confinement Decisions.*

53. Zimring, Franklin, and Gordon Hawkins (October 1988) "The New Mathematics of Imprisonment." *Crime and Delinquency* 34(4), p. 431.

54. Harrison, Paige M., and Allen J. Beck (2002) *Prisoners in 2001.* Washington, D.C.: U.S. Department of Justice, Office of Justice Programs, Bureau of Justice Statistics.

55. Ibid.

56. Harrison, Paige M., and Allen J. Beck (2003) *Prisoners in 2002*. Washington, D.C.: U.S. Department of Justice, Office of Justice Programs, Bureau of Justice Statistics.

57. Harrison and Beck, *Prisoners in 2001*.

58. Harrison and Beck, *Prisoners in 2002*.

59. The other state usually included in this group is Florida, since these four are by far the largest state prison systems in the country. Florida, however, actually grew by 1.1%.

60. Harrison and Beck, *Prisoners in 2001*.

61. Harrison and Beck, *Prisoners in 2002*.

62. Harrison, Paige M., and Jennifer C. Karberg (May 2004) *Prison and Jail Inmates at Midyear 2003*. Washington, D.C.: U.S Department of Justice, Office of Justice Programs, Bureau of Justice Statistics.

63. Harrison and Beck, *Prisoners in 2002*.

64. Snell, Tracy (2001) *Capital Punishment 2000*. Washington, D.C.: U.S. Department of Justice, Office of Justice Programs, Bureau of Justice Statistics.

65. Beck, Allen J., Jennifer C. Karberg, and Paige M. Harrison (2002) *Prison and Jail Inmates at Midyear 2001*. Washington, D.C.: Bureau of Justice Statistics, U.S. Department of Justice, Office of Justice Programs.

66. Barbee, Andrew, Lisa Carruth, and Michelle Munson (2002) *Adult and Juvenile Correctional Population Projections, FY 2003–2008*. Criminal Justice Policy Council, Austin, Texas.

67. Harrison and Beck, *Prisoners in 2001*.

68. Beck, Allen, and Paige Harrison (2001) *Prisoners in 2000*. Washington, D.C.: Bureau of Justice Statistics, U.S. Department of Justice, Office of Justice Programs.

69. Harrison and Beck, *Prisoners in 2002*.

70. Harrison and Karberg, *Prison and Jail Inmates at Midyear 2003*.

71. California Department of Corrections, *Spring 2002 Population Projections*.

72. See Beck and Harrison, *Prisoners in 2000*; and Beck, Karberg, and Harrison, *Prison and Jail Inmates at Midyear 2001*.

73. Harrison and Karberg, *Prison and Jail Inmates at Midyear 2003*.

74. Harrison and Karberg, *Prison and Jail Inmates at Midyear 2003*.

75. Criminal Justice Estimating Conference (February 16, 2004) Executive Summary. Tallahassee: Florida State Legislature. Available at www.state.fl.us/edr/Conferences/CriminalJustice/ES02162004Cj1.pdf.

76. Currie, Elliot (1998) *Crime and Punishment in America*. New York: Henry Holt & Co., p. 6.

77. Hoffman, David (October 8, 1998) "Bush Attacks Dukakis as the 'Furlough King'; Republican Seeks to Direct Attention Away from Quayle's Debate Performance." *Washington Post*.

78. Parenti, *Lockdown America*, p. 60.

79. Part I crimes include, murder, rape, robbery, and aggravated assault.

80. Ditton and Wilson, *Truth in Sentencing in State Prisons.*

81. Ibid.

82. Garland, David (2001) *The Culture of Control: Crime and Social Order in Contemporary Society.* Chicago: University of Chicago, p. 199.

83. Caplow, T., and J. Simon (1999) "Understanding Prison Policy and Population Trends." In M. Tonry and J. Petersilia (eds.) *Crime and Justice.* Vol. 26: *Prisons.* Chicago: University of Chicago Press, p. 79.

84. Ibid.

85. Tonry, Michael (2004) *Thinking about Crime: Sense and Sensibility in American Culture.* New York: Oxford University Press, p. 70.

86. Ibid., p. 138.

87. Austin, James, and Garry Coventry (2001) *Emerging Issues on Privatized Prisons.* Washington, D.C.: U.S. Department of Justice, Office of Justice Programs, Bureau of Justice Assistance.

88. Ibid.

89. Ibid., p. ix.

90. Ibid., p. 29.

91. Ibid. Though the authors don't conclude that private prisons are more violent than public prisons, their data seem to suggest that is likely the case.

92. Ibid., p. 38.

93. Hoover's online, available at www.hoovers.com/corrections-corporation-of-america.

94. See The Sentencing Project, "Prison Privatization and the Use of Incarceration," for a more detailed relationship between ALEC and private corrections companies. Report available at www.sentencingproject.org.

95. Parenti, *Lockdown America*, p. 220.

96. See Austin and Coventry, *Emerging Issues on Privatized Prisons,* for a discussion on the speed in which private companies can build prisons, compared to government building projects, and how they have built prisons on spec.

97. McDonald, Douglas C., Elizabeth Fournier, and Malcolm Russell-Einhorn (1998). *Private Prisons in the United States: An Assessment of Current Practice.* Cambridge, MA: Abt Associates Inc.

98. Bureau of Justice Statistics (1999) *Expenditure and Employment Statistics. Selected Statistics.* Justice Expenditure and Employment Extracts. Tables 2 and 7. Available at www.ojp.usdoj.gov/bjs; and Bauer, Lynn (May 2004) *Justice Expenditure and Employment in the United States, 2001.* Washington, D.C.: U.S. Department of Justice, Office of Justice Programs, Bureau of Justice Statistics.

99. Clear, "Incarceration, Social Capital, and Crime," p. 312.

100. Morain, Dan (March 15, 2002) "Davis to Close State's Privately Run

Prisons; funding: Elected with the Help of $2.3 Million for guards' Union, Governor Includes Plan in Budget." *Los Angeles Times*, p. A1.

100. Morain, Dan (March 15, 2002) "Davis to Close State's Privately Run Prisons; Funding: Elected with the Help of $2.3 Million for Guards' Union, Governor Includes Plan in Budget." *Los Angeles Times*, p. A1; "Prison Guard Clout Endures" (April 1, 2002) *Los Angeles Times*, p. B10; Warren, Jennifer (August 21, 2000) "When He Speaks, They Listen: In 20 Years, Don Novey Has Built the Once Powerless California Prison Guards Union into One of the Most Influential and Richest Forces in State Politics." *Los Angeles Times*, p. 1.

102. Morain, "Davis to Close State's Privately Run Prisons," p. A1; "Prison Guard Clout Endures," p. B10.

103. Morain, "Davis to Close State's Privately Run Prisons," p. A1.

104. Hernandez, Raymond (December 31, 1999) "Pataki Assents to Pension Rise for Jail Guards." *New York Times*, p. B1.

105. Austin and Coventry, *Emerging Issues on Privatized Prisons*, p. ix.

106. Stephan, James J. (1999) *State Prison Expenditures in 1996*. Washington, D.C.: U.S. Department of Justice, Office of Justice Programs, Bureau of Justice Statistics.

107. National Association of State Budget Officers (NASBO) (Summer 2001) *2000 State Expenditure Report*. Washington, D.C., p. 62.

108. Ibid., p. 94.

109. Stephan, *State Prison Expenditures in 1996*

110. NASBO, *2002 State Expenditure Report*, p. 64, This figure is derived by subtracting the $891 million in capital expenses that NASBO includes in its overall estimate of $38.5 billion for total state spending on prisons.

111. Clear, "Incarceration, Social Capital, and Crime," p. 236.

112. Whitley, Tyler (August 30, 2002) "Southside Rallied for Prisons." *Virginia Times Dispatch*.

113. King, Ryan S., Marc Mauer, and Tracy Huling (2003) *Big Prisons, Small Towns: Prison Economics in Rural America*. Washington, D.C.: The Sentencing Project.

114. Mauer, *Race to Incarcerate*, p. 10.

115. Langan and Levin, *Recidivism of Prisoners Released in 1994*.

116. Washington State Department of Corrections (April 2002) "Recidivism: Historical Review of Returns to Prison." Recidivism Briefing Paper No. 20. Olympia, WA.

117. California Department of Corrections (March 14, 2002) "Recidivism Rates within One and Two Year Follow-up Periods for Felons Paroled to California Supervision." Sacramento: Office of Correctional Planning.

118. Pennsylvania Department of Corrections (2002) "Recidivism, 1996–2000." Harrisburg, PA.

119. Langan and Levin, *Recidivism of Prisoners Released in 1994*.

120. Elkins, Mike, and Jide Olagundoye (2001) "The Prison Population in 2000: A Statistical Review." Home Office, London, England.

121. Langan and Levin, *Recidivism of Prisoners Released in 1994.*

122. California Department of Corrections (2001) *California Prisoners and Parolees 2001.* Sacramento: Office of Correctional Planning, tables 33, 34, 35, 36, 38, and 42.

123. Kansas Sentencing Commission (2002) *Kansas Sentencing Commission Annual Report FY 2001: Analysis of Sentencing Guidelines in Kansas,* p. 28.

124. California Department of Corrections, *Historical Trends, 1983–2003.* Sacramento: Offender Information Services Branch, Data Analysis Unit, table 5.

125. Kansas Sentencing Commission, *Kansas Sentencing Commission Annual Report FY 2001,* p. 59.

126. Greenwood, Peter W., Karyn E. Model, C Peter Rydell, and James Chiesa (1996) *Diverting Children from a Life of Crime: Measuring Costs and Benefits.* Santa Monica, CA: Rand Corporation.

NOTES TO CHAPTER 3

1. National Conference of State Legislators (NCSL) (July 2002) *State Budget and Tax Actions: 2002 Preliminary Report.* Washington, D.C.

2. National Association of State Budget Officers (NASBO) and the National Governors Association (NGA) (2002) *Fiscal Survey of States.* Washington, D.C., p. ix.

3. Ibid., p. 1.

4. Ibid., p. 2.

5. National Governors Association (NGA) and the National Association of State Budget Officers (NASBO) (June 2003) *The Fiscal Survey of States.* Washington, D.C., p. ix.

6. NCSL, *State Budget and Tax Action: 2002.*

7. Ibid.

8. NASBO and NGA, *Fiscal Survey of the States.*

9. NCSL, *State Budget and Tax Action: 2002.*

10. Ibid.

11. National Conference of State Legislators (2003) *State Budget and Tax Actions 2003.* Washington, D.C. Available at www.ncsl.org/programs/fiscal/presbta03.htm.

12. NGA and NASBO, *Fiscal Survey of the States.*

13. Ibid.

14. Ibid.

15. NCSL, *State Budget and Tax Action: 2002,* p. 3.

16. National Conference of State Legislators, *State Fiscal Update, June 2002.* Washington, D.C. Available at www.ncsl.org/programs/fiscal/sfo2002.htm.

17. NASBO and NGA, *Fiscal Survey of the States.*

18. Ibid., p. 9.

19. NGA and NASBO, *Fiscal Survey of the States.*

20. Ibid.

21. Ibid.

22. National Association of State Budget Officers (NASBO) (Summer 2001) *2000 State Expenditure Report.* Washington, D.C.

23. NASBO and NGA, *Fiscal Survey of the States.*

24. NASBO, *2000 State Expenditure Report.*

25. NGA and NASBO, *Fiscal Survey of the States.*

26. NASBO and NGA, *Fiscal Survey of the States.*

27. Ibid.

28. NASBO (2004) *Budgeting Amid Fiscal Uncertainty: Ensuring Budget Stability by Focusing on the Long Term,* Washington, D.C. p. 5.

29. McNicol, Elizabeth (May 12, 2004) "States Face Continuing Fiscal Problems—Evidence from Recent Reports." Washington, D.C.: Center on Budget and Policy Priorities, p. 1.

30. Ibid.

31. Broder, John M. (January 5, 2004) "Despite Signs of Economic Recovery, States' Budgets Are Still Reeling." *New York Times,* p. A1.

32. National Conference of State Legislators (2002), *State Fiscal Update, April 2002.* Washington, D.C.

33. Wilhelm, Daniel F., and Nicholas R. Turner (2002) *Is the Budget Crisis Changing the Way We Look at Sentencing and Incarceration?* New York: Vera Institute of Justice.

34. Keitch, Ryan (July 22, 2002) "Bills Awaiting Approval could Add Prison Costs." *Indianapolis Star.*

35. Wilhelm and Turner, *Budget Crisis.*

36. Wool, Jon, and Don Stemen (March 2004) *Changing Fortune or Changing Attitudes: Sentencing and Corrections in 2003.* New York: Vera Institute of Justice.

37. Wilhelm and Turner, *Budget Crisis,* p. 3.

38. Harrison, Paige M., and Allen J. Beck (2002) *Prisoners in 2001.* Washington, D.C.: U.S. Department of Justice, Office of Justice Programs, Bureau of Justice Statistics. The national average for states per 100,000 incarceration rate is 422, and Louisiana's rate is 800.

39. Shuler, Marsha (May 3, 2001) "Senators Vote to Relax Prison Terms." *Baton Rouge Advocate.*

40. See Wilhelm and Turner, *Budget Crisis;* and Greene, Judith, and Vincent Schiraldi (2002) *Cutting Correctly: New Prison Policies for Times of Fiscal Crisis.* Washington, D.C.: Center for Juvenile and Criminal Justice.

41. McGill, Kevin (April 12, 2001) "Saving Money on Prisons: Will It Be Politically Costly?" *Associated Press.*

42. Butterfield, Fox (September 2, 2001) "States Ease Laws on Time in Prison." *New York Times.*

43. McGill, Kevin (May 23, 2001) "Foster Pushes for Bill Removing Some Minimum Sentences." *Associated Press.*

44. Harrison and Beck, *Prisons in 2001.*

45. Greene and Schiraldi, *Cutting Correctly.*

46. Butterfield, "States Ease Laws."

47. Ibid.

48. See King, Ryan S., and Marc Mauer (2002) *State Sentencing and Corrections Policy in an Era of Fiscal Restraint.* Washington, D.C.: The Sentencing Project; Greene and Schiraldi, *Cutting Correctly*; and Wilhelm and Turner, *Budget Crisis,* for a full and detailed discussion of the changes in state sentencing policies and other reform efforts.

49. Greene, Judith (2003) *Positive Trends in State-Level Sentencing and Corrections Policy.* Washington, D.C.: Families against Mandatory Minimums.

50. Butterfield, Fox (November 10, 2003) "With Cash Tight, States Reassess Long Jail Terms." *New York Times.* Available at www.nytimes.com/2003/11/10/national/10PRIS.html?hp=&pagewanted=print&position=.

51. Ibid.

52. Wool and Stemen, *Changing Fortune or Changing Attitudes.*

53. Butterfield, "States Ease Laws."

54. *Sourcebook of Criminal Justice Statistics* (2002) Table 2.1: "Attitudes toward the Most Important Problem Facing the Country." Available at www.albany.edu/sourcebook/1995/pdf/21.pdf.

55. See Madriz, Esther (1997) *Nothing Bad Happens to Good Girls: Fear of Crime in Women's Lives.* Berkeley: University of California Press; and Beckett, Katherine (1997) *Making Crime Pay: Law and Order in Contemporary American Politics.* New York: Oxford University Press.

56. See The Sentencing Project. "Crime, Punishment and Public Opinion: A Summary of Recent Studies and Their Implications for Sentencing Policy." Washington D.C. Available at www.sentencingproject.org/pdfs/1005.pdf.

57. Peter D. Hart Research Associates, Inc. (2002) *The New Politics of Criminal Justice.* Washington, D.C.

58. Ibid., p. 3.

59. See also Sentencing Project, "Crime, Punishment and Public Opinion."

60. Peter D. Hart Associates, *New Politics of Criminal Justice,* p. 14.

61. *Sourcebook of Criminal Justice Statistics* (2002) The Gallup Poll. Table 2.0007: "Attitudes toward Approaches to Lowering Crime in the US." Albany: University of Albany, p. 131.

62. Peter D. Hart Associates, *New Politics of Criminal Justice,* p. 20.

63. Ibid., p. 23.

64. Ibid., p. 19.

65. Ibid., pp. 35, 37, 41.

66. Ibid., pp. 44–45.

67. The Field Poll Release #2020, "Spending Cuts Preferred over Tax Increases to Reduce State Budget Deficit. Low Confidence in Governor and Legislature to Resolve Deficit Properly, Similar to Public Sentiment in 1993." Compiled December 28, 2001. San Francisco: The Field Institute.

68. Peter D. Hart Associates, *New Politics of Criminal Justice*, p. 69.

69. Ibid., p. 69.

70. Cullen, Francis T., Bonnie S. Fischer, and Brandon Applegate (2000) "Public Opinion about Punishment and Corrections." In Michael Tonry (ed.) (2000) *Crime and Justice: A Review of the Research*. Vol. 27. Chicago: University of Chicago Press, p. 8.

71. See California Campaign for New Drug Policies (2002) *Basic Facts: Substance Abuse and Crime Prevention Act of 2000*. Available at www.drugreform.org.

72. Ferrell, David, and Jennifer Warren (November 13, 2000) "For Many, Plan to Help Addicts Touched Home." *Los Angeles Times*.

73. Ibid.

74. Ibid.

75. Ibid.

76. California Campaign for New Drug Policies, *Basic Facts*.

77. California Legislative Analysts Office. *Proposition 36: Drug Treatment Program. Initiative Statute*. Available at www.lao.ca.gov/initiatives/2000/36_11_2000.

78. Wren, Christopher S. (April 21, 1999) "Arizona Finds Cost Savings in Treating Drug Offenders." *New York Times*.

79. Ibid.

80. Arizona Supreme Court, Administrative Office of the Court, Adult Probation Services Division" (November 2001) *Drug Treatment and Education Fund, Annual Report FY 1999*. Phoenix.

81. Ibid.

NOTES TO CHAPTER 4

1. New York Police Department (NYPD) (2004) *CompStat*. Available at www.nyc.gov/html/nypd/pdf/chfdept/cscity.pdf. Since NYPD CompStat numbers go through 2003, they are used here for the most recent statistics available for crime in New York City. However, in the rest of this chapter, 2001 numbers will be used for national and other city comparisons since they are the most recent data available at this writing.

2. Federal Bureau of Investigation (FBI) (1993–2002) *Uniform Crime Reports*. Available at www.fbi.gov/ucr/ucr.htm.

3. NYPD, *CompStat*.

4. See Bratton, William, with Peter Knobler (1998) *Turnaround: How America's Top Cop Reversed the Crime Epidemic.* New York: Random House; Kelling, George L., and Catherine M. Coles (1996) *Fixing Broken Windows: Restoring Order and Reducing Crime in Our Communities.* New York: Simon and Schuster; and Silverman, Eli B. (1999) *NYPD Battles Crime: Innovative Strategies in Policing.* Boston: Northeastern University Press.

5. See Curtis, Richard (1998) "The Improbable Transformation of Inner-City Neighborhoods: Crime, Violence, Drugs and Youth in the 1990's." *Journal of Criminal Law and Criminology* 88, pp. 1233–1276.

6. See Karmen, Andrew (2001) *New York Murder Mystery: The True Story behind the Crime Crash of the 1990s.* New York: New York University Press; and Fagan, Jeffrey, Franklin E. Zimring, and June Kim (1998) "Declining Homicide in New York City: A Tale of Two Trends." *Journal of Criminal Law and Criminology* 88(4), pp. 1277–1323.

7. See Eck, John, and Edward Maguire (2000) "An Economic Model of Recent Trends in Violence." In Alfred Blumstein and Joel Wallman (eds.) *The Crime Drop in America.* New York: Cambridge University Press.

8. Mauer, Marc (June 20, 2003) "Comparative International Rates of Incarceration: An Examination of Causes and Trends." Available at www.sentencingproject.org/pdfs/pub9036.pdf.

9. Pastore, Ann L., and Kathleen Maguire (eds.) (2003) *Sourcebook of Criminal Justice Statistics.* Table 6.27. Available at www.albany.edu/sourcebook/1995/pdf/t627.pdf.

10. Department of Justice (1995) "State and Federal Prisons Report Record Growth during Last 12 Months." Press release, December 3; and Paige, Harrison M., and Allen J. Beck (2003) *Prisoners in 2002.* Washington, D.C.: U.S. Department of Justice, Office of Justice Programs, Bureau of Justice Statistics. Available at www.ojp.usdoj.gov/bjs/pub/press/pam95.pr.

11. Bauer, Lynn, and Steven D. Owens (2004) *Justice Expenditure and Employment in the United States, 2001.* Washington, D.C.: U.S. Department of Justice, Office of Justice Programs, Bureau of Justice Statistics.

12. See Block, Michael K. (1997) "Supply Side Imprisonment Policy." In *Two Views on Imprisonment Policies. Presentations from the 1996 Annual Research and Evaluation Conference in Washington, DC.* Washington, D.C.: Office of Justice Programs, National Institute of Justice; Clear, Todd (1996) "Backfire: When Incarceration Increases Crime." *Journal of the Oklahoma Criminal Justice Research Consortium* 3, pp. 7–17; Mauer, Marc (1999) *Race to Incarcerate.* New York: New Press; Petersilia, Joan (1999) "Parole and Prisoner Reentry in the United States." In Michael Tonry and Joan Petersilia (eds.) *Prisons.* Chicago: University of Chicago Press; Tonry, Michael H. (1995) *Malign Neglect: Race, Crime and Punishment in America.* New York: Oxford University Press; Zimring, Franklin E., and Gordon Hawkins (1995) *Incapacitation: Penal Confinement and the Restraint of Crime.*

Studies in Crime and Public Policy. New York: Oxford University Press; and Zimring, Franklin E., and Gordon Hawkins (1997) *Crime Is Not the Problem: Lethal Violence in America.* New York: Oxford University Press.

13. For the purposes of this analysis, the crime decline measures to be used will be the official numbers from the FBI's Uniform Crime Reporting system. Although the measures from the *National Crime Victimization Survey* are likely a more accurate portrait of crime in America, these victimization studies do not exist at the city level. Since much of this chapter involves comparing national and local crime reduction trends, the only way to do this uniformly is to use the FBI *Uniform Crime Report* numbers for both New York City and the rest of the country.

14. See Bennet, William J., John J. DiIulio, and John P. Waters (1996) *Body Count: Moral Poverty . . . and How to Win America's War against Crime and Drugs.* New York: Simon and Schuster; and Block, "Supply Side Imprisonment Policy."

15. Spelman, William (2000) "The Limited Importance of Prison Expansion." In Alfred Blumstein and Joel Wallman (eds.) *The Crime Drop in America.* New York: Cambridge University Press.

16. Firestone, David (June 9, 2001) "US Figures Show Prison Population Is Now Stabilizing," *New York Times.*

17. Federal Bureau of Investigation (FBI) (1988–1992) *Uniform Crime Reports.* Available at www.fbi.gov/ucr/ucr/htm.

18. Bureau of Justice Statistics *Key Crime and Justice Facts at a Glance.* Available at www.ojp.usdoj.gov/bjs/glance.htm.

19. The 1994 Crime Bill appropriated $8.8 billion for the hiring of 100,000 police officers and appropriated $9.7 billion for new prison construction (U.S. Department of Justice, October 24, 1994).

20. Federal Bureau of Investigation (FBI) (1989–1993) *Uniform Crime Reports.* Available at www.fbi.gov/ucr/ucr.htm.

21. See Jacobson, Michael (2001) "From the 'Back' to the 'Front': The Changing Character of Punishment in New York City." in John Mollenkopf and Ken Emerson (eds.) *Rethinking the Urban Agenda: Reinvigorating the Liberal Tradition in New York City and Urban America.* New York: Century Foundation Press, p. 173.

22. Beck, Allen J. and Darrell K. Gilliard (1995) *Prisoners in 1994.* Washington, D.C.: U.S. Department of Justice, Office of Justice Programs, Bureau of Justice Statistics; and Harrison, Paige M., and Allen J. Beck (2002) *Prisoners in 2001.* Washington, D.C.: U.S. Department of Justice, Office of Justice Programs, Bureau of Justice Statistics.

23. State of New York Department of Correctional Services (2002) *Characteristics of Inmates Discharged 2000.* Albany: Division of Program Planning, Research and Evaluation.

24. New York State Division of Criminal Justice Services (DCJS). *Criminal*

Justice Indicators. Available at criminaljustice.state.ny.us/crimnet/ojsa/areastate/ areast.htm.

25. Beck and Gilliard, *Prisoners in 1994*; and Harrison, Paige M., and Allen J. Beck (2002). *Prisoners in 2001.* Washington, D.C.: U.S. Department of Justice, Office of Justice Programs, Bureau of Justice Statistics.

26. All city jail figures are in fiscal years (July–June), since calendar-year figures are unavailable.

27. *Mayor's Management Reports* (1993–2001). New York: Office of the Mayor, Office of Operations.

28. For a description of this system, see McGuire, Philip G. (2000) "The New York Police Department Compstat Process." In Victor Goldsmith, Philip G. McGuire, John H. Mollenkopf, and Timothy A. Ross (eds.) *Analyzing Crime Matters: Frontiers of Practice.* Thousand Oaks, CA: Sage Publications.

29. This initiative took effect in 1991. The Safe Streets/Safe City program raised revenue through increased property and personal income taxes to add police officers as well as provide funding for education and other criminal justice programs.

30. *Executive Budget of the City of New York* (New York Fiscal Years 1993–2001). New York: Office of the Mayor, Office of Management and Budget.

31. The NYPD records higher numbers of misdemeanor arrests than the New York State Division of Criminal Justice Services. Since all other arrest, indictment, and conviction data used in this chapter are from DCJS, its misdemeanor numbers will be used for uniformity. If the NYPD numbers were used, the increase in misdemeanor arrests would be even more telling than the trend based on the DCJS data.

32. DCJS, *Criminal Justice Indicators.*

33. New York City Criminal Justice Agency (1994) *Semi-Annual Report for the Second Half of 1993.* New York: Criminal Justice Agency.

34. Indictment figures include Supreme Court Informations (SCIs). An SCI is essentially an agreement by the defendant to skip the indictment stage and proceed directly to Supreme Court.

35. DCJS, *Criminal Justice Indicators.*

36. New York City Department of Correction, Population Research Unit (1999). Personal correspondence.

37. *Mayor's Management Reports.*

38. New York City Department of Correction, Population Research Unit, personal correspondence.

39. *Mayor's Management Reports.*

40. New York City Department of Correction, Population Research Unit, personal correspondence.

41. In addition to the population reduction from the new mix of felony and

misdemeanor cases, the city has shrunk its state-ready and parole-violator population. The changing nature of arrests contributed significantly to the decline, but these other factors contributed to the drop in population as well.

42. DCJS, *Criminal Justice Indicators.*

43. Ibid.

44. Beck and Gilliard, *Prisoners in 1994;* and Harrison and Beck, *Prisoners in 2001.*

45. DCJS, *Criminal Justice Indicators.*

46. State of New York Department of Correctional Services (1999) *Characteristics of Inmates Discharged 1997.* Albany: Division of Program Planning, Research and Evaluation.

47. All length-of-stay figures are from the New York State Department of Correction.

48. DCJS, *Criminal Justice Indicators.*

49. San Diego Police Department Web site. *San Diego Historical Crime Actuals, 1950–2003.* Available at www.sannet.gov/police/pdf/ucractuals.pdf.

50. Butterfield, Fox (March 4, 2000). "Cities Reduce Crime and Conflict without New York Style Hardball." *New York Times,* p. A1.

51. Ibid.

52. Crime Analysis Unit, San Diego Police Department, June 18, 2004. Data was sent by the Department to the author per request.

53. Office of the Attorney General, State of California, Department of Justice, Criminal Justice Statistics Center, 2004 Available at justice.hdcdojnet.state .ca.us/cjsc_stats/prof02/index.htm.

54. Langan, Patrick A., and Jondi M. Brown (January 1997) *Felony Sentences in State Courts, 1994.* Washington D.C.: U.S. Department of Justice, Office of Justice Programs, Bureau of Justice Statistics; and Durose, Matthew R., and Patrick A. Langan (June 2003) *Felony Sentences in State Courts, 2000.* Washington D.C.: U.S. Department of Justice, Office of Justice Programs, Bureau of Justice Statistics.

55. U.S. Department of Justice, Office of Justice Programs, Bureau of Justice Statistics (June 19, 2004) *Crime and Justice Data Online: Crime Trends.* Available at bjsdata.ojp.usdoj.gov/dataonline/Search/Crime/Crime.cfm.

56. National Governors Association (NGA) and the National Association of State Budget Officers (NASBO) (June 2003) *The Fiscal Survey of States.* Washington D.C.

57. Gainsborough, Jenni, and Marc Mauer (2000) *Diminishing Returns: Crime and Incarceration in the 1990's.* Washington, D.C.: The Sentencing Project.

58. Spelman, William (2000) "What Recent Studies Do (and Don't) Tell Us about Imprisonment and Crime." In Michael Tonry (ed.) (2000) *Crime and Justice: A Review of Research.* Vol. 27. Chicago: University of Chicago Press, p. 481.

NOTES TO CHAPTER 5

1. Hughes, Timothy A., Doris James Wilson, and Allen J. Beck (2001) *Trends in State Parole, 1990–2000.* Washington, D.C.: U.S. Department of Justice, Office of Justice Programs, Bureau of Justice Statistics.

2. Zimring, Franklin E., and Gordon Hawkins (1995) *Incapacitation: Penal Confinement and the Restraint of Crime.* New York: Oxford University Press, p. 7.

3. See Simon, Jonathan (1993) *Poor Discipline: Parole and the Social Control of the Underclass, 1890–1990.* Chicago: University of Chicago Press; Rothman, David J. (1971) *The Discovery of the Asylum: Social Order and Disorder in the New Republic.* Boston: Little, Brown; and Rothman, David J. (1980) *Conscience and Convenience: The Asylum and Its Alternatives in Progressive America.* Boston: Little, Brown.

4. Friedman, Lawrence M. (1993) *Crime and Punishment in American History.* New York: Basic Books, pp. 304–305.

5. Glaze, Lauren E. (2003) *Probation and Parole in the United States, 2002.* Washington, D.C.: U.S. Department of Justice, Office of Justice Programs, Bureau of Justice Statistics.

6. Ibid.

7. U.S. Department of Justice, Office of Justice Programs, Bureau of Justice Statistics, *Reentry Trends in the U.S.: Releases from State Prison.* Available at www.ojp.usdoj.gov/bjs/reentry/releases.htm.

8. Travis, Jeremy, and Sarah Lawrence (2002) *Beyond the Prison Gates: The State of Parole in America.* Washington, D.C.: The Urban Institute, Washington, D.C.

9. Ibid.

10. Ibid.; and Glaze, *Probation and Parole in the United States, 2002.*

11. Glaze, *Probation and Parole in the United States, 2002.*

12. Ibid.

13. California budget and "total felons under supervision" figures are from *California Department of Correction Facts, Third Quarter 2002,* available at www.cdc.state.us/Factsht.htm. Mississippi budget and "total felons under supervision" figures are from *Mississippi Department of Corrections Monthly Fact Sheet,* and the budget figures are from *Mississippi Department of Corrections Schedule of Costs by Category,* available at www.mdoc.state.ms.us. The total figures for California include prisoners and parolees, and the Mississippi figures include prisoners, parolees, and probationers.

14. Travis and Lawrence, *Beyond the Prison Gates,* p. 18.

15. Hughes, Wilson, and Beck, *Trends in State Parole.*

16. If instead of having parole violators make up 70% of its prison admissions in 2001 it had Texas's percentage of 29%, there would be 52,000 fewer parole violators entering California prisons. At an average length of stay of 160

days, this translates into almost 22,800 beds (see California Department of Corrections [2001] *California Prisoners and Parolees, 2001.* Sacramento: Office of Correctional Planning). At an average cost of $30,000 per bed, this is a total cost of $684 million annually. Since this is a "fully loaded" cost, that is, it includes a variety of fixed or relatively fixed costs such as upper-level management and power, the actual budget savings from a reduction of this size would be somewhat less than this figure.

17. Calculated by removing California's approximately 89,000 parole violators in 2001 from the national number of 215,450 and dividing that by the national number of state prison admissions in 2001, 601,270 less California's prison admissions of 127,328.

18. Harrison, Paige M., and Jennifer C. Karberg (May 2004) *Prison and Jail Inmates Midyear 2003.* Washington, D.C.: U.S. Department of Justice, Office of Justice Programs, Bureau of Justice Statistics.

19. Travis and Lawrence, *Beyond the Prison Gates.*

20. Langan, Patrick A., and David J. Levin (2002) *Recidivism of Prisoners Released in 1994.* Washington, D.C.: Department of Justice, Office of Justice Programs, Bureau of Justice Statistics.

21. Personal communication with Michael Eisenberg of the Texas Criminal Justice Policy Council, September 3, 2002. It is important to note here that the data from the Texas Criminal Justice Policy Council on technical parole violators is different from the BJS data. According to the Texas Criminal Justice Policy Council (the official statistics-gathering agency for corrections in Texas until it was disbanded in 2003), there were closer to 2,400 technical parole violators admitted to prison in 2001 as opposed to the more than 13,000 shown by BJS. Since I could not reconcile these numbers, for the purpose of national comparisons I use the BJS numbers, but to illustrate trends internal to Texas over time I rely on the numbers from the staff at the Texas Criminal Justice Policy Council.

22. Harrison, Paige M., and Allen J. Beck (2003) *Prisoners in 2002.* Washington, D.C.: U.S. Department of Justice, Office of Justice Programs, Bureau of Justice Statistics.

23. Bonczar, Thomas P., and Tracy L. Snell (2003) *Capital Punishment 2002.* Washington, D.C.: U.S. Department of Justice, Office of Justice Programs, Bureau of Justice Statistics.

24. Personal communication with Michael Eisenberg.

25. Hughes, Wilson, and Beck, *Trends in State Parole.*

26. Petersilia, Joan (1999) "Parole and Prisoner Reentry in the United States." In Michael Tonry and Joan Petersilia (eds.) (1999) *Prisons.* Chicago: University of Chicago Press, p. 501.

27. Ibid., p. 507.

28. Ibid.

29. Currie, Elliot (1998) *Crime and Punishment in America.* New York: Henry Holt & Co., p. 52.

30. Feeley, Malcolm, and Jonathan Simon (1992) "The New Penology: Notes on the Emerging Strategy of Corrections and Its Implications." *Criminology* 30, pp. 449–474.

31. Simon, Jonathan (1993) *Poor Discipline: Parole and the Social Control of the Underclass, 1890–1990,* Chicago: University of Chicago Press, p. 201.

32. Garland, David (2001) *The Culture of Control: Crime and Social Order in Contemporary Society.* Chicago: University of Chicago Press, p. 192.

33. Rhine, Edward, William Smith, and Ronald Jackson (1991) *Paroling Authorities: Recent History and Current Practices.* Laurel, MD: American Correctional Association.

34. Holt, Norman (1998) "The Current State of Parole in America." In Joan Petersilia (ed.) (1998) *Community Corrections: Probation, Parole, and Intermediate Sanctions.* New York: Oxford University Press, pp. 28–41.

35. Simon, *Poor Discipline,* p. 193.

36. Lynch, Mona (1998) "Waste Managers? The New Penology, Crime Fighting, and Parole Agent Identity." *Law and Society Review* 32, pp. 839–869.

37. Blumstein, Alfred, and Allen J. Beck (2004) "Reentry as a Transient State between Liberty and Recommitment." In Travis, Jeremy, and Christy Visher (eds.) (2005 forthcoming) *Prisoner Reentry and Public Safety in America.* New York: Cambridge University Press.

38. Ibid.

39. Travis, Jeremy (2001) "But They All Come Back: Rethinking Prisoner Reentry." Washington, D.C.: U.S. Department of Justice, Office of Justice Programs, National Institute of Justice.

40. See, for instance, many of the reports done by the Urban Institute on the issue of prisoner reentry. In addition, the Vera Institute of Justice now has a large technical assistance program that provides states with expertise in a number of areas, including prisoner reentry and parole.

41. Horn, Martin (2001) "Rethinking Sentencing." *Corrections Management Quarterly* 5, pp. 34–40.

42. Ibid., p. 36.

43. Ibid., p. 37.

44. Ibid.

45. Ibid., p. 36.

46. Petersilia, "Parole and Prisoner Reentry," pp. 479–530.

47. Ibid., pp. 515–516.

48. Petersilia, Joan (2003) *When Prisoners Come Home: Parole and Prisoner Reentry.* New York: Oxford University Press.

49. Personal communication with Martin Horn, August 31, 2002.

50. Travis, Jeremy (May 22, 2002) "Thoughts on the Future of Parole." Remarks delivered at the Vera Institute of Justice, New York.

51. Ibid.

52. Ibid.

53. See Nelson, Marta, and Jennifer Trone (2000) "Why Planning for Release Matters." New York: Vera Institute of Justice.

54. Travis, "Thoughts on the Future of Parole."

55. Ibid.

56. Austin, James (June 2001) "Prisoner Reentry: Current Trends, Practices and Issues." *Crime and Delinquency* 47(3).

57. The Legal Action Center (2004) *After Prison: Roadblocks to Reentry, A Report on State Legal Barriers Facing People with Criminal Records.* New York.

NOTES TO CHAPTER 6

1. Interview with Dan Wilhelm, Director of the Vera Institute of Justice's State Sentencing and Corrections Program, conducted on August 5, 2003.

2. Harrison, Paige M., and Allen J. Beck (2002) *Prisoners in 2001.* Washington, D.C.: U.S. Department of Justice, Office of Justice Programs, Bureau of Justice Statistics, p. 5.

3. Martin, John, and Tim Kalish (October 2, 2002) "Governor Says State Committed to Helping Leflore Co. Economy." *Greenwood Commonwealth.* Available at www.zwire.com/site/news.

4. *Historical Trends: 1982–2002.* Sacramento: California Department of Corrections Offender Information Services Branch, Data Analysis Unit.

5. Hughes, Timothy A., Doris James Wilson, and Allen J. Beck (2001) *Trends in State Parole, 1990–2000.* Washington, D.C.: U.S. Department of Justice, Office of Justice Programs, Bureau of Justice Statistics; and Bureau of Justice Statistics, National Prisoner Statistics.

6. Ibid.

7. See McDonald, Douglas C., Elizabeth Fournier, and Malcolm Russell-Einhorn (1998) *Private Prisons in the United States: An Assessment of Current Practice.* Cambridge, MA: Abt Associates Inc.; and Austin, James, and Garry Coventry (2001) *Emerging Issues on Privatized Prisons.* Washington, D.C.: U.S. Department of Justice, Office of Justice Programs, Bureau of Justice Statistics.

8. See, for example, Aos, Steve, Polly Phipps, Robert Barnoski, and Roxanne Lieb (2001) *The Comparative Costs and Benefits of Programs to Reduce Crime.* Seattle: Washington State Institute for Public Policy.

9. See, for example, Buck, Maria (2000) *Getting Back to Work: Employment Programs for Ex-Offenders.* Philadelphia: Public Private Ventures.

10. Sullivan, Eileen, Milton Mino, Katherine Nelson, and Jill Pope (2002)

Families as a Resource in Recovery from Drug Abuse: An Evaluation of La Bodega de la Familia. New York: Vera Institute of Justice.

11. There is quite a bit of controversy over the meaning of "technical" parole violators in California. While there is no disagreement that these are parolees who are returned to prison with no new conviction charges, CDOC has long claimed that many of these violations actually involved new crimes but were "disposed" as technical violations, since it is easier and faster to send a parolee back to prison for a technical violation than to go through the process of trying a new case. In fact, Jeremy Travis of the Urban Institute conducted a preliminary analysis of CDOC data that showed as many as 47,000 of the technical violations also had new arrests; see Travis, Jeremy (2003) *Parole in California, 1980–2000: Implications for Reform.* Washington, D.C.: Urban Institute. Amazingly, there were 78 arrests of parolees for homicide, 524 for robbery, and 384 for rape and sexual assault where the case was disposed through a technical violation process. On its face, this seems highly suspect. It is one thing for a district attorney to dispose of a low-level misdemeanor offense through a technical violation process. It is quite another to dispose of a homicide through this same process, where the average length of stay for a technical violation is only slightly more than four months. Clearly, more work needs to be done to sort out the "pure technical" violations from ones that involve new arrests. The state needs to investigate whether or how alleged homicide charges are disposed through the parole violation process.

12. California Department of Corrections (2003) *Historical Trends: 1982–2002.* Sacramento: Offender Information Services Branch, Data Analysis Unit.

13. California Youth and Adult Correctional Agency, Department of Corrections (2003) *California Prisoners and Parolees, 2002.* Sacramento: Office of Correctional Planning, Offender Information Services Branch, Data Analysis Unit, Table 9.

14. California Department of Finance (January 2004) *Governor's Budget, 2004–2005.* Sacramento.

15. Ibid.

16. Morgante, Michelle (June 15, 2004) "More Winning Parole under Schwarzenegger." *Associated Press.* Available at customwire.ap.org/dynamic/stories/S/SCHWARZENEGGER_PAROLE?SITE=APWEB&SECTION=HOME&TEMPLATE=DEFAULT.

17. California Campaign for New Drug Policies, Proposition 36 Quick Facts, 2004. Available at www.drugreform.org/prop36/results.tpl.

18. Baldassare, Mark (2003) *PPIC Statewide Survey: Special Survey on the California State Budget.* San Francisco: Public Policy Institute of California.

19. Broder, John M. (July 2, 2003) "As California Borrows Time, Other States Adopt Short Term Budgets." *Los Angeles Times.* Available at www.nytimes.com/2003/07/02/national/02STAT.html?pagewanted=print&position.

20. National Governors Association (NGA) and the National Association of State Budget Officers (NASBO) (2003) *The Fiscal Survey of States*. Washington, D.C.

21. Ibid., Table A-6, p. 31.

22. Ibid., Table A-5, p. 29.

23. Ibid., Table A-2, p. 22.

24. Ibid., Table A-8, pp. 35–40, and Table 5, p. 6.

25. Broder, "California Borrows Time."

26. Morain, Dan, and Jennifer Warren (January 22, 2003) "Battle Looms over Prison Spending in State Budget." *Los Angeles Times*.

27. Legislative Analyst's Office (May 17, 2004) *Overview of the 2004–2005 May Revision*. Sacramento, California. Available at www.lao.ca.gov/2004/may_revision/011704_may_revision.pdf.

28. Morain and Warren, "Battle Looms over Prison Spending."

29. California Youth and Adult Correctional Agency, *California Prisoners and Parolees 2001*, Table 42.

30. Ibid.

31. Travis, *Parole in California*, p. 8. The Little Hoover Commission is an independent state oversight agency that has as its mission the investigation of state government operations and promoting the efficient delivery of government services.

32. Ibid., p. 9.

33. California Youth and Adult Correctional Agency, *California Prisoners and Parolees 2001*, Table 42.

34. Travis, *Parole in California*, p. 9.

35. California Youth and Adult Correctional Agency, *California Prisoners and Parolees 2001*, Table 42.

36. Calculation is made by taking the difference of the average lengths of stay for the drug use and possession and miscellaneous crimes, or 134.2 days and 60 days—a savings of 74.2 days. These savings are multiplied by all 24,085 cases and divided by 365 to calculate the number of annual bed savings. For this category, that savings is 4,896 beds. The same methodology applies to the 11,556 purely technical violators who have an average length of stay of 128.1 days. This bed savings equals 2,156 beds, for a total bed savings of 7,052. An annual cost per prison bed of $27,000 is used to calculate savings. This includes the $26,690 per bed that CDOC reports on its Web site, plus a $310 per prisoner estimate for additional costs not reflected in the corrections budget, such as hospital in-patient health care for prisoners.

37. Calculation derived by reducing by 10% the number of parolees returned for new convictions (16,011) and conservatively assuming a two-year length of stay for these parolees sentenced for another felony; reducing the total number of those sent back to prison for technical violations who were allegedly

engaged in criminal behavior (47,151) by 10%, and using the lengths of stay found in Table 42 of the CDOC *Prisoners and Parolees in 2001* report (except for those categories for which I already assumed a decreased length in the first scenario—I used the newly reduced length of stays to avoid double counting the savings); and reducing the 11,556 purely technical violators by 50%, and using the newly assumed 60-day length of stay. The per-bed savings remains at $27,000.

38. Travis, Jeremy (2003) "Reflections on Parole: Meeting the Challenges of Today." Keynote speech for the Association of Paroling Authorities International Annual Conference, St. Louis, Missouri.

39. Petersilia, Joan (2003) *When Prisoners Come Home: Parole and Prisoner Reentry.* New York: Oxford University Press.

40. Austin, James (2001) "Prisoner Reentry: Current Trends, Practices and Issues." *Crime and Delinquency* 47(3), pp. 314–334.

41. Travis, "Reflections on Parole," p. 11.

42. Horn, Martin (2001) "Rethinking Sentencing." *Corrections Management Quarterly* 5.

43. California Department of Corrections (2004) *Spring 2004 Population Projections.* Sacramento, Table C, p. 4.

44. California Department of Finance (May 2004) *Governor's Budget May Revision, 2004–2005.* Sacramento. Available at www.dof.ca.gov/HTML/BUD_DOCS/May_Revision_04_www.pdf.

45. Warren, Jennifer (January 21, 2004) "California Guards Tell of Retaliation for Informing; Whistle-Blowers Testify before Senate Panel on How Their Reports of Misconduct at State Prisons Are Received." *Los Angeles Times,* p. B1.

46. From *The Field Poll* (June 10, 2004). Available at field.com/fieldpoll online/subscribers/RLS2121.pdf.

47. Austin, James, Eric Cadora, and Michael Jacobson (2003) *Building Bridges: From Conviction to Employment.* New York: Council of State Governments, Criminal Justice Programs.

48. Harrison and Beck, *Prisoners in 2002.*

49. Ibid.

50. Ibid.

51. Ditton, Paula M., and Doris James Wilson (1999) *Truth in Sentencing in State Prisons.* Washington, D.C.: U.S. Department of Justice, Office of Justice Programs, Bureau of Justice Statistics.

52. Austin, Cadora, and Jacobson, *Building Bridges.*

53. Ibid.

54. Glaze, Lauren E. (2003) *Probation and Parole in the United States, 2002.* Washington, D.C.: U.S. Department of Justice, Office of Justice Programs, Bureau of Justice Statistics.

55. Austin, Cadora, and Jacobson, *Building Bridges.*

56. Ibid.

57. Testimony of Governor John Rowland to Joint Appropriations and Judiciary Committees (April 3, 2003). Hartford, Connecticut.

58. Herszenhom, David (December 22, 2002) "How Did a Rich State Get So Poor?" *New York Times.*

59. Haigh, Susan (June 6, 2003) "State's Spending Habits Changing as Crisis Deepens." *New Haven Register.* Available at www.newhavenregister.com/site/news.cfm?newsid=9294688&BRD=1281&PAG=461&dept_id=517515&rfi=6.

60. NGA and NASBO, *Fiscal Survey of States,* Tables 5 and 6, pp. 6–7.

61. Ibid., Table A-5, p. 29.

62. Herszenhom, "How Did a Rich State Get So Poor?"

63. NGA and NASBO (April 2004) *The Fiscal Survey of States,* Washington, D.C.

64. In 2002, Michael Thompson asked James Austin and me to provide technical assistance, through CSG, to states that were eventually selected as demonstration sites. The selected states wound up being Connecticut and Louisiana. In both states, Dr. Austin already had professional relationships with the corrections agencies and was well known as a respected and reliable consultant who worked with prisons on classification systems, population projections, and information systems. His reputation not only made a huge difference in gaining access to data in these states but also lent a huge amount of legitimacy to the project.

65. Austin, Cadora, and Jacobson, *Building Bridges.*

66. Ibid., pp. 5–6.

67. The cost calculations were done using a figure of $50 a day per prison bed. This compares to the DOC's figure of $75 a day. A far lower figure was used both to be conservative and realistic and to recognize that prison systems don't save the average cost per bed when there are marginal reductions in beds. Since the average costs also include a variety of fixed costs that don't change with marginal reductions, such as the cost of the Commissioner and Deputy Commissioners and a variety of other support services, these costs should not be included in what "true" budget savings would result from reductions in population.

68. Cowan, Allison Leigh (August 1, 2003) "Plan to Transfer More Inmates Draws Criticism in Connecticut." *New York Times.* Available at www.nytimes.com/2003/08/01/nyregion/01CONN.html?pagewanted=print&position=.

69. There are a host of national models of all of these kinds of programs. The Center for Employment Opportunities in New York City and the Safer Foundation in Chicago are both well known employment readiness, training, and placement programs. Neighborhood Justice is another program in New York City, a recent recipient of a Harvard Innovation award, that works with parolees and their families on addiction issues.

70. Harrison, Paige M., and Allen J. Beck (2003) *Prisoners in 2002.* Washington, D.C.: U.S. Department of Justice, Office of Justice Programs, Bureau of Justice Statistics.

71. Ibid.

72. Ibid.

73. Hughes, Wilson, and Beck, *Trends in State Parole*; and Bureau of Justice Statistics, National Prisoner Statistics, 2001.

74. Ibid.

75. Travis, Jeremy, and Sarah Lawrence (2002) *Beyond the Prison Gates: The State of Parole in America.* Washington, D.C.: The Urban Institute, p. 19.

76. Louisiana Department of Public Safety and Corrections. "Incarceration Only: Admissions and Releases Comparison 1994–2002." Available at www .corrections.state.la.us./Statistics/BB.htm.

77. Naro, Wendy (2002) "Ten Year Adult Secure Population Projection 2002–2012." Report prepared for the Louisiana Department of Public Safety and Corrections, the Institute on Crime Justice and Corrections, George Washington University, Washington, D.C., Table 2, p. 11. Since this study uses a different methodology than the one used to collect the national BJS statistics, these numbers are somewhat different than the BJS numbers. For purposes of analyzing detailed prison, probation, and parole numbers over time and in a consistent fashion, these data will be used.

78. Ibid.

79. Ibid.

80. Ibid., Table 6, p. 24. The average lengths of stay are calculated by taking the numbers of different categories of technical violator and waiver cases and their associated lengths of stay, found on Table 6, and aggregating them by summing up the total months served for all technical and waiver violators and dividing by the total number of technical and waiver violators.

81. Ibid., Table 6, p. 25.

82. Ibid., Table 6, p. 24.

83. Proctor, Bernadette D., and Joseph Dalaker (2002) *Poverty in the United States: 2001.* Washington, D.C.: U.S. Department of Commerce, U.S. Census Bureau, Table 4, p. 10. Available at www.census.gov/prod/2002pubs/ p60-219.pdf.

84. U.S. Bureau of the Census. *State and County QuickFacts: Louisiana.* Available at quickfacts.census.gov/qfd/states/22000.html.

85. State legislative and governor affiliation available at www.statescape .com/Resources/Resources.asp.

86. Naro, "Ten Year Adult Secure Population Projection."

87. Ibid.

88. Gill, James (August 1, 2003) "Honesty Makes a Shaky Campaign Plat-

form." *Times Picayune.* Available at www.nola.com/news/t-p/gill/index.ssf?/base/news-01/1059715665301460.xml.

89. The $23-per-day figure raises a host of other issues that revolve around corrections practice: What kind of environment, services, and security can be provided for $8,400 annually? This is 43% less than the $12,000 annual cost of a Louisiana Department of Correction prison bed, which in itself is among the lowest per-prisoner spending in the United States. It is unimaginable that anything above and beyond a cell, some security, and (hopefully) three meals a day is provided by the sheriffs at $23 a day—especially since this figure has some level of "profit" built into it.

90. Louisiana Department of Public Safety (2003) "Sheriffs Payments Projection FY 2002–2003." Available at www.corrections.state.la.us./Statistics/BB.htm.

91. Figures supplied by the Louisiana Office of Planning and Budget, August 5, 2003.

92. NGA and NASBO, *Fiscal Survey of States.*

93. National Conference of State Legislators (NCSL) (2003) *State Budget and Tax Actions 2003.* Washington, D.C. Available at www.ncsl.org/programs/fiscal/presbta03.htm.

94. NGA and NASBO (April 2004) *The Fiscal Survey of States.* Washington, D.C.

95. See Petersilia, *When Prisoners Come Home.* Petersilia writes that instruments that try to predict who will recidivate and who will not are right about 70% of the time (p. 190).

96. NCSL, *State Budget and Tax Actions 2003.*

97. Barrouquere, Brett (June 3, 2003) "Juvenile Justice Reform Approved." *2theadvocate.* Available at 2theadvocate.com/ns-search/stories/060303/leg_juvenile001.shtml?NS-search-set=/3f327/aaaa045353279b8&NS-doc-offste=O&.

98. Personal interview with Senator Don Cravins, conducted on March 27, 2004.

99. Staff Bayoubuzz (May 24, 2004) "Louisiana Governor Blanco Makes Three Appointments to Department of Public Safety and Corrections." Available at www.bayoubuzz.com/articles.aspx?aid=1680.

NOTES TO CHAPTER 7

1. "Justice Kennedy against Minimum Prison Terms" (August 11, 2003) CNN.com Law Center. Available at www.cnn.com/2003/LAW/08/11/prison.terms.ap.

2. Greenhouse, Linda (June 24, 2004) "High Court Justice Supports Bar

Plan to Ease Sentencing." *New York Times.* Available at www.nytimes.com/ 2004/06/24/politics/24sentence.html.

3. Harrison, Paige M., and Allen J. Beck (2003) *Prisoners in 2002.* Washington, D.C.: U.S. Department of Justice, Office of Justice Programs, Bureau of Justice Statistics.

4. Bonczar, Thomas P., and Allen J. Beck (2003) *Lifetime Likelihood of Going to State or Federal Prison.* Washington, D.C.: U.S. Department of Justice, Office of Justice Programs, Bureau of Justice Statistics.

5. Cullen, Francis T., Bonnie S. Fischer, and Brandon Applegate (2000) "Public Opinion about Punishment and Corrections." In Michael Tonry (ed.) (2000) *Crime and Justice: A Review of the Research.* Vol. 27. Chicago: University of Chicago Press.

6. Campbell, Robin (2003) *Dollars and Sentences.* New York: Vera Institute of Justice and the National Conference of State Legislatures, p. 12.

7. Ibid.

8. Andrews, Tara, and Vincent Shiraldi (June 21, 2003) "GOP Leads the Way on Drug Policy Reform." *Baltimore Sun.* Available at www.justicepolicy .org/article.php?id=209.

9. This is precisely the method employed by the Vera Institute of Justice's State Sentencing and Corrections program. The program, which assists states with both diagnosing their correctional systems and helping to create strategies and plans for reform, employs a number of national "associates" who are current practitioners or legislators around the country. The theory of the program is that, depending on the issues a state is confronting, Vera will deploy other active professionals who have faced many of the same issues and managed to successfully implement reform programs. Thus, if a state is considering creating a sentencing commission, Vera might send current sentencing commission directors, along with legislators from other states that have gone through the process of reform. This type of peer-to-peer consulting can provide both substantive and political momentum to a state struggling with correctional reform.

10. Personal interview with Senator Don Cravins, June 29, 2004.

11. Wacquant, Loic (2002) "Four Strategies to Cut Carceral Costs: On Managing Mass Imprisonment in the United States." *Studies in Political Economy* 18 (Spring), pp. 19–30.

12. Tonry, Michael (1996) *Sentencing Matters.* New York: Oxford University Press, p. 5.

Bibliography

American Civil Liberties Union (December 9, 2003) *A Question of Innocence.* Available at www.aclu.org/DeathPenalty/DeathPenalty.cfm?ID=93168c=65.

American Correctional Association's Web Site's Legislative Position statements. Available at www.corrections.com/aca/government.

Andrews, Tara, and Vincent Schiraldi (June 21, 2003) "GOP Leads the Way on Drug Policy Reform." *Baltimore Sun.* Available at www.justicepolicy.org/article.php?id=209.

Aos, Steve, Polly Phipps, Robert Barnoski, and Roxanne Lieb (2001) *The Comparative Costs and Benefits of Programs to Reduce Crime.* Seattle: Washington State Institute for Public Policy.

Arizona Supreme Court, Administrative Office of the Court, Adult Probation Services Division (November 2001) *Drug Treatment and Education Fund, Annual Report FY 1999.* Phoenix.

Austin, James (June 2001) "Prisoner Reentry: Current Trends, Practices and Issues." *Crime and Delinquency* 47(3).

Austin, James, and Garry Coventry (2001) *Emerging Issues on Privatized Prisons.* Washington, D.C.: U.S. Department of Justice, Office of Justice Programs, Bureau of Justice Assistance.

Austin, James, Eric Cadora, and Michael Jacobson (2003) *Building Bridges: From Conviction to Employment.* New York: Council of State Governments, Criminal Justice Programs.

Austin, James, John Clark, Patricia Hardyman, and D. Allen Henry (October 1999) "The Impact of 'Three Strikes and You're Out.'" *Punishment and Society* 1(2).

Baldassare, Mark (2003) *PPIC Statewide Survey: Special Survey on the California State Budget.* San Francisco: Public Policy Institute of California.

Barbee, Andrew, Lisa Carruth, and Michelle Munson (2002) *Adult and Juvenile Correctional Population Projections, FY 2002–2007.* Criminal Justice Policy Council, Austin, Texas.

Barrouquere, Brett (June 3, 2003) "Juvenile Justice Reform Approved." *2theadvocate.* Available at 2theadvocate.com/ns-search/stories/060303/leg_juvenile001.shtml?NS-search-set=/3f327/aaaa045353279b8&NS-doc-offste=O&.

Bauer, Lynn, and Steven D. Owens (2004) *Justice Expenditure and Employment in the United States, 2001.* Washington, D.C.: U.S. Department of Justice, Office of Justice Programs, Bureau of Justice Statistics.

Beck, Allen J. (2000) *Prisoners in 1999.* Washington, D.C.: U.S. Department of Justice, Office of Justice Programs, Bureau of Justice Statistics.

——— (April 2000) *State and Federal Prisoners Returning to the Community: Findings from the Bureau of Justice Statistics.* Presented at the First Re-Entry Initiative Cluster Meeting, Washington, D.C.

Beck, Allen J., and Darrell K. Gilliard (1995) *Prisoners in 1994.* Washington, D.C.: U.S. Department of Justice, Office of Justice Programs, Bureau of Justice Statistics.

Beck, Allen J., and Paige M. Harrison (2001) *Prisoners in 2000.* Washington, D.C.: Bureau of Justice Statistics, U.S. Department of Justice, Office of Justice Programs. Also Bureau of Justice Statistics Data online. *Violent Crime Totals.* Available at www.ojp.usdoj.gov/bjs.

Beck, Allen J., and Jennifer C. Karberg (2001) *Prison and Jail Inmates at Midyear 2000.* Washington, D.C.: U.S. Department of Justice, Office of Justice Programs, Bureau of Justice Statistics.

Beck, Allen, and Bernard Shipley (1989) *Recidivism of Prisoners Released in 1983.* Washington, D.C.: Bureau of Justice Statistics, U.S. Department of Justice, Office of Justice Programs.

Beck, Allen J., Jennifer C. Karberg, and Paige M. Harrison (2002) *Prison and Jail Inmates at Midyear, 2001.* Washington, D.C.: Bureau of Justice Statistics, U.S. Department of Justice, Office of Justice Programs.

Beckett, Katherine (1997) *Making Crime Pay: Law and Order in Contemporary American Politics.* New York: Oxford University Press.

Beckett, Katherine, and Bruce Western (1999) "How Unregulated Is the US Labor Market? The Penal System as a Labor Market Institution." *American Journal of Sociology* 104, pp. 1030–1060.

"Before Being Sentenced to Die, Killer Disrupts a Courtroom." *New York Times* (September 27, 1996), p. A16.

Bennet, William J., John J. DiIulio, and John P. Waters (1996) *Body Count: Moral Poverty . . . and How to Win America's War against Crime and Drugs.* New York: Simon and Schuster.

Block, Michael K. (1997) "Supply Side Imprisonment Policy." In *Two Views on Imprisonment Policies. Presentations from the 1996 Annual Research and Evaluation Conference in Washington, DC.* Washington, D.C.: Office of Justice Programs, National Institute of Justice.

Blumenstein, Alfred, and Allen J. Beck (2004) "Reentry as a Transient State between Liberty and Recommitment." In Jeremy Travis and Christy Visher (eds.) (2005 forthcoming) *Prisoner Reentry and Public Safety in America.* New York: Cambridge University Press.

Bonczar, Thomas P. (2003) *The Prevalence of Imprisonment in the U.S. Population, 1974–2001,* Washington, D.C.: U.S. Department of Justice, Office of Justice Programs, Bureau of Justice Statistics.

Bonczar, Thomas P., and Allen J. Beck (2003) *Lifetime Likelihood of Going to State or Federal Prison.* Washington, D.C.: U.S. Department of Justice, Office of Justice Programs, Bureau of Justice Statistics.

Bratton, William, with Peter Knobler (1998) *Turnaround: How America's Top Cop Reversed the Crime Epidemic.* New York: Random House.

Broder, John M. (July 2, 2003) "As California Borrows Time, Other States Adopt Short Term Budgets." *Los Angeles Times.* Available at www.nytimes.com/2003/07/02/national/02STAT.html?pagewanted=print&position.

——— (January 5, 2004) "Despite Signs of Economic Recovery States' Budgets Are Still Reeling." *New York Times.*

Buck, Maria (2000) *Getting Back to Work: Employment Programs for Ex-Offenders.* Philadelphia: Public Private Ventures.

Bureau of Justice Statistics. *Crime and Victim Statistics. Summary Findings.* Available at www.ojp.usdoj.gov/bjs/cvict.htm#summary.

——— (1999) *Expenditure and Employment Statistics. Selected Statistics.* Justice Expenditure and Employment Extracts. Available at www.ojp.usdoj.gov/bjs.

——— (2004) *Four Measures of Serious Violent Crime.* Available at www.ojp.usdoj.gov/bjs/glance/tables/4meastab.htm.

——— *Key Crime and Justice Facts at a Glance.* Available at www.ojp.usdoj.gov/bjs/glance.htm.

——— *Key Facts at a Glance: Correctional Populations. Number of Persons under Correctional Supervision.* Available at www.ojp.usdoj.gov/bjs/.

——— *National Prisoner Statistics, Data Series (NPS-1).* Available at www.ojp.usdoj.gov/bjs/abstract/cpusst.htm.

——— *Prison Statistics: Summary of Findings.* Available at www.ojp.usdoj.gov/bjs/prisons.htm.

——— *Probation and Parole Statistics, Summary of Findings.* Available at www.ojp.usdoj.gov/bjs/pandp.htm.

Butterfield, Fox (March 4, 2000) "Cities Reduce Crime and Conflict without New York Style Hardball." *New York Times,* p. A1.

——— (September 2, 2001) "States Ease Laws on Time in Prison." *New York Times.*

——— (November 10, 2003) "With Cash Tight, States Reassess Long Jail Terms." *New York Times.* Available at www.nytimes.com/2003/11/10/national/10PRIS.html?hp=8pagewanted=print&position=.

California Attorney General, State Department of Justice Web Site. Available at justice.hdcdojnet.state.ca.us/cjsc_stats/prof00/index.

California Campaign for New Drug Policies. *Basic Facts: Substance Abuse and Crime Prevention Act of 2000.* Available at www.drugreform.com.

California Department of Corrections (2001) *California Prisoners and Parolees 2001.* Sacramento: Office of Correctional Planning.

────── (March 14, 2002) "Recidivism Rates within One and Two Year Follow-up Periods for Felons Paroled to California Supervision." Sacramento: Office of Correctional Planning.

────── *Spring 2002 Population Projections, 2002–2007.* Available at www.cdc .state.ca.us/pdf/S02Pub.pdf.

────── (2003) *Historical Trends: 1982–2002.* Sacramento: Offender Information Services Branch, Data Analysis Unit.

────── (2003) *Spring 2003 Population Projections.* Sacramento.

California Department of Corrections Data Analysis Unit. *Historical Trends, 1979–1999* and *California Department of Corrections Facts.* Available at www .cdc.state.ca.us.

California Department of Corrections Facts, Third Quarter 2002. Available at www .cdc.state.us/Factsht.htm.

California Department of Corrections Web Site. Available at www.corr.ca.gov/ CDC/facts_figures.asp.

California Department of Finance (May 2004) *Governor's Budget May Revision, 2004–2005.* Sacramento. Available at www.dof.ca.gov/HTML/BUD_ DOCS/May_Revision_04_www.pdf.

California Legislative Analysts Office (2000) *Proposition 36: Drug Treatment Program. Initiative Statute.* Available at www.lao.ca.gov/initiatives/2000/36_ 11_2000.

California Youth and Adult Correctional Agency, Department of Corrections (2001) *California Prisoners and Parolees, 2001.* Sacramento: Office of Correctional Planning, Offender Information Services Branch, Data Analysis Unit.

Campbell, Robin (2003) *Dollars and Sentences.* New York: Vera Institute of Justice and the National Conference of State Legislatures.

Caplow, T., and J. Simon (1999) "Understanding Prison Policy and Population Trends." In M. Tonry and J. Petersilia (eds.) *Crime and Justice.* Vol. 26: *Prisons.* Chicago: University of Chicago Press.

Chancer, Lynn, and Pamela Donovan (1994) "A Mass Psychology of Punishment: Crime and the Futility of Rationally Based Approaches." *Social Justice* 21(3) (Fall).

Christie, Nils (1981) *Limits to Pain.* New York: Oxford University Press.

Clear, Todd R. (1994) *Harm in American Penology: Offenders, Victims and Their Communities.* Albany: State University of New York Press.

────── (1996) "Backfire: When Incarceration Increases Crime." *Journal of the Oklahoma Criminal Justice Research Consortium* 3, pp. 7–17.

Clear, Todd, and George Cole (2000) *American Corrections.* Belmont, CA: Wadsworth Publishing Co.

Clear, Todd, and Dina Rose (1999) *When Neighbors Go to Jail: Impact on Attitudes about Formal and Informal Social Control: Summary of a Presentation.* Washington, D.C.: U.S. Department of Justice, Office of Justice Programs, National Institute of Justice.

Clear, Todd, Dina Rose, and Judith Ryder (2000) *Drugs, Incarceration and Neighborhood Life: The Impact of Reintegrating Offenders into the Community.* Washington, D.C.: U.S. Department of Justice, Office of Justice Programs, National Institute of Justice.

Corbett, Ronald P. Jr., Bernard L. Fitzgerald, and James Jorday (1998) "Boston's Operation Nightlight: An Emerging Model for Police-Probation Partnerships." In Joan Petersilia (ed.) (1998) *Community Corrections: Probation Parole and Intermediate Sanctions.* New York: Oxford University Press.

Cowan, Allison Leigh (August 1, 2003) "Plan to Transfer More Inmates Draws Criticism in Connecticut." *New York Times.* Available at www.nytimes.com /2003/08/01/nyregion/01CONN.html?pagewanted=print&position=.

Criminal Justice Estimating Conference (2003) Tallahassee: Florida State Legislature. Available at www.state.fl.us/edr/Conferences/Criminal_Justice/ cj2.pdf.

Cullen, Francis T., Bonnie S. Fischer, and Brandon Applegate (2000) "Public Opinion about Punishment and Corrections." In Michael Tonry (ed.) (2000) *Crime and Justice: A Review of the Research.* Vol. 27. Chicago: University of Chicago Press.

Cullen, F. T., and P. Gendreau (2000). "Assessing Correctional Rehabilitation: Policy, Practice, and Prospects." In J. Horney (ed.), *Criminal Justice 2000.* Vol. 4: *Policies, Processes, and Decisions of the Criminal Justice System* (pp. 109–175). Washington, D.C.: National Institute of Justice, U.S. Department of Justice.

Currie, Elliot (1998) *Crime and Punishment in America.* New York: Henry Holt & Co.

Curtis, Richard (1998) "The Improbable Transformation of Inner-City Neighborhoods: Crime, Violence, Drugs and Youth in the 1990's." *Journal of Criminal Law and Criminology* 88, pp. 1233–1276.

DeParle, Jason (October 8, 2001) "A Mass of Newly Laid-Off Workers Will Put Social Safety Net to the Test." *New York Times,* National Desk.

Department of Justice (1995) *State and Federal Prisons Report Record Growth during Last 12 Months.* Press release, December 3.

DiIulio, John (March 12, 1999) "Two Million Prisoners Are Enough," *Wall Street Journal,* A14.

Ditton, Paula, and Doris James Wilson (1999) *Truth in Sentencing in State Prisons.* Washington D.C.: U.S. Department of Justice, Office of Justice Programs, Bureau of Justice Statistics.

Dugan, Molly (July/August 2000) "Census Dollars Bring Bounty to Prison Towns." *Chicago Reporter.*

Durose, Matthew R., and Patrick A. Langan (June 2003) *Felony Sentences in State*

Courts, 2000. Washington, D.C.: U.S. Department of Justice, Office of Justice Programs, Bureau of Justice Statistics.

Echols, Alice (1989) *Daring to Be Bad: Radical Feminism in America, 1967–1975.* Minneapolis: University of Minnesota Press.

Eck, John, and Edward Maguire (2000) "An Economic Model of Recent Trends in Violence." In Alfred Blumstein and Joel Wallman (eds.) *The Crime Drop in America.* New York: Cambridge University Press.

Egan, Timothy (February 28, 1999) "War on Crack Retreats, Still Taking Prisoners." *New York Times,* p. A1.

Elkins, Mike, and Jide Olagundoye (2001) "The Prison Population in 2000: A Statistical Review." Home Office, London, England. Available at www.homeoffice.gov.uk/rds/pdfs/r154.pdf.

Executive Budget of the City of New York (New York Fiscal Years 1993–2001). New York: Office of the Mayor, Office of Management and Budget.

Fagan, Jeffrey, Franklin E. Zimring, and June Kim (1998) "Declining Homicide in New York City: A Tale of Two Trends." *Journal of Criminal Law and Criminology* 88(4), pp. 1277–1323.

Federal Bureau of Investigation (1988–2000) *Uniform Crime Reports.* Available at www.fbi.gov/ucr/ucr/htm.

Feeley, Malcolm, and Jonathan Simon (1992) "The New Penology: Notes on the Emerging Strategy of Corrections and Its Implications." *Criminology* 30, pp. 449–474.

Ferrell, David, and Jennifer Warren (November 13, 2000) "For Many, Plan to Help Addicts Touched Home." *Los Angeles Times.*

The Field Poll (2002) "Spending Cuts Preferred over Tax Increases to Reduce State Budget Deficit. Low Confidence in Governor and Legislature to Resolve Deficit Properly, Similar to Public Sentiment in 1993." Compiled December 28, 2001. San Francisco: Field Institute.

Fine, Michele, et al. (2002) "Changing Minds: The Impact of College in a Maximum Security Prison," The Graduate Center of the City of New York and Women in Prison at the Bedford Hills Correctional Facility.

Firestone, David (June 9, 2001) "US Figures Show Prison Population Is Now Stabilizing." *New York Times.*

Friedman, Lawrence M. (1993) *Crime and Punishment in American History.* New York: Basic Books.

Gabel, Katherine, and Denise Johnston (1997) *Children of Incarcerated Parents.* Lanham, MD: Lexington Books.

Gaes, Gerald G., Timothy J. Flanagen, Laurence L. Motiuk, and Lynn Stewart (1999) "Adult Correctional Treatment." In Joan Petersilia and Michael Tonry (eds.) (1999) *Prisons.* Chicago: University of Chicago Press.

Gainsborough, Jenni, and Marc Mauer (2000) *Diminishing Returns: Crime and Incarceration in the 1990's.* Washington, D.C.: The Sentencing Project.

Gallup Organization, Inc., The (2003) *The Gallup Poll.* Available at www.gallup .com/poll/topics/death_pen.asp.

Garland, David (1990) *Punishment and Modern Society: A Study in Social Theory.* Oxford: Clarendon Press.

——— (2001) *The Culture of Control: Crime and Social Order in Contemporary Society.* Chicago: University of Chicago Press.

——— (ed.) (2001) *Mass Imprisonment: Social Causes and Consequences.* New York: Sage.

Gendreau, Paul, and Robert Ross (1987) "Revivification of Rehabilitation: Evidence from the 1980's." *Justice Quarterly* 4(3), pp. 349–407.

Gendreau, Paul, Francis T. Cullen, and James Bonta (1998) "Intensive Rehabilitation Supervision: The Next Generation in Community Corrections?" In Joan Petersilia (ed.) (1998) *Community Corrections: Probation Parole and Intermediate Sanctions.* New York: Oxford University Press.

Gifford, Sidra Lea (February 2002) *Justice Expenditures and Employment in the United States, 1999.* Washington, D.C.: Bureau of Justice Statistics, U.S. Department of Justice, Office of Justice Programs.

Gill, James (August 1, 2003) "Honesty Makes a Shaky Campaign Platform." *Times Picayune.* Available at www.nola.com/news/t-p/gill/index.ssf?/ base/news-01/1059715665301460.xml.

Glaze, Lauren E. (2002) *Probation and Parole in the United States, 2001.* Washington, D.C.: U.S. Department of Justice, Office of Justice Programs, Bureau of Justice Statistics.

——— (2003) *Probation and Parole in the United States, 2002.* Washington, D.C.: U.S. Department of Justice, Office of Justice Programs, Bureau of Justice Statistics.

Greenberg, David (January 2001) "Novus Ordo Saeclorum? A Commentary on Downes, and on Beckett and Western." *Punishment and Society* 3(61), pp. 81–93.

Greene, Judith (2003) *Positive Trends in State-Level Sentencing and Corrections Policy.* Washington, D.C.: Families against Mandatory Minimums.

Greene, Judith, and Vincent Schiraldi (2002) *Cutting Correctly: New Prison Policies for Times of Fiscal Crisis.* Washington, D.C.: Center for Juvenile and Criminal Justice.

Greenhouse, Linda (June 24, 2004) "High Court Justice Supports Bar Plan to Ease Sentencing." *New York Times.* Available at www.nytimes.com/2004/ 06/24/politics/24sentence.html.

Greenwood, Peter W., Karyn E. Model, C. Peter Rydell, and James Chiesa (1996) *Diverting Children from a Life of Crime: Measuring Costs and Benefits.* Santa Monica, CA: Rand Corporation.

Haigh, Susan (July 6, 2003) "State's Spending Habits Changing as Crisis Deepens." *New Haven Register.* Available at www.newhavenregister.com/

site/news.cfm?newsid=9294688&BRD=1281&PAG=461&dept_id=517515 &rfi=6.

Harer, Miles D. (1994) *Recidivism among Federal Prison Releases in 1987: A Preliminary Report.* Federal Bureau of Prisons, Washington, D.C.

Harrison, Paige M., and Allen J. Beck (2002) *Prisoners in 2001.* Washington, D.C.: U.S. Department of Justice, Office of Justice Programs, Bureau of Justice Statistics.

——— (2003) *Prisoners in 2002.* Washington, D.C.: U.S. Department of Justice, Office of Justice Programs, Bureau of Justice Statistics.

Harrison, Paige M., and Jennifer Karberg (2003) *Prison and Jail Inmates at Midyear 2002.* Washington, D.C.: U.S. Department of Justice, Office of Justice Programs, Bureau of Justice Statistics.

——— (May 2004) *Prison and Jail Inmates at Midyear 2003.* Washington, D.C.: U.S. Department of Justice, Office of Justice Programs, Bureau of Justice Statistics.

Hernandez, Raymond (December 31, 1999) "Pataki Assents to Pension Rise for Jail Guards." *New York Times,* p. B1.

Herszenhom, David (December 22, 2002) "How Did a Rich State Get So Poor?" *New York Times.*

Hoffman, David (October 8, 1998) "Bush Attacks Dukakis as the 'Furlough King'; Republican Seeks to Direct Attention Away from Quayle's Debate Performance." *Washington Post.*

Holt, Norman (1998) "The Current State of Parole in America." In Joan Petersilia (ed.) (1998) *Community Corrections: Probation, Parole, and Intermediate Sanctions.* New York: Oxford University Press.

Horn, Martin (2001) "Rethinking Sentencing." *Corrections Management Quarterly* 5, pp. 34–40.

Hughes, Timothy A., Doris James Wilson, and Allen Beck (2001) *Trends in State Parole, 1990–2000.* Washington, D.C.: Bureau of Justice Statistics, U.S. Department of Justice, Office of Justice Programs.

Huling, Tracy (May 10, 2000) "Prisoners of the Census." *Mother Jones.*

International Center for Prison Studies. "Prison Briefs for France, Italy, Germany, the Netherlands, Spain, Australia and South Africa," Available at www.prisonstudies.org.

Irwin, John, and James Austin (1997) *It's About Time: America's Imprisonment Binge.* Belmont, CA: Wadsworth.

Jacobson, Michael (2001) "From the 'Back' to the 'Front': The Changing Character of Punishment in New York City." In John Mollenkopf and Ken Emerson (eds.) *Rethinking the Urban Agenda: Reinvigorating the Liberal Tradition in New York City and Urban America.* New York: Century Foundation Press.

Jenkins, David H., Jennifer Pendry, and Stephen J. Steurer (1993) *A Post Release*

Follow-up of Correctional Education Program Completers Released in 1990–1991. Maryland Department of Education.

"Justice Kennedy against Minimum Prison Terms" (August 11, 2003) CNN.com Law Center. Available at www.cnn.com/2003/LAW/08/11/prison.terms .ap.

Kaminer, Wendy. (1995) *It's All the Rage: Crime and Culture.* Reading, MA: Addison-Wesley.

Kansas Sentencing Commission (2002) *Kansas Sentencing Commission Annual Report FY 2001: Analysis of Sentencing Guidelines in Kansas.*

Karmen, Andrew (2001) *New York Murder Mystery: The True Story behind the Crime Crash of the 1990s.* New York: New York University Press.

Keitch, Ryan (July 22, 2002) "Bills Awaiting Approval Could Add Prison Costs." *Indianapolis Star.*

Kelling, George L., and Catherine M. Coles (1996) *Fixing Broken Windows: Restoring Order and Reducing Crime in Our Communities.* New York: Simon and Schuster.

King, Ryan S., and Marc Mauer (August 2001) *Aging behind Bars: "Three Strikes" Seven Years Later.* Washington D.C.: The Sentencing Project. Available at www.sentencingproject.org.

——— (2002) *State Sentencing and Corrections Policy in an Era of Fiscal Restraint,* Washington, D.C.: The Sentencing Project.

King, Ryan S., Marc Mauer, and Tracy Huling (2003) *Big Prisons, Small Towns: Prison Economics in Rural America.* Washington, D.C.: The Sentencing Project.

Langan, Patrick A., and John M. Brown (January 1997) *Felony Sentences in State Courts, 1994.* Washington, D.C.: U.S. Department of Justice, Office of Justice Programs, Bureau of Justice Statistics.

Langan, Patrick, and David Levin (2002) *Recidivism of Prisoners Released in 1994.* Washington, D.C.: Bureau of Justice Statistics, U.S. Department of Justice, Office of Justice Programs.

Lawrence, Sarah, Daniel P. Mears, Glen Dubin, and Jeremy Travis (2002) *Practice and Promise of Prison Programming.* Washington, D.C.: Urban Institute.

Leaf, Robin, Robin Arthur Lurigio, and Nancy Martin (1998) "Chicago's Project Safeway: Strengthening Probation's Links with the Community." In Joan Petersilia (ed.) (1998) *Community Corrections: Probation Parole and Intermediate Sanctions.* New York: Oxford University Press.

Legal Action Center, The (2004) *After Prison: Roadblocks to Reentry, A Report on State Legal Barriers Facing People with Criminal Records.* New York.

Legislative Analyst's Office (May 17, 2004) *Overview of the 2004–2005 May Revision.* Sacramento, CA. Available at www.lao.ca.gov/2004/may_revision/ 011704_may_revision.pdf.

LeonHardt, David (November 4, 2001) "Recession: Almost Official." *New York Times,* Final, Section 4, p. 2.

Los Angeles Probation Department Web site: probation.co.la.ca.us/adult/aspecial.html.

Louisiana Department of Public Safety and Corrections. "Incarceration Only: Admissions and Releases Comparison 1994–2002." Available at www.corrections.state.la.us./Statistics/BB.htm.

Louisiana Department of Public Safety (2003) "Sheriffs Payments Projection FY 2002–2003." Available at www.corrections.state.la.us./Statistics/BB.htm.

Lynch, Mona (1998) "Waste Managers? The New Penology, Crime Fighting, and Parole Agent Identity." *Law and Society Review* 32, pp. 839–869.

Madriz, Esther (1997) *Nothing Bad Happens to Good Girls: Fear of Crime in Women's Lives.* Berkeley: University of California Press.

Martin, John, and Tim Kalish (October 2, 2002) "Governor Says State Committed to Helping Leflore Co. Economy." *Greenwood Commonwealth.* Available at www.zwire.com/site/news.

Martinson, Robert (1974) "What Works? Questions and Answers about Prison Reform." *Public Interest* 35, pp. 22–54.

—— (1979) "New Findings, New Views: A Note of Caution Regarding Sentencing Reform." *Hofstra Law Review* 7, pp. 242–258.

Mauer, Marc (1999) *The Crisis of the Young African American Male and the Criminal Justice System.* Prepared for the U.S. Commission of Civil Rights, Washington, D.C., April 15–16. Available at www.sentencingproject.org.

—— (1999) *Race to Incarcerate.* New York: New Press.

—— (June 30, 2003) "Comparative Rates of Incarceration: An Examination of Causes and Trends." Washington, D.C.: The Sentencing Project. Available at www.sentencingproject.org/pdfs/pub9036/pdf.

Mauer, Marc, and Meda Chesney-Lynd (eds.) (2003) *Invisible Punishment: The Collateral Consequences of Mass Imprisonment.* New York: New Press.

Mayor's Management Reports (1993–2001). New York: Office of the Mayor, Office of Operations.

Mayor's Management Report (February 2002). New York: Office of the Mayor, Office of Operations.

McAdam, Doug (1988) *Freedom Summer.* New York: Oxford University Press.

McDonald, Douglas C., Elizabeth Fournier, and Malcolm Russell-Einhorn (1998) *Private Prisons in the United States: An Assessment of Current Practice.* Cambridge, MA: Abt Associates Inc.

McGill, Kevin (April 12, 2001) "Saving Money on Prisons: Will It Be Politically Costly?" *Associated Press.*

—— (May 23, 2001) "Foster Pushes for Bill Removing Some Minimum Sentences." *Associated Press.*

McGuire, Phillip G. (2000) "The New York Police Department Compstat Process." In Victor Goldsmith, Philip G. McGuire, John H. Mollenkopf, and

Timothy A. Ross (eds.) *Analyzing Crime Matters: Frontiers of Practice.* Thousand Oaks, CA: Sage Publications.

MacKenzie, D. L. (1997) "Criminal Justice and Crime Prevention." In L. W. Sherman, D. Gottfredson, D. MacKenzie, J. Eck, P. Reuter, and S. Bushway (eds.), *Preventing Crime: What Works, What Doesn't, What's Promising* (pp. 9.1–9.76). Washington, D.C.: National Institute of Justice.

McNicol, Elizabeth (May 12, 2004) "States Face Continuing Fiscal Problems—Evidence from Recent Reports." Washington, D.C.: Center on Budget and Policy Priorities.

Miller, Jerome (1996) *Search and Destroy: African-American Males in the Criminal Justice System.* New York: Cambridge University Press.

Miller, Ted R, Mark A. Cohen, and Brian Wiersema (1996) *Victim Costs and Consequences: A New Look.* Washington, D.C.: U.S. Department of Justice, National Institute of Justice.

Mississippi Department of Corrections Monthly Fact Sheet. Available at www.mdoc.state.ms.us.

Mississippi Department of Corrections Schedule of Costs by Category. Available at www.mdoc.state.ms.us.

Morain, Dan (March 15, 2002) "Davis to Close State's Privately Run Prisons; Funding: Elected with the Help of $2.3 Million for Guards' Union, Governor Includes Plan in Budget." *Los Angeles Times,* p. A1.

Morain, Dan, and Jennifer Warren (January 22, 2003) "Battle Looms over Prison Spending in State Budget. *Los Angeles Times.*

Morgan, Terry, and Stephen D. Marrs (1998) "Richmond, Washington's SMART Partnership for Police and Community Corrections." In Joan Petersilia (ed.) (1998) *Community Corrections Probation Parole and Intermediate Sanctions.* New York: Oxford University Press.

Morgante, Michelle (June 15, 2004) "More Winning Parole under Schwarzenegger." *Associated Press.* Available at customwire.ap.org/dynamic/stories/S/SCHWARZENEGGER_PAROLE?SITE=APWEB&SECTION=HOME&TEMPLATE=DEFAULT.

Morris, Aldon (1984) *The Origins of the Civil Rights Movement: Black Communities Organized for Change.* New York: Free Press.

Morris, Norval (1974) *The Future of Imprisonment.* Chicago: University of Chicago Press.

Mumola, Christopher (2000) *Incarcerated Parents and Their Children.* Washington, D.C.: U.S. Department of Justice, Office of Justice Programs, Bureau of Justice Statistics.

Naro, Wendy (2002) "Ten Year Adult Secure Population Projection 2002–2012." Report prepared for the Louisiana Department of Public Safety and Corrections, the Institute on Crime Justice and Corrections, George Washington University, Washington, D.C.

National Advisory Commission on Criminal Justice Standards and Goals (1973) *A National Strategy to Reduce Crime: Final Report*. Washington, D.C.: Government Printing Office.

National Association of State Budget Officers (NASBO) (Summer 2001) *2000 State Expenditure Report*. Washington, D.C., p. 62.

National Association of State Budget Officers and the National Governors Association (2002) *Fiscal Survey of States*. Washington, D.C.

—— (2004) *Budgeting Amid Fiscal Uncertainty: Ensuring Budget Stability by Focusing on the Long Term*. Washington, D.C.

National Conference of State Legislators (July 2002) *State Budget and Tax Actions: 2002 Preliminary Report*. Washington, D.C.

—— (2002) *State Fiscal Update, April 2002*, Washington, D.C.

—— (2002) *State Fiscal Update, June 2002*. Available at www.ncsl.org/programs/ fiscal/sfo2002.htm.

—— (2003) *State Budget and Tax Actions 2003*. Washington, D.C. Available at www.ncsl.org/programs/fiscal/presbta03.htm.

National Governors Association and the National Association of State Budget Officers (June 2003) *The Fiscal Survey of States*. Washington, D.C.

National Governors Association and National Association of State Budget Officers (April 2004) *The Fiscal Survey of States*. Washington, D.C.

Nelson, Marta, and Jennifer Trone (2000) "Why Planning for Release Matters." New York: Vera Institute of Justice.

The New Politics of Criminal Justice: A Research and Messaging Report for The Open Society Institute (February 2002). Peter D. Hart Research Associates, Inc.

New York City Criminal Justice Agency (1994) *Semi-Annual Report for the Second Half of 1993*. New York: Criminal Justice Agency.

New York City Department of Correction, Population Research Unit (1999). Personal correspondence.

New York Police Department (NYPD) (2002) *CompStat*. Available at www.nyc .gov/html/nypd/html/pct/cspdf.html.

New York State Division of Criminal Justice Services (DCJS) (1900–2002). *Criminal Justice Indicators*. Available at criminaljustice.state.ny.us/crimnet.

Office of the Attorney General, State of California, Department of Justice, Criminal Justice Statistics Center (2004). Available at justice.hdcdojnet.state.ca .us/cjsc_stats/prof02/index.htm.

Open Society Institute (1997) *Education as Crime Prevention: Providing Education to Prisoners*. Research Brief, Occasional Paper Series No. 2. New York: OSI Center on Crime Communities and Culture.

Padgett, Tania, and James Toedtman (November 1, 2001) "Evidence Points to Recession: Economy Shrinks at Fastest Rate in Decade." *Newsday*, p. A45.

Parenti, Christian (1999) *Lockdown America: Police and Prisons in the Age of Crisis*. New York: Verso.

Pastore, Ann L., and Kathleen Maguire (eds.) (2000) *Sourcebook of Criminal Justice Statistics*. Available at http://www.albany.edu/sourcebook.

Pennsylvania Department of Corrections (2002) "Recidivism, 1996–2000." Harrisburg, PA.

Peter D. Hart Research Associates, Inc. (2002) *The New Politics of Criminal Justice*. Washington, D.C.

Petersilia, Joan (1998) "The Current State of Probation, Parole and Intermediate Sanctions." In Joan Petersilia (ed.) *Community Corrections: Probation Parole and Intermediate Sanctions*. New York: Oxford University Press.

——— (1999) "Parole and Prisoner Reentry in the United States." In Michael Tonry and Joan Petersilia (eds.) (1994) *Prisons*. Chicago: University of Chicago Press.

——— (2003) *When Prisoners Come Home: Parole and Prisoner Reentry*. New York: Oxford University Press.

——— (ed.) (1998) *Community Corrections: Parole, Probation and Intermediate Sanctions*. New York: Oxford University Press.

"Prison Guard Clout Endures" (April 1, 2002) *Los Angeles Times*, p. B10.

Probation and Parole in the United States, 2000. Press release. Washington, D.C.: U.S. Department of Justice, Office of Justice Programs, Bureau of Justice Statistics. Available at www.ojp.usdoj.gov/bjs/.

Proctor, Bernadette D., and Joseph Dalaker (2002) *Poverty in the United States: 2001*. Washington, D.C.: U.S. Department of Commerce, U.S. Census Bureau. Available at www.census.gov/prod/2002pubs/p60-219.pdf.

Reiman, Jeffrey (2000) *The Rich Get Richer and the Poor Get Prison: Ideology, Class and Criminal Justice*. Boston: Allyn & Bacon.

Rhine, Edward, William Smith, and Ronald Jackson (1991) *Paroling Authorities: Recent History and Current Practices*. Laurel, MD: American Correctional Association.

Riveland, Chase (1999) "Prison Management Trends, 1975–2025." In Michael Tonry and Joan Petersilia (1999) *Prisons*. Chicago: University of Chicago Press.

Rose, Dina R., and Todd Clear (1998) "Incarceration, Social Capital and Crime: Implications for Social Disorganization Theory." *Criminology* 36(3), pp. 441–480.

Rose, Dina R., Todd R. Clear, and Judith A. Ryder (2001) "Addressing the Unintended Consequences of Incarceration through Community-Oriented Services at the Neighborhood Level." *Corrections Management Quarterly* 5(3).

Rothman, David J. (1971) *The Discovery of the Asylum: Social Order and Disorder in the New Republic*. Boston: Little, Brown.

——— (1980) *Conscience and Convenience: The Asylum and Its Alternatives in Progressive America*. Boston: Little, Brown.

Rudolph, Alexander, and Jacquelyn Gyamerah (September 28, 1997) "Differential Punishment of African Americans and Whites Who Possess Drugs: A Just Policy or a Continuation of the Past?" *Journal of Black Studies,* pp. 97–111.

San Diego Police Department Web Site. *San Diego Historical Crime Actuals, 1950–2001.* Available at www.sannet.gov/police/stats/index.shtml.

The Sentencing Project (1985–1998) "Crime, Punishment and Public Opinion: A Summary of Recent Studies and Their Implications for Sentencing Policy," Washington, D.C.

——— (1970–2003) *Facts about Prisons and Prisoners.* Available at www.sentencingproject.org.

——— (1984–2001) "Prison Privatization and the Use of Incarceration." Report available at www.sentencingproject.org.

——— (1998) *US Surpasses Russia as World Leader in Rate of Incarceration.* Available at www.sentencingproject.org/brief/usvsrus.pdf.

Shichor, D., and D. K. Sechrest (eds.) (1996) *Three Strikes and You're Out: Vengeance as Public Policy.* Thousand Oaks, CA: Sage.

Shuler, Marsha (May 3, 2001) "Senators Vote to Relax Prison Terms." *Baton Rouge Advocate.*

Silverman, Eli B. (1999) *NYPD Battles Crime: Innovative Strategies in Policing.* Boston: Northeastern University Press.

Simon, Jonathan (1993) *Poor Discipline: Parole and the Social Control of the Underclass, 1890–1990.* Chicago: University of Chicago Press.

Slevin, Peter (February 18, 2001) "Prison Firms Seek Inmates and Profits." *Washington Post,* p. A3.

Snell, Tracy (2001) *Capital Punishment 2000.* Washington, D.C.: U.S. Department of Justice, Office of Justice Programs, Bureau of Justice Statistics.

——— (n.d.) *Women in Prison: Survey of State Prison Inmates, 1991.* Washington, D.C.: U.S. Department of Justice, Office of Justice Programs, Bureau of Justice Statistics.

Sourcebook of Criminal Justice Statistics (2002). Available at www.albany.edu/sourcebook/1995/pdf/21.pdf.

Spelman, William (2000) "The Limited Importance of Prison Expansion." In Alfred Blumstein and Joel Wallman (eds.) *The Crime Drop in America.* New York: Cambridge University Press.

——— (2000) "What Recent Studies Do (and Don't) Tell Us about Imprisonment and Crime." In Michael Tonry (ed.) (2000) *Crime and Justice: A Review of Research.* Vol. 27. Chicago: University of Chicago Press.

Staff Bayoubuzz (May 24, 2004) "Louisiana Governor Blanco Makes Three Appointments to Department of Public Safety and Corrections." Available at www.bayoubuzz.com/articles.aspx?aid=1680.

State of California Department of Corrections Offender Information Services Branch, Estimates and Statistical Analysis Section, Data Analysis Unit (2000) *California Prisoners and Parolees 2000.* Available at www.cdc.state.ca.us.

State of New York Department of Correctional Services (1999) *Characteristics of Inmates Discharged 1997.* Albany: Division of Program Planning, Research and Evaluation.

――― (2002) *Characteristics of Inmates Discharged 2000.* Albany: Division of Program Planning, Research and Evaluation.

State Prison Expenditures, 1996. Washington, D.C.: U.S. Department of Justice, Office of Justice Programs, Bureau of Justice Statistics.

Stephan, James J. (1999) *State Prison Expenditures in 1996.* Washington, D.C.: U.S. Department of Justice, Office of Justice Programs, Bureau of Justice Statistics.

Steurer, Stephen J., Linda Smith, and Alice Tracy (2001) *OCE/CEA Three State Recidivism Study.* Correctional Educational Association.

Stevenson, Richard W. (November 27, 2001) "Economists Make It Official: U.S. Is in a Recession." *New York Times,* Business/Financial Desk.

Substance Abuse and Mental Health Services Administration (2003) *Results from the 2002 National Survey on Drug Use and Health: National Findings.* Rockville, MD: Office of Applied Studies, NHSDA Series H-22, DHHS Publication No. SMA03-3836.

Sullivan, Eileen, Milton Mino, Katherine Nelson, and Jill Pope (2002) *Families as a Resource in Recovery from Drug Abuse: An Evaluation of La Bodega de la Familia.* New York: Vera Institute of Justice.

Testimony of Governor John Rowland to Joint Appropriations and Judiciary Committees (April 3, 2003). Hartford, Connecticut.

Tonry, Michael (1994) "Racial Politics, Racial Disparities and the War on Crime." *Crime and Delinquency* 40(4), pp. 475–494.

――― (1995) *Malign Neglect: Race, Crime and Punishment in America.* New York: Oxford University Press.

――― (1996) *Sentencing Matters.* New York: Oxford University Press.

――― (2004) *Thinking about Crime: Sense and Sensibility in American Culture.* New York: Oxford University Press.

Tonry, Michael, and Norval Morris (1990) *Between Prison and Probation: Intermediate Punishments in a Rational Sentencing System.* New York: Oxford University Press.

Tonry, Michael, and Joan Petersilia (1999) "American Prisons." In Michael Tonry and Joan Petersilia (eds.) (1999) *Prisons.* Chicago: University of Chicago Press.

――― (eds.) (1999) *Prisons.* Chicago: University of Chicago Press.

Tournier, Pierre W. (2002) "The Prisons of Europe, Prison Population Inflation and Prison Overcrowding." Centre de Recherches Sociologiques sur le Droit et les Institutions Penales, France.

Travis, Jeremy (2001) "But They All Come Back: Rethinking Prisoner Reentry." Washington, D.C.: U.S. Department of Justice, Office of Justice Programs, National Institute of Justice.

——— (May 22, 2002) "Thoughts on the Future of Parole." Remarks delivered at the Vera Institute of Justice, New York.

——— (2003) *Parole in California, 1980–2000: Implications for Reform.* Public hearing on parole reform, Little Hoover Commission, February 27.

——— (2003) "Reflections on Parole: Meeting the Challenges of Today." Keynote speech for the Association of Paroling Authorities International Annual Conference, St. Louis, Missouri.

Travis, Jeremy, and Sarah Lawrence (2002) *Beyond the Prison Gates: The State of Parole in America.* Washington, D.C.: The Urban Institute.

U.S. Bureau of the Census (2000) *State and County QuickFacts: Louisiana.* Available at quickfacts.census.gov/qfd/states/22000.html.

U.S. Department of Justice, Office of Justice Programs, Bureau of Justice Statistics (June 19, 2004) *Crime and Justice Data Online: Crime Trends.* Available at www.bjsdata.ojp.usdoj.gov/dataonline/Search/Crime/Crime.cfm.

——— *Reentry Trends in the U.S.: Releases from State Prison.* Available at www.ojp.usdoj.gov/bjs/reentry/releases.htm.

The Vera Institute of Justice (January 1996) *Unintended Consequences of Incarceration: Papers from a Conference Organized by Vera,* Available at www.vera.org/publications.

Wacquant, Loic (2001) "Deadly Symbiosis: When Ghetto and Prison Meet and Merge." *Punishment and Society* 3(1).

——— (2001) "Deadly Symbiosis: When Ghetto and Prison Meet and Mesh." In David Garland (ed.) *Mass Imprisonment: Social Causes and Consequences.* London: Sage.

——— (2002) "Four Strategies to Cut Carceral Costs: On Managing Mass Imprisonment in the United States." *Studies in Political Economy* 18 (Spring), pp. 19–30.

Walker, Samuel (1998) *Sense and Nonsense about Crime and Drugs.* 4th ed., Belmont CA: Wadsworth Publishing Co.

Warren, Jennifer (August 21, 2000) "When He Speaks, They Listen: In 20 Years, Don Novey Has Built the Once Powerless California Prison Guards Union into One of the Most Influential and Richest Forces in State Politics." *Los Angeles Times*, p. 1.

——— (January 21, 2004) "California Guards Tell of Retaliation for Informing: Whistle-Blowers Testify before Senate Panel on How Their Reports of Misconduct at State Prisons Are Received." *Los Angeles Times*, p. B1.

Washington State Department of Corrections (April 2002) "Recidivism: Historical Review of Returns to Prison." Recidivism Briefing Paper No. 20. Olympia, WA.

Weekly Report of Population as of Midnight September 18, 2002. Sacramento: California Department of Corrections Offender Information Services Branch, Data Analysis Unit.

Western, Bruce, and Katherine Beckett (January 1999) "How Unregulated Is the U.S. Labor Market? The Penal System as a Labor Market Institution." *American Journal of Sociology* 104(4).

Whitley, Tyler (August 30, 2002) "Southside Rallied for Prisons." *Virginia Times Dispatch.* Interview with Wilhelm, Daniel F., Director of the Vera Institute of Justice's State Sentencing and Corrections Program conducted on August 5, 2003.

Wilhelm, Daniel F., and Nicholas R. Turner (2002) *Is the Budget Crisis Changing the Way We Look at Sentencing and Incarceration?* New York: Vera Institute of Justice.

Wool, Jon, and Don Stemen (March 2004) *Changing Fortune or Changing Attitudes: Sentencing and Corrections in 2003.* New York: Vera Institute of Justice.

Wren, Christopher S. (April 21, 1999) "Arizona Finds Cost Savings in Treating Drug Offenders." *New York Times.*

Young, Jock (2003) "Merton with Energy, Katz with Structure: The Sociology of Vindictiveness and the Criminology of Transgression." *Theoretical Criminology* 7(3).

Zedlewski, Edwin W. (July 1987) *Making Confinement Decisions.* Washington, D.C.: National Institute of Justice.

Zimring, Franklin, and Gordon Hawkins (October 1988) "The New Mathematics of Imprisonment," *Crime and Delinquency* 34(4).

——— (1991) *The Scale of Imprisonment.* Chicago: University of Chicago Press.

——— (1995) *Incapacitation: Penal Confinement and the Restraint of Crime.* New York: Oxford University Press.

——— (1997) *Crime Is Not the Problem: Lethal Violence in America.* New York: Oxford University Press.

Index

An "f" following a page number indicates that the information appears in a figure on the page. An "n" indicates that the information is in an endnote on the page. The number following the "n" is the note's number.

About the Author

MICHAEL JACOBSON has over twenty years of government service. He was formerly the Commissioner of the New York City Departments of Correction and Probation and a Deputy Budget Director for the City of New York, serving in the Koch, Dinkins, and Giuliani administrations. He is currently President of the Vera Institute of Justice, Professor of Criminology in the Department of Law, Police Science, and Criminal Justice Administration at John Jay College of Criminal Justice, and Professor of Sociology at the Graduate Center of the City University of New York.